WORLD POLITICS

PROSPECTS AND CHALLENGES FOR

SECOND EDITION

STEPHEN M. HILL

ALI R. ABOOTALEBI

Kendall Hunt

publishing company

To Polly and Oliver, SMH
To Katayun and Mickael, ARA

Contents

Preface

With so many introductory texts to choose from, one might wonder why we decided to write yet another—a question we often asked ourselves during the lengthy writing process! There are essentially two reasons we believed the effort was warranted, both of which have emerged from our experience of teaching more than 30 combined years of introductory world politics courses.

First, we saw a need for an introductory text that is both accessible and engaging to students who are taking world politics as a general education class at a liberal arts college. Though we might wish that all our students would continue to study upper-division courses in our discipline, reality and experience have taught us that for most this will not be the case. Despite this, we feel the overwhelming majority of introductory texts in the field, in an understandable attempt to appeal to as broad a range of courses as possible, tend to 'cram' in too much content and detail and thereby overwhelm the novice. We have therefore structured and written this text in a fashion designed to encourage the general education student to better engage with the material. We hope this will have a commensurate impact on their enjoyment of, and appreciation for, the discipline.

Second, we wanted to help our students fully appreciate the importance of engaging in the core theoretical debates of our discipline. Theory, of course, can be a frightening word for any college student. This fear can be exacerbated by the seemingly indecipherable jargon that is used by many so-called "introductory" texts. Nevertheless, engaging in the great theoretical debates of the field is essential for any student trying to make sense of how the world works. Therefore, this text tries to reduce students' fear by taking them on a methodical journey through the development and application of three of the central theories of the discipline. Though we hope students will pursue further study and eventually be exposed to even more theoretical perspectives, we believe that our principal goal in an introductory class should be to provide our students with the intellectual skills and knowledge required to become lifelong learners in the field of world politics. We have therefore favored the systematic discussion, application, and evaluation of three core theories over the temptation to cover all theories within the discipline.

We have also tried to make the importance of the theoretical debates in the discipline more tangible to our students by engaging them in the foreign policy choices that the United States (US) must make in areas such as international security, international organizations, and law and international economics. In our experience, students have always developed a better understanding of the larger theoretical debates in the discipline when they realize that informed foreign policy decisions can only be made on the basis of theoretical assumptions about how the world works. This point is reiterated throughout the text. Thus, rather than rely on additional texts to elicit discussion and help students apply the discipline's theoretical insights (which generally makes the conceptual and theoretical debates of the discipline more tangible for them), we have made the foreign policy challenges facing the US a systematic component of our text. Although debates on US foreign policy are therefore only used as a means to encourage students to apply theoretical perspectives and engage with the broader issues in world politics, we nevertheless acknowledge that such an approach may lessen the book's attractiveness to some instructors teaching in other countries. Despite this, we believe it is the best way to engage our students here in the US.

Acknowledgments

We owe a great deal of gratitude to all our family members and friends for the love and support they provided throughout this project, in particular, our spouses, Dr. Polly Hashmi (Hill) and Katayun Kasiri (Abootalebi). Christopher Sharples provided invaluable comments on our drafts. The book would also not have been possible without sabbatical and research support provided to both authors through the Office of Research and Sponsored Programs at the University of Wisconsin–Eau Claire.

We also owe a debt of gratitude to those working for our publisher, in particular our acquisitions editor, Jeffrey Huemoeller, who remained both patient and supportive despite many missed deadlines. We would also like to thank our production editors, Beth Trowbridge and Linda Chapman.

Finally, we would like to express our appreciation to the students that have attended our classes at UW–Eau Claire over so many years and who have continued to motivate, inspire, and challenge us in the classroom.

Stephen M. Hill
Ali R. Abootalebi

Introduction

Image © Elenarts, 2013. Used under license from Shutterstock, Inc.

CHAPTER OUTLINE

1.0 What Is World Politics?

As in any discipline, the first thing we must do is define the subject we are going to study. This requires us to answer the fundamental question: What is "world politics"? If you have ever glanced across a library or college bookstore bookshelf containing introductory texts like this one, you may have already noticed that some are entitled *Introduction to World Politics*, while others have titles such as *Introduction to International Relations* or *Introduction to Global Politics*. What is the difference? In most cases, very little! The terms *world politics*, *international relations*, and *global politics* tend to be used interchangeably.

However, despite being commonly used as synonyms, differences do exist between these concepts. For instance, **international relations (IR)** is a discipline that specifically studies the interactions between states. As we will emphasize throughout this text, the terms of our field of study have developed over many decades (and even centuries) and thus the terms used are not always what we might think are most accurate. For example, IR, which became an independent discipline of study in the aftermath of World War I (1914–1918), might be more accurately called "inter-state relations."

Studying world politics as IR is akin to studying American politics by studying the interactions of the principal public institutions of American government; the presidency, the Congress, and the Supreme Court. Most scholars argue that limiting the study of American politics like this ignores not only other important actors (such as trade unions, businesses, and individuals), but also important issues of analysis (e.g., Why are there so many millionaires in Congress?). So too with world politics: Other actors and important issues may be omitted from one's analytical approach (e.g., Are the poor countries of the world being exploited within the capitalist world economy?).

It is usually in an attempt to be more inclusive of these additional actors and issues that some texts adopt the term *global politics*. This term also tends to be used to reflect the changing world in which we live, one that is becoming increasingly "globalized" through a process, not surprisingly, called "globalization." However, the nature and extent of globalization remains hotly contested. Is it a new phenomenon or simply an old process in a new guise? Are we living in a new and fundamentally different era of "globalized" politics? Or is the nature of world politics still essentially the same as it has always been? To remain neutral in these debates, this text has adopted the title of *Introduction to World Politics*. We thus hope to allow you, the reader, to determine the answers to the above questions.

Finally, although we have adopted the more inclusive term of *world politics*, we remain cognizant of the fact that we cannot provide an adequate analysis of all the actors and relationships that exist in world politics in a single text, especially one that is designed as an introduction! We will therefore be concentrating most on the interactions of the most powerful actors in world politics, states, while hopefully providing you with an insight into the importance of other actors and the debates that have ensued around them.

1.1 How Is World Politics Studied?

There are three principal ways in which world politics can be studied. The first way is to study it historically. This usually entails studying the causes of momentous events (e.g., World War I), the importance of certain periods of time (e.g., the Cold War) or the impact of influential individuals (e.g., Adolf Hitler or Mahatma Gandhi). The historians who conduct such work do so with a meticulous eye for detail and are always concerned with the rich complexity and uniqueness of their accounts. For example, a historian studying the causes of World War I will be cognizant of the fact that many of the countries that fought that war no longer exist; that the leaders who made the fateful decisions leading to war are no longer alive; and that those leaders were operating in social, political, and economic environments that have since changed dramatically. Historians therefore seek to give the best description or explanation for the events they cover and do not seek to generalize from those accounts. In other words, an historian of World War I will not try to use his or her explanation for the cause of that war to explain the start of all wars throughout history, or perhaps even the 20th century!

The second way to study world politics is to philosophize about it. Philosophers are concerned less with studying **empirical** (what can be observed) evidence and more with addressing the fundamental questions of world politics through the application of reason and rational argument. Many of the classical philosophers are still studied in our field because they reasoned about these essential questions, including, How selfish is human nature? What should be the relationship between a state's government and its citizenry? What obligations do individuals and states hold toward one another? The contribution of these classical philosophers, including Niccolo Machiavelli, Thomas Hobbes, and Immanuel Kant, will become fully apparent when we cover the principal theories of world politics in the next chapter. However, even today, moral and political philosophers continue to make significant contributions to the field by continuing to debate the older questions, as well as addressing newer ones, like, When is it ethical to violate a state's **sovereignty** to protect its citizens from human rights abuses?

The third way in which world politics is studied is the social scientific approach utilized by many political scientists. It differs from the historical approach in that it begins with a generalization—from which a **hypothesis** can be **deduced**. That hypothesis is then tested against empirical evidence to determine whether it is true or false. This process is the *scientific method*, which is common to all the natural and social sciences. For example, a generalization that all wars are caused by the competition over power could lead to the deduction of a hypothesis that WWI was caused by British fears that Germany was becoming too powerful. The political scientist will then look for empirical evidence to prove (validate) or disprove (reject) this hypothesis. If it is disproven, the generalization may be discarded, or at least amended in some way. If it is proven, then further hypotheses will be deduced; for example, was World War II also caused by similar fears of a more powerful Germany? Or was the Cold War between the United States and USSR fueled by the competition for power (and not by ideological differences)? These hypotheses, in turn, are tested against empirical evidence and the cycle continues.

The principal approaches of the historian, philosopher, and political scientist to the study of world politics are, therefore, fundamentally distinct. The philosopher applies reason to the fundamental questions of world politics, while the historian and political scientist base their analyses on empirical observation (their own or others). However, while the historian concentrates on providing an analysis or narrative of a specific event(s) or time period(s), the political scientist searches for the best theory to explain phenomena that occur across a significant time period and/or geographical space. By building on the theories proposed by others before us, we can thus hope to cumulatively produce an ever-greater understanding of how the world works.

Although we will be emphasizing this social scientific approach to theory testing in this text, it is important to acknowledge the contributions made to the field by philosophers and historians. For example, historians provide a vital service to political scientists, as it is they who produce the "history," or empirical evidence, against which our theories can be tested. History is thus our "laboratory"—we can "experiment" by producing hypotheses and testing them against history (there will be further discussion of this in Chapter 2). The challenge for you as new students of world politics will be to decide which of the competing theories in world politics is best, a challenge that begins with an explanation of those theories in Chapter 2.

1.2 What Actors Exist in World Politics?

Before we can debate which of these theories is correct, we must first define the terminology we are going to use, so that we can at least be sure that we are referring to the same things. This terminology is also used as a form of shorthand within our discipline, just as terms like "test tube," "reaction," and "product" are used in chemistry. If you were unfamiliar with these basic terms of chemistry, it would be very difficult for you to relate the importance of your experiment to your colleagues. This is equally true in world politics. Learning the basic terms and concepts of world politics is a prerequisite to the effective communication of your thoughts and ideas and thus your meaningful participation in the debates of the discipline!

An *actor* is essentially any entity that has a notable influence in world politics. In general, scholars of world politics recognize two types of such actors. These are **non-state actors** and **states.** Non-state actors come in various forms. The smallest is the **individual**. Traditionally, the discipline of world politics has only paid attention to individuals who led governments or who were influential within them. However, with the development of modern technologies, like the Internet and Twitter, private individuals are influencing world politics in ever-increasing ways. Whether it is a political dissident in China or an al Qaeda operative in Afghanistan, modern technology is enabling individuals to communicate their messages across the globe. Individuals can even threaten the security of powerful states, through acts of terrorism, or simply by hacking into their secure electronic networks. Wealthy individuals, such as CNN's founder Ted Turner or Microsoft's Bill Gates, or the world's wealthiest person, Carlo Slim, can use their wealth to help with worthy global causes and/or buy political influence. Individuals are thus gaining increasing attention in the study of world politics.

Other forms of non-state actor include **nongovernmental organizations (NGOs)** and **multinational corporations (MNCs)**. As will be explained in Chapter 4, there are two principal types of NGO: those that operate *within* individual state borders and those that operate *across* state borders. Because those in the latter category operate across state borders, they are often called **transnational NGOs (TNGOs)**. Any actor, whether a local-government body, NGO, or company, that influences the foreign policies of a state in which they operate, but does not operate across state borders themselves, can be defined as a **sub-state** actor.

MNCs are, by their very nature, transnational actors. They are companies that conduct business across state borders, in many cases globally. As is the case with all the different actors in world politics, scholars disagree about their relative degree of importance and whether their influence is, on the whole, desirous or destructive. This debate will be covered in Chapter 5.

The final principal non-state actors in world politics are **intergovernmental organizations (IGOs)**. These are organizations that are composed of state members, but still operate (to some degree) independently of those states. Perhaps the best-known example of this is the United Nations. Although it is an IGO composed of 193 member-states, it also has a Secretary-General (presently Ban Ki Moon) who is expected to represent the "peoples of the United Nations" and not just the interests of its state-members. Together, TNGOs and IGOs make up another category of actor in world politics, **international organizations (IOs)**. The debates over the roles and influence of IOs in world politics will be covered in Chapter 4.

As one can tell from the classification of actors in Table 1.1 below, in world politics there are essentially two types of actor, states and other actors that are *not* states! This dichotomy is a reflection of the relative importance that states are awarded by most scholars of world politics. The fact that you have probably read the term *state* numerous times in this text alone and never once stopped to ask what it is, suggests that it is a term you are already familiar with. However, that does not necessarily mean you actually know what a state is, or what is required to become one. We will thus try to answer these questions in the next section.

Table 1.1 Types of Actors in World Politics

Non-State Actors	**Type**	**Examples**
Individuals, NGOs	sub-state	Members of government, companies, cities and other government bodies, private individuals
MNCs	transnational	Coca Cola, Toyota, Royal-Dutch Shell
TNGOs (IO)	transnational	Amnesty International, Greenpeace, Human Rights Watch
IGOs (IO)	intergovernmental	United Nations, North Atlantic Treaty Organization, World Trade Organization

1.2.1 What Is a State?

The simplest definition of a state is a sovereign entity possessing a permanent population, a defined territory, a government, and the capacity to enter into relations with other states. These four criteria were established in the Montevideo Convention on the Rights and Duties of States, which was signed by 19 states in 1933 (the Montevideo Convention simply codified what had already become customary international law [see Chapter 4]). Once these criteria have been fulfilled, all that is left is for the aspiring state is to be recognized by already existing states, thereby gaining **international recognition**.

Any entity that aspires to statehood and possesses at least some of the criteria required is called a **quasi-state**. Examples of quasi-states include Palestine, Taiwan, and Kurdistan. As we shall see in the discussion box on Palestine, many argue that each of the quasi-states mentioned here actually possess the four criteria required for statehood. If this is true, it means that statehood is not guaranteed simply by meeting these criteria. In fact, some existing states might not meet the criteria quite as well as some of these so-called quasi-states. For example, Vatican City is a state, despite being located within Rome, the capital city of Italy. It may also lack what one might expect of a state in terms of a permanent population and government. For these reasons many believe the Vatican to be no more than a religion or TNGO masquerading as a state. Yet, today it has formal diplomatic relations with more states than any other in our international system.

The example of the Vatican thus highlights the importance of international recognition. If existing states are willing to recognize you, you may not need to achieve all four of the Montevideo criteria. Equally, you may acquire all four of the criteria and still not receive international recognition. This leads to apparent double standards. For example, the United States recognized Kosovo as an independent state in 2008, but continues to deny the same recognition to the Palestinian Authority, despite the latter's protestations of also having met the necessary criteria (see discussion box).

DISCUSSION BOX

Should the United States Recognize Palestine as a State?

In 2011 the Palestinian Authority (PA) attempted to gain recognition as a sovereign state by joining the United Nations. President Abbas argued not only that Palestine had met all four of the Montevideo Convention criteria, but that Palestinian statehood would also bring the U.S.-supported goal of a two-state solution to the Israeli–Palestinian conflict closer to fruition. He argued that statehood would be the fulfillment of the Palestinian right to self-determination. (Abbas 2011). Though not successful in achieving full membership, one year later 138 states in the UN General Assembly actually voted in favor of recognizing the State of Palestine as a "non-member observer state."

However, David B. Rivkin and Lee A. Casey, two former Justice Department lawyers during the Reagan and George H. W. Bush administrations, have both argued against U.S. recognition of Palestine on the grounds that the four Montevideo Convention criteria have still not been met. They argue that the PA had "neither a permanent population nor a defined territory (both being the subject of ongoing if currently desultory negotiations), nor does it have a government with the capacity to enter into relations with other states. . . . The PA does not control any part of the West Bank to the exclusion of Israeli authority, and it exercises no control at all in the Gaza Strip" (Rivkin 2011).

Do you think the PA has met all four of the Montevideo Convention criteria? Do you think the PA has a "right" to become a state if, or when, it does so? Or do you think the United States should take other considerations into account before recognizing it, such as how Palestinian statehood might affect the security of Israel and the United States, or the impact that Palestinian statehood might have on the Israeli–Palestinian peace process?

Sometimes the process of international recognition can be a speedy one. In these cases the most powerful states in the international system recognize the new state and establish formal diplomatic relations with it. The aspiring state will then tend to apply to join the United Nations (UN). As will be explained in more detail in Chapter 4, states seeking to join the UN must first be recommended by the Security Council (on which the United States, United Kingdom, France, China, and Russian Federation serve as permanent members with veto power) and achieve a two-thirds majority vote in the General Assembly, the body in which all 193 current members may vote. As only states can join the UN, being allowed to accede to it in this way effectively means that you are being recognized as a state by the vast majority of the international system, including its most powerful members.

Unfortunately for some, the process of international recognition is much more contentious. In these cases there tends to be significant disagreement over whether the aspiring state should be recognized. For instance, Kosovo has been recognized by the United States, France, and the UK. However, China and Russia both refuse to recognize it. As long as this is the case, Kosovo will never be able to join the UN. Nevertheless, as of the end of 2017, Kosovo had been recognized by 115 UN member-states, including 23 members of the European Union. Is Kosovo thus now a state? If your tendency is to answer in the affirmative because the United States has recognized Kosovo, we must ask what has made the United States the final arbiter in the process of international recognition. For instance, Russia and China have both recognized the Palestinian Authority, but the United States has not. Would the Palestinian Authority still not be a state even if every other state in the international system recognized them but the United States?

As one can see, the process of international recognition can be contentious and difficult to adjudicate. There is no independent international judicial body tasked with deciding which aspiring states should be recognized and at what point (i.e., which states have recognized them and how many) they may have officially achieved their statehood. Nevertheless, once they reach this elusive point, they become a sovereign state. Nor is there any independent body that can adjudicate when a state may have lost its sovereignty. States that are no longer able to fulfill some of their basic responsibilities, such as controlling their territory or providing public services, are often called failing or **failed states**. Nevertheless, although states like Somalia and Afghanistan may be labeled as such, they still retain their international recognition as sovereign states. But what is sovereignty? Once again, we have a concept that is ubiquitous in the discussion of world politics, yet one that usually remains undefined. The next section will thus explore the nature and development of the concept of sovereignty.

1.2.2 What Is Sovereignty?

Sovereignty is one of the oldest and most important norms of behavior in world politics. In fact, as we will see in the following section, our modern international system is commonly dated to the birth of the concept of state sovereignty in 1648. A common definition of sovereignty, or what might be more accurately called **absolute sovereignty**, is the right of a state (or government) to do whatever it wishes within its own borders. The sovereign state is thus often referred to as having a monopoly on the use of force. This means the right to use force belongs to the state alone—non-state actors do not possess the right to use violence. For example, the state can draft ordinary citizens to serve in a national army and, if necessary, order them to kill in the service of the state. Any non-state actor that organizes to use violence in this way will normally be condemned by the state as criminal, and its members will be prosecuted for the violent crimes they commit. Sovereignty also allows states to tax their citizens as the ultimate representative of the people. There are no corporations, TNGOs, IGOs, or individuals with such sovereign rights, and acts of violence or the illegitimate expropriation of national resources by corporations, for example, would also be considered criminal and punishable by the state.

The acceptance of sovereignty means that all states are legally equal, a concept called **sovereign equality**. Thus, just as individual American citizens have legal rights and duties regardless of how wealthy, strong, or large they may be, the same is true of states.

Preemptive War: In international law it is legal for a State to use force in order to defend itself against an 'imminent' attack. This right to 'self- defense' is enshrined in Art. 55 of the UN Charter. However, as the threat from Iraq in 2003 was not deemed to be 'imminent', most analysts believed it was instead a case of **preventive war**. Obviously, the distinction between preemption and prevention depends on how impending the threat is perceived to be.

The principal rights and duties of states concerning sovereignty involve noninterference in each other's internal affairs. These rights and duties are outlined explicitly at the beginning of the UN Charter, which is the foremost document on issues involving sovereignty in international law (see Chapter 4). The founding members of the UN ensured that the principle of noninterference was enshrined in the first chapter of the Charter. Chapter I Article 2 (4) the Charter states that "[all] members shall refrain in their international relations from the threat or use of force against the *territorial integrity or political independence* of any state." In Chapter 1 Article 2 (7), it even ensures that the UN itself will not interfere in the sovereignty of its member states, when it states that "[nothing] contained in the present Charter shall authorize the United Nations to intervene in matters which are essentially within the *domestic jurisdiction* of any state."

When the founding members of the UN met to compose the organization's Charter in 1945, they were perhaps understandably focused on preventing a repeat of World War II, which they believed had started with German violations of state sovereignty in Europe during the 1930s. At first glance, it would thus appear that this concern had led the founding members of the UN to enshrine the concept of absolute sovereignty in the UN's Charter. However, at the end of Chapter I Article 2 (7), they also included a significant caveat to absolute sovereignty, essentially stating that the right to sovereignty of the UN's member-states could not prevent "the application of enforcement measures under Chapter VII" of the Charter. This means the UN Security Council (the only body that can enact Chapter VII enforcement measures) can vote to take enforcement action to restore international peace and security, including the violation of state sovereignty, whenever it believes it to be necessary.

As one can see from the above discussion, absolute sovereignty does not exist in its purest form. No state can legally prevent interference in its internal affairs if it is mandated by the UN Security Council under Chapter VII. However, it is debatable whether absolute sovereignty has ever existed. From the very beginning of our modern international system, states have interfered in the sovereignty of other states, especially when they believed those other states to be a threat (or future threat) a threat to their security. For example, the right of self-defense (now enshrined in Article 51 of the UN Charter), another legal right of states in our international system, has always presumed a right of **preemption**, a state's right to defend itself against an imminent attack, even if the military forces of the threatening state have not yet crossed its border. This type of challenge to absolute sovereignty continues to exist and new ones are being increasingly added to the list.

1.2.3 What Is the Future of State Sovereignty?

Much of the discussion that this text hopes to elicit will involve you forming an opinion about what you think the nature of sovereignty should be in the future. Do you believe the United States should aspire to absolute sovereignty? Or do you think the United States should "pool" its sovereignty in order to integrate economically and politically with other states? When do you think it is legitimate for the United States to interfere in the sovereignty of other states and vice versa? Hopefully one of the theories of world politics we are going to debate will help guide you in your answer to these questions. However, even at this stage, we can begin to recognize the centrality of sovereignty to the major issues in world politics.

As highlighted at the end of the previous section, the first area of world politics in which questions over sovereignty arise is **international security**. Traditionally, international security studies have focused on issues involving threats to the security (or even survival) of states. These threats generally arise from other states. For example, the United States may feel threatened by China's ongoing military modernization. Is it a violation of Chinese sovereignty if the United States spies on China's military buildup? If so, do you think it is wrong to do so? If the United States promotes democracy in China in the belief that a democratic China would no longer threaten it, is this also a violation of Chinese sovereignty? Would it be legitimate for the United States to preempt the growing threat from China's military expansion by attacking first?

Another issue of international security issues involving questions of sovereignty is that of nuclear proliferation. Nuclear proliferation involves the spread of nuclear weapons to more and more states around the world, including those with which the United States has had unfriendly relations. For example, the United States continues to accuse Iran of trying to build a nuclear weapon (contrary to international commitments for it not to do so; see Chapter 3) and, along with Israel, has threatened to use military force to stop it from doing so. Are these threats a violation of Iranian sovereignty? Reza Nasri, an international lawyer, argues that the "threat of force" against a sovereign member of the United Nations is illegal (and therefore illegitimate) under international law, because it violates Article 2 (4) of the UN Charter, which as we know from the previous section, commits member-states not to use or *threaten* the use of force against another member-state. Such threats can only be legally made by the UN Security Council under Chapter VII of the UN Charter. Do you agree with him?

Terrorism is another issue of international security in which the debate over sovereignty plays a central role. Since September 11, 2001, the United States has been fighting what the George W. Bush administration called a "global war on terror." Although the Obama administration preferred not to use this phrase, it continued to use (and expand) many of the counterterrorism tactics utilized by its predecessor, including the use of armed drone strikes on suspected terrorists in foreign countries. Most of those drone strikes took place in Pakistan, a country that insists that it has never given permission for the United States to conduct such strikes (Pakistan Warns US Drone Strikes Are 'Red Line' 2013). If this is true, are such drone strikes a violation of Pakistani sovereignty? If the Trump administration decides that they are necessary to protect national security, do you believe that they should continue even if they are a violation of Pakistani sovereignty?

Other issues that have traditionally been located outside the area of international security, but are increasingly being included within it, include issues of human rights and environmental destruction. Deciding whether and when states should intervene to protect human rights in other states obviously depends on one's perspective of sovereignty. If states have absolute sovereignty, they possess the right to do whatever they wish within their own borders, including committing large-scale human rights abuses. If they do not, then the question becomes what type and scale of human rights abuses warrants intervention by other states. Chapter 4 of this text explains the expansion of international law in the areas of human rights and international criminal law (to prosecute individuals who commit human rights atrocities). Do you believe that absolute sovereignty should be sacrificed in favor of the universal protection of basic human rights through these laws?)

Environmental destruction also poses significant challenges to the concept of absolute sovereignty. Pollution of the air and water is not contained by national borders. Individual states cannot control the production of greenhouse gases alone and thus cannot prevent global climate change by themselves. What should states do if others continue to destroy their environment and refuse to participate in international cooperative efforts to deal with the problem? Do states have the right to pollute their rivers with industrial run-off, even when those rivers run into seas shared with other states? Do states have the right to cut down as many trees as they would like to, regardless of the effects that might have on global greenhouse gas accumulation? When do you believe states have the right to intervene in the sovereignty of other states to protect the environment?

We can also see how sovereignty is central to the discussion of another area of world politics; **international political economy** (IPE). IPE is the study of the interplay between politics and economics in world politics. For example, we might ask whether you believe the United States and other states should pool their sovereignty in order to achieve greater economic prosperity and political cooperation. As we will see in Chapter 4, many of the states in Europe have joined together in a supranational organization, the European Union, in an attempt to integrate their economies and thereby achieve greater international peace and prosperity. This has resulted in political and economic decisions normally made at the national level being made at a regional (European) level. Do you believe the United States should follow in the same path and seek regional economic and political integration? Do you believe the United States should pool its sovereignty in a supranational body, perhaps a North American Union?

Similarly, in Chapter 5 of this text you will see questions arising over whether poor countries in the developing world are having their sovereignty violated by states like the United States and international institutions like the World Bank and International Monetary Fund. The latter organizations often place restrictions on government spending when they provide states with loans. Do you believe this is a violation of a state sovereignty?

As already mentioned, answering these numerous questions about sovereignty in a consistent fashion will require you to explore the theoretical debates in world politics covered in the next chapter. Before we do so, however, we must first define and explore the "system" in which states operate.

1.3 What Is an International System?

As with the terms *state* and *sovereignty*, this text has already utilized the concept of an "international system" on a number of occasions, and once again, you may have assumed you know what is meant by it. Perhaps the reason you have not questioned it is that you are already very familiar with it. The concept of a "system" is common to many academic disciplines. In high school you probably studied the human circulatory system in biology or the solar system in physics. And if you've ever played in (or watched) a football game, you have probably already heard discussion of offensive and defensive systems.

The reason the term *system* is common to all of these cases is that it conveys the same concept. A system is defined as *a group of interacting, interrelated, or interdependent elements forming a complex whole.* For example, the solar system is composed of the Sun and a number of planets, moons, and other bodies that are all interdependent (meaning they affect one another). We also use the term *system* because we know that its elements do not interact randomly. Instead, there is an ordered regularity to the behavior of these elements because of invisible forces like gravity. Once we have identified these forces and recognized that these celestial bodies form a system, we can then make sense of it. It is only because we have recognized it a system that we can predict that the Earth will orbit the Sun every 365 days and that Halley's Comet will be visible from Earth approximately every 75 years.

Similarly, in the case of our international system, when we use the concept of a system we recognize that the elements (states) within it are interacting, interrelated, and interdependent. We are also acknowledging that there is some ordered regularity to the behavior of states in the system, just as there is in the behavior of the planets in our solar system. It is this ordered regularity that allows us to theorize about why states behave as they do. How could one ever hope to generate a theory that explains completely random behavior? Scientists thus tend to first identify regular patterns of behavior and then theorize about their causes. The recognition of regular patterns of behavior in our solar system eventually led to the generation of the theory of gravity. As we will see in Chapter 2, the discipline of world politics has not yet formed a consensus on the principal causes of the regular patterns of behavior we have identified in our international system. We will thus be debating three different theories that each attempt to explain this behavior, beginning in the next chapter.

1.3.1 What Existed before Our Modern International System?

So far we have defined and explored the concepts of the state, sovereignty, and the international system. We have done so because it is impossible to have an informed debate about world politics without referencing these basic concepts. A truly informed debate, however, requires not only that you know what these concepts are, but also how they were created. For instance, it is important to recognize that these concepts were not created recently by some designated architects of world politics, but have instead evolved over many centuries.

The manner in which world politics has evolved proves that the creation of our international system was not preordained. Rather, it is the result of numerous momentous decisions and pivotal events in world history. Understanding what existed before our international system can therefore not only enlighten us as to how these concepts were generated, but also to how alternative political groupings and structures might have been more prevalent today if other paths had been taken. In essence, if our international system has not always existed, why should we assume that it always will? Furthermore, will the future of world politics look anything like its past?

Although the international system we live in today is truly global, its origins lie in the political development of Western Europe over the past two millennia. During that time three principal forms of political organization have existed. The first is the **city-state system**. The most prominent example of this existed in Ancient Greece during the Classical Greek period (500–300 B.C.E.). In this system, independent city-states acted in very similar fashion to states in the international system we know today. They conducted trade, joined alliances, and fought wars with one another, all in a system without a higher authority. As we will see in the next chapter, the Ancient Greek historian, Thucydides, provides us with an account of one of the greatest of these wars; one fought between the city-states of Athens and Sparta in the 5th century B.C.E.

The second principal form of political organization witnessed in Europe (and other regions of the world) is the **empire**. Rather than a system of interdependent independent states, an empire is defined by control and domination. For example, the Roman Empire (50 B.C.E.–450 C.E.), which at its peak stretched from the northern borders of England, all the way across Europe to Syria and Egypt in the Middle East and North Africa, was based on complete subjugation to Roman rule. Some empires continued to exist even after the birth of our modern state system. For example at their peaks, the Ottoman Empire (1301–1922) and Russian Empire (1721–1917) each controlled vast territories and populations across Europe and Asia.

Although no one expects a return to this type of territorial empire, as we will see in the next chapter, there are many scholars of world politics who argue that the United States is dominating our modern state system through its economic and military dominance or **hegemony**. Although hegemonic control is principally indirect (sometimes direct, as in the invasions of Afghanistan and Iraq), the results, they argue, are the same: the exploitation of the subjugated peoples for the benefit of the **imperial** power. Do you think that U.S. hegemony exists today? If so, is U.S. hegemony different from the empires that have existed before it? Is U.S. hegemony a good or bad force in world politics?

The last of the three principal types of political organization that existed before our modern international system is the **feudal system** of medieval Europe. It emerged from the ruins of the Roman Empire and reached its zenith between the 9th and 15th centuries. Out of the ruins of the centrally controlled large Roman Empire grew a plethora of smaller units, including fiefdoms, principalities, duchies, and monarchies. Within this decentralized feudal system existed a complex web of relationships based principally on land ownership and kinship ties. At the top of the socioeconomic hierarchy was the king, prince, or lord who owned the land (fief). These "rulers" would offer all, or parts, of their land to vassals in return for military service. At the bottom of socioeconomic hierarchy were the serfs and peasants, who despite composing by far the largest demographic group in feudal society, possessed hardly any rights at all. If the fief was sold, the peasants and serfs were sold along with it. Although not technically slavery, their plight was little better.

The one centralizing force in European politics at this time was the Catholic Church. The Church was highly integrated into the feudal system (many of its bishops possessed fiefdoms), and ultimate political and religious authority lay with the Papacy in Rome. For example, when Charlemagne was crowned as Emperor of the Holy Roman Empire (the greatest attempt during this era to unify Western Europe under a single secular authority) in 800 C.E., the crown was placed upon his head by Pope Leo III.

Similarly, when the Crusades took place in the 12th and 13th centuries, they were conducted under Papal authority. Church doctrine also provided the moral framework for feudal society and helped justify its highly stratified nature. "One pledged fealty to one's lord in part out of respect for the lord's position in the Great Chain of Being (social hierarchy with the Pope at its pinnacle). Indeed, the vassal's lord could simply be understood as the local representative of the Lord of all Creation. All aspects of the [feudal] social system were [thus] ultimately legitimated by God" (Duvall 2003).

Although sovereignty, together with the separation of church and state, are now almost universally accepted principles in Western societies, other regions of the world are still enmeshed in the discussion of whether a higher religious authority than the state should exist. For example, some in the global Muslin community (or *Ummah*) still argue for the (re-) establishment of a pan-Islamic religious ruler (or *Caliphate*) who would play a similar role to that of the medieval papacy.

1.3.2 How Did Our Modern International System Emerge?

Our modern international system is obviously different from the three principal alternatives described above. It differs from the Classical Greek city-state system in that it is global and is composed of much larger units—states. It differs from empire in that it is anarchic—there is no higher authority than the sovereign state. It also differs from the feudal system because it is composed principally of sovereign states. So how did our modern international system emerge? When did the concept of the sovereign state emerge and how did it beat out the rival political units that have competed with it to become the truly global phenomenon it is today?

The date most often cited in the world politics literature for the birth of sovereignty and (consequently) the starting point of our modern international system is 1648. This date marks the culmination of the Thirty Years War, a devastating conflict that was primarily fought in Central Europe, but that at some point involved all of the major powers of the region. Composed of two treaties, the **Peace of Westphalia** that ended the war is commonly cited as having diminished the power of the Papacy and Holy Roman Emperor by (for the first time) establishing sovereign independent political units that could decide for themselves which religion they would adopt. It is because of this that out modern international system is often referred to as a **Westphalian system** of sovereign states. The notion of independent states free of external interference is also often referred to as **Westphalian sovereignty**.

Recent scholarship, however, has cast doubt on the Westphalian origins of sovereignty. For example, Andreas Osiander argues that it is a myth that the Peace of Westphalia established sovereignty, noting that the peace agreement is "silent on the issue of sovereignty. . . . It does not refer to any corollary of sovereignty either, such as non-intervention. It does not deal with the prerogatives of the [Holy Roman Emperor], nor does it mention the Pope" (Osiander 2001, 266). Stephen Krasner concurs, noting that the Peace of Westphalia "had little or nothing to do with conventional notions of sovereignty" (Krasner 2001, 232).

So, if the Peace of Westphalia was not the incubator of sovereignty that we have come to believe, when and how was the concept established? For Krasner and Osiander the origins of the modern notion of sovereignty lie not in international (peace) agreements, but in the writings of legal theorists. Krasner emphasizes the writings of the 17th century scholar, Emer de Vattel, and for this reason refers to the concept as *Westphalian/Vattelian sovereignty*, while Osiander places greater emphasis on the writings of 19th- and 20th-century legal theorists. Both agree also that the conquest of the sovereign state over other forms of political organization was a gradual process that involved a significant amount of serendipity. Krasner argues that states were simply able to take greater advantage of the "wealth and military power generated by technological and commercial changes that took place during the Middle Ages . . . [and] . . . were better able to promote economic development, fight wars and extract resources," among other things (Krasner 2001, 241). Osiander, on the other hand, highlights later developments, in particular the triumvirate of the French Revolution, the onset of industrialization, and the growth of the unifying phenomena of nationalist ideology, which together worked to make the sovereign state the most popular form of political organization in world politics (Osiander 2001, 281).

It was also these three phenomena (together with the American Revolution) that led to the connection of the state with the nation—creating the concept of the **nation-state**. A nation is a cultural grouping composed of people who identify with one another in some way, usually through a common language, religion, and/or shared traditions. Whether the idea of the nation or the state came first in world politics is still contested among historians, but in general one can see that, before and during the 18th century, states tended to create national identities to encourage their citizenry to defend their sovereign territory and pay taxes toward the cost of doing so. At this point states were forming nations. The American and French revolutions in the late 18th century thus helped forge the idea of national identity because both revolutionary groups made appeals to their respective nations to rise up against injustice. It was also after these events that state sovereignty began to be perceived as resting in the will of the people, rather than in divinely appointed monarchs—a concept now called **popular sovereignty**. These events precipitated a period of time during which more and more "nations" began to claim sovereignty on the basis of a right to "national" independence and self-determination. Perhaps the best examples of these were the creation of the modern states of Germany and Italy around 1870.

The trend of nations forming states that had begun with the American and French revolutions continued until the mid-20th century and the end World War II in 1945. At this point the trend returned to states trying to forge national identities, mostly in Asia and Africa, where new states were formed from the remnants of the old European colonial empires. Many of these new states had had their borders drawn by European colonial administrators who had given no consideration to the identities and allegiances of the people who lived within them. At the birth of their national independence many of these states were thus left with populations with multiple ethnic identities and languages (sometimes numbering in the hundreds and thousands) and no sense of national identity or national loyalty. Calling such states nation-states was (and in some cases continues to be) a misnomer.

Nationalism (a political ideology that promotes an individual's strong identification with a nation) has taken two general forms in world politics. The first is **ethnic nationalism**. In this variant, membership of a nation is determined by your ethnic identity. Can you trace your ancestry to an ethnic/national group? Do you share a common language or religious affiliation with the ethnic/national group? The second variant is **civic nationalism**. In this variant, membership of

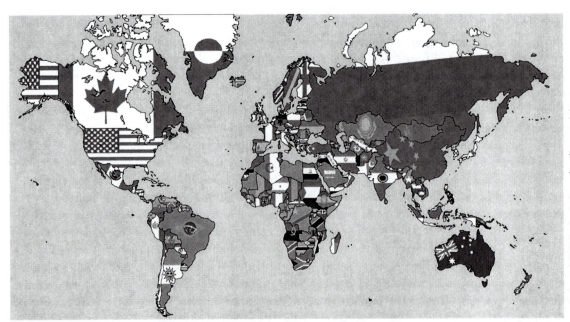

Figure 1.1. The world map with all states and their national flags.

the nation is not determined by ethnic identity, but the person's commitment to shared ideals, laws, and values. For example, becoming an American does not require that you trace your ancestry to the United States or that you belong to a particular religion. Rather, the American naturalization process requires only that you declare your belief in (and commit to defend) the constitution of the United States, which embodies the values, laws, and ideals of the American nation.

Since the foundation of the concept of the sovereign (nation)-state, state leaders have promoted **patriotism** (love of and devotion to one's country) as a means to engender national unity. This sense of unity was/is important to encourage ordinary citizens to volunteer to fight to protect and promote the state's interests (as well as pay the taxes that are necessary to pay for such action). Although intimately connected, patriotism is not the same as nationalism. As we will see in Chapter 3, nationalism has often been a cause of conflict and war because it tends to be exclusionary—nationalists desire their nation's independence and will often see their own nation as superior to others. Patriotism is more inclusive because it celebrates the national identity of the state, regardless of whether it is composed of many nations. Patriotism is therefore more often found in civic-nationalist states and nationalism in ethno-nationalist states.

Today, most states are perhaps best described not as nation-states, but as multi-nation-states. Although we know the United States has a national identity, we still recognize that it is composed of multiple ethnic identities and even (in the case of Native Americans) nations. For this reason, it is simpler and more accurate to call them states, as this text will continue to do.

1.4 What Is Power?

There is perhaps no more ubiquitous a term in world politics than **power**. You have probably heard it used constantly in discussions on television and read it numerous times in newspaper articles. The most important questions in our field appear to either concern it directly or imply a knowledge of it, including questions such as Is the United States a declining power? Does the rise of Chinese power threaten the United States? Can the United States eliminate terrorism?

Despite its popularity and importance, scholars of world politics have often shied away from detailed considerations of what power actually is (Smith 2012). It is simply easier to talk about the power that states possess (and how they might use it) than to analyze the nature of power itself. However, as with the other fundamental concepts that we have covered in this text, power is simply too important to treat in such a superficial manner.

Even the most prominent scholar on power in world politics, Joseph Nye, acknowledges that, despite its popularity, the concept of power remains "surprisingly elusive and difficult to measure." This makes it similarly difficult to reach a consensus on an appropriate definition. Nevertheless, he also argues that "such problems do not make the concept meaningless," no more than "love" should be considered meaningless simply because we cannot say "I love you 3.6 times more than I love something else" (Nye, The Future Of Power 2011, 3). Therefore, despite the difficulties involved, we must continue to strive for a better understanding of what power is and how it might/should be used, so that we can feel confident discussing it in the context of our debates in world politics.

Perhaps the best place to begin our analysis is to discuss the elements of power. When most people think of power in world politics, they think primarily of the military and economic power possessed by states. These first two elements of power are the easiest to understand because they are the most tangible; they are the easiest to see and measure. Military power tends to be measured in terms of the size of a state's military (army, naval, air) forces, including the number and types of soldiers, tanks, planes, and ships it possesses. Economic power tends to be measured in terms of economic variables, such as a state's Gross Domestic Product (GDP), and the natural resources at its disposal. Nevertheless, the more tangible elements of power still contain less-tangible resources that significantly affect a state's military and economic power, such as military morale and its population's levels of patriotism and intelligence.

The third element of power is composed principally of intangible factors, including the ideas, values, culture, and policies that states possess or adopt. Unlike the military and economic elements of power, these resources cannot be used to coerce others into changing their behavior. Military power is normally used to *coerce* others through the threat and use of physical force. Economic power is used to coerce others primarily through the imposition of economic (negative) sanctions or economic (positive) inducements. When power is used to coerce others in this way, it is generally referred to as **hard power**. The third element of power is not capable of such coercion, but instead relies on the ability to *attract* others to behave in certain ways. This ability to "pull" (to get them to want what you want) others, rather than "push" (compel them to do what you want) them, is referred to as **soft power** (Nye, The Future Of Power 2011, 20). The major components of a state's soft power are thus how pleasing its culture is to others, whether its values are thought to be attractive and consistently practiced, and whether its policies are seen as inclusive and legitimate (Nye, Get Smart 2009).

Along with the three elements of power described above, we can also recognize four essential qualities of power. The first is that power is *relational*: The possession and exercise of power only makes sense in terms of how it affects some other actor (McClurg 2010). We can only truly measure the power possessed by one actor if it is measured in relation to that possessed by another. It makes no sense to call yourself the most powerful person on an island if you are the only person on it!

The second quality of power is that it is *dynamic* (subject to relative change). Technological innovation, economic development, and war are all examples of factors in world politics that can cause relative changes in power. For example, the United States was the first state to build and use a nuclear bomb in 1945, which generated a significant shift in relative international power. Power was then rebalanced when the USSR tested one of its own in 1949. Today, China is a great deal more powerful than it was during the Cold War, due to its recent economic growth and development, whereas the Russian Federation is now much less powerful than it was when the USSR still existed. Relative power has changed in this way consistently throughout history, so much so that some scholars argue that there is a "law of uneven growth" operating in our international system (Walt 1981, 94). This means that all powerful states will eventually see their relative power rise and fall.

The third quality of power is one that is has become apparent already in our discussion; it is composed of both *intangible* and *tangible* elements. Scholars who have (and continue) to try to accurately measure the amount of power that states possess tend to concentrate on the tangible elements. This makes sense, because they are the most easily measured. However, as we have already seen, even the most tangible resources like military power have significant intangible elements that can affect their effectiveness. History is replete with examples of larger armies being defeated by less numerical foes simply because they had better generals. How can one measure such intangibles as leadership?

The fourth quality of power is that it is *contextual*; its effectiveness depends on the context in which it is being used. Your professor may be able to use the hard power of grade sanctions and inducements to make you sit and listen to them teach, but he or she will not be able to use that power to skip the line at lunchtime! The term used to describe how easily power resources can be transferred and utilized from one context (or issue-area) to another is **fungibility**. Some highly fungible power resources, like money, can be utilized in many contexts. For example, your professor might pay you to sit and listen to her teach and bribe someone financially to allow her to cut in line for lunch. The authority (soft power) a professor possesses may also encourage you to allow them to cut in line, but how well will it work with someone who doesn't know (or respect) them? You can probably already tell that hard power tends to be more fungible than soft power, but that doesn't mean it is always the most effective (see discussion box). So, now that we know the essential elements and qualities of power, is it possible to form a definition that encompasses all of them? Power, just like all the concepts we have covered so far, is contested, so there can be no surprise that its definition is too! We might therefore look at some of the best examples. Perhaps the easiest definition to remember is that power is the ability to get others to do what you want them to do (and not to do what you don't want them to do). Nye prefers the more eloquent definition of power as "the capacity to do things and in social situations to affect others to get the outcomes we want" (Nye, The Future Of Power 2011, 5). Hans Morgenthau, a famous scholar of world politics with

DISCUSSION BOX

What Is the Correct Balance of Hard and Soft Power?

In 2003, Joseph S. Nye coined the term **smart power** to argue that states need more than either hard or soft power alone in order to achieve their foreign policy goals in the 21st century. Smart power thus requires the adoption of "smart strategies that combine the tools of both hard and soft power" (Nye, Get Smart 2009).

Nye argues that soft power is becoming increasingly important in our modern international system. In the 21st century even the most powerful states will be unable to achieve the main foreign policy goals alone. For example, ensuring international financial stability and limiting global climate change are both vital to the future prosperity and safety of Americans, but the United States needs global cooperation to achieve them. The United States thus needs to maintain coalitions or networks of supporting states and non-state actors in these issue areas, something only soft power can achieve effectively (Nye, The Future Of Power 2011, 218–219).

However, in 2017 the estimated budgets of the US Department of Defense and Department of State were 575 billion and 50 billion respectively. In light of Nye's arguments, do you think this is a "smart" balance? What do you think the correct balance should be?

whom you will become familiar in the next chapter, described power as "anything that establishes and maintains the power of man over man . . . from physical violence to the most subtle psychological ties by which one mind controls another" (Morgenthau 1965, 9). Each of these definitions conveys the same message about the nature and uses of power.

Key Terms

absolute sovereignty
city-state system
civic nationalism
deduction
empire
empirical
ethnic nationalism
failed state
feudal system
fungibility
hard power
hegemony
hypothesis
Imperial
individual
intergovernmental organization (IGO)
international organization (IO)
international political economy (IPE)
international recognition
International relations
international security

multinational corporation (MNC)
nationalism
nation-state
nongovernmental organization (NGO)
non-state actor
patriotism
Peace of Westphalia
popular sovereignty
power
preemption
quasi-state
smart power
soft power
sovereignty
sovereign equality
state
sub-state actor
transnational nongovernmental organization (TNGO)
Westphalian sovereignty
Westphalian system

2

Theories and Foreign Policies

Image © Elenarts, 2013. Used under license from Shutterstock, Inc.

CHAPTER OUTLINE

2.0 Why Are Theories Important?

Imagine that you are campaigning to become president of the United States. You are about to conduct a televised debate with your opponent on foreign policy. To do well, you will need to formulate positions on a whole range of important issues, and you will have to explain your reasoning to the audience in order to convince them you are correct. Should the United States allow North Korea to keep its nuclear weapons? Should the United States seek to spread democracy in the Middle East? Is China a growing threat to the United States? Should the United States increase its foreign aid to Africa? Should the United States continue its embargo of Cuba when China is one of its greatest trading partners? These are just some of the questions you will face. To be persuasive, you will have to convince the audience that you can make sense of all these different issues and the factors that influence them. In other words, you will have to convince them that you understand how the world works.

Is this actually possible? The world is such a large place, full of different states, cultures and organizations! Of all the historical and contemporary information that is available to you, how can you identify what is important to know from that which is superfluous? To do so we must think theoretically. A **theory** is composed of a set of interrelated statements or assumptions that explain a recurring phenomenon. In world politics, such phenomena include wars or periods of peace, rising prosperity, or increasing economic disparities between states. Theories of world politics thus act like a highlighter pen through history—they help us identify the information that is important. They act like a relief map, showing us the important features of world politics and how they are connected. Of course, if we can explain why a phenomenon recurs, we can use that information to help us avoid it (as in the case of war) or bring it about (as in the case of economic prosperity). This is the connection between theory and foreign policy and we will analyze this connection further in the next chapter.

2.1 How Can We Judge Theories?

So, how can we know which theory is best? Of course, the best theory will be the one that is most **accurate**—the one that truly explains how the world works. However, as we will see, in world politics there are a number of contending theories, all of which claim to be the most accurate. So how can we decide between them? The best way is to test them against empirical evidence. In the hard sciences, like chemistry and physics, a great deal of testing takes place in the laboratory. The goal is to recreate an experiment time and time again, thus constantly reproducing the same results under the same conditions. In this way a theory can be verified or discredited. Scientists can also remove and add components to test their individual effects. However, in the social sciences, and particularly in world politics, this is often impossible. For example, how can we test the hypothesis that Adolf Hitler was responsible for WWII? One way would be to recreate all the conditions in the world that existed in the 1930s and just leave out Hitler. If WWII starts again, Hitler could not have been its cause. Although this may seem a ridiculous suggestion, it helps explain why there are still a number of competing theories in world politics. The quest for us as students of world politics is thus to test our theories and answer **counterfactuals**, like the one posited above, despite the limitations of our discipline.

Other qualities of a theory that are deemed important include how **parsimonious** it is and its explanatory **range**. Parsimony is a measure of simplicity. The more parsimonious a theory is, the

Table 2.1   Qualities of Theories

Quality of Theory	Explanation
Accuracy	How well does it explain world politics?
Parsimony	How simple is it?
Range	How much behavior does it explain?
Prediction	Can it predict future events?

simpler it is. This is often referred to as the principle of **Occam's Razor**, after the 14th-century English philosopher, William of Ockham. A theory's explanatory range is a measure of how much behavior it purports to explain. A theory of world politics is therefore a theory with a much greater range than a theory of youth crime in inner cities.

A final quality that is often cited is a theory's ability to **predict** the future. If a theory can accurately explain why states have gone to war in the past and why they are at war in the present, then maybe it can predict which (and when) states will go to war in the future. A theory with such predictive qualities would naturally be valued more than one without them.

To summarize, the best theory of world politics will be the one that is the most accurate, for that will be the one that best explains world politics. It will therefore make the best foundation for a successful foreign policy. Of two theories with equal accuracy and range, the most parsimonious is best. Finally, of two theories with equal accuracy, range, and parsimony, the one with the greatest predictive qualities is best (see Table 2.1).

2.2 Contending Theories of World Politics

There are many theories of world politics. For example, more recently generated theories include Feminism and Constructivism. Unfortunately, an introductory course like this one does not have the time to cover all the theories of world politics that we would like. This text will therefore concentrate on providing you with a firm understanding of the oldest and most prominent theories in the field. Hopefully, you will use this as a foundation to take more specialized courses in the future.

The three oldest and most prominent theories of world politics are *Realism, Liberalism,* and the *Radical Approach*. Proponents of each theory argue that theirs explains world politics the best and will therefore make the best foundation for a successful foreign policy. The challenge for you as a student of world politics is to compare and contrast these theories, to judge them by the criteria we have established, and to decide for yourself which one you think is best. The importance of this task cannot be overstated. The theory you support will act as the foundation for your foreign policy proposals. If the United States adopts the wrong policies, it could lead to economic decline, war, and global insecurity!

Of these theories, the oldest is **Realism**. As we will see, its origins date back to the writings of a Greek historian in the 5th century B.C.E., Thucydides. Liberalism, on the other hand, dates back to at least the Enlightenment period of the 17th and 18th centuries. The Radical Approach has its beginnings in the mid-19th century.

The rest of this chapter will thus provide an explanation of these theories. For each theory, four questions will be asked:

1. What are the basic assumptions of the theory?
2. How has the theory evolved?
3. How does the theory explain world politics?
4. Which levels of analysis does the theory operate on?

By asking these questions, we can begin to understand their similarities and differences and start the process of testing and assessing them.

2.3 Theories and Levels of Analysis

Although each of the three theories we are about to discuss differs fundamentally on how it explains world politics, the theories do share certain commonalities. As first documented by a now famous Realist scholar, Kenneth Waltz, the theories that scholars have proposed to explain phenomena in world politics, like war and peace, have tended to do so on at least one of three *levels of analysis* (Waltz 1957). These three levels are the individual (first), the state (second), and the international (third). What Waltz intuitively noticed was that despite the fact that theories may focus on different causes of those phenomena, they still tend to look for those cause(s) in the nature of the individual, in the nature of the state, or in the nature of international system.

For example, some theories will explain the major events in world politics as the outcome of decisions by individual state leaders. They might blame World War II on the evil behavior of one individual, Adolf Hitler. Or they might blame the decision of Joseph Stalin, the leader of the then Soviet Union, to sign a non-aggression pact with Hitler in 1939 and thus embolden him to invade France. Or they might suggest that the reason conflict and war has been so prevalent throughout history is that human nature is selfish or aggressive. All of these theories operate on the individual level of analysis in explaining the phenomena in question.

Other theories will focus on causes found that the state level. For example, a theory might propose that democratic states are less aggressive than dictatorships. Another theory might propose that states with capitalist economies act more imperially than those without. Another might suggest that the nature of states is just like human nature, in that it too is selfish and aggressive. All these theories focus on the nature of the state and thus operate on the state level of analysis in order to explain the phenomena in question.

Finally, some theories might argue that the principal causes of the phenomena we are seeking to explain are not to be found in the nature of the individual, or of the state, but instead in the nature (or level) of the international system. For example, some theories might suggest that it is the anarchic nature of our international system that leaves states and individuals feeling vulnerable and scared, and it is this fear that motivates states to behave aggressively. Other theories might suggest that increasing economic disparities in world politics are being caused by the global spread of capitalism. As these theories focus on the nature of the international system, they are said to operate on the international (or systemic) level of analysis.

Each of the three theories we are about to discuss locate the principal causes of phenomena in world politics on at least one of these three levels of analysis. In fact, we will find that each theory actually tends to focus on more than one level. This suggests that phenomena in world politics, like war, peace, and poverty, have more than one cause and that these causes can interact to produce the phenomena in question.

Perhaps the best way to clarify something that may seem at this point to be quite complex and difficult to comprehend is to learn about each of the three theories we are concerned with and try to identify on which levels of analysis it operates. Doing so will allow us to clarify the assumptions on which each theory is based and thus help us to identify the information we may need in order to prove or disprove each theory.

2.4 Introduction to Realism

Realism has historically been the most dominant theory of world politics. Although the term *Realism* was only coined in the early 20th century, its contemporary adherents claim that many prominent historians, philosophers, and political leaders throughout history have espoused its basic tenets. As this section will explain, these figures date back as far as the 5th century B.C.E.

2.4.1 Basic Assumptions of Realism

1. Human nature is selfish.
2. States are the only important actors in world politics.

3. States are unitary and rational actors.
4. The international system is anarchic.
5. States want to survive and will therefore seek to maximize their power.

2.4.2 The Evolution of Realism

Thucydides, the ostensible father of Realism, wrote an account of the second Peloponnesian War (431–404 b.c.e.), which was fought between the two most powerful city-states of Ancient Greece (Hellas), Athens and Sparta. Thucydides had been an Athenian general, but in the midst of the war he was deemed to have failed in his duties and, as punishment, was exiled from his home city-state for 20 years. Fortunately, rather than fading into obscurity, Thucydides decided to use his time in exile to write a historical account of the war he had fought in, a war that was to eventually affect the whole Hellenic system and last for 27 years. For the Greeks it was the equivalent of a modern world war. Unlike his predecessors, however, Thucydides was not content to look for the cause of conflicts in the whims of the Gods. Instead, by traveling, interviewing, and recording events, he sought to ascertain the cause of the war in the actions and decisions of the men involved. For this reason, he is also known as one of the founders of modern scientific historical studies.

Figure 2.1. Thucydides.

The end product of this odyssey for Thucydides was his *History of the Peloponnesian Wars*. This book is a seminal one for Realists because in explaining the cause of the Second Peloponnesian War, they believe Thucydides unearthed truths about the behavior of states that are still relevant today. So what did Thucydides believe caused the war? His answer was "*the rising power of Athens and the fear it instilled in Sparta.*"

This explanation tells us that Thucydides did not believe that differences in the political systems or social orders of Athens and Sparta had caused the war. Sparta was an **authoritarian** and militaristic state. It was led by two kings, both chosen from among the city's noble families. All its male citizens entered military service at the age of 7. When leaving for battle, Spartan mothers would tell their sons, "with your shield, or on it," meaning that they must return victorious or dead. Sparta was also an agrarian state that, with all its male citizens in military service, depended on the work of tens of thousands of slaves (helots). Athens, on the other hand, was a much more **democratic** state. All of its male citizens could vote in its Assembly, which met regularly to decide on a broad range of government policies, including military operations. The Assembly was also responsible for electing 10 generals each year to lead the Athenian government, and it could hold each of them accountable for his actions throughout their tenure. Unlike Sparta, which was located in the middle of the Peloponnesian peninsula, Athens was located on the coast. This encouraged it to become a sea-faring state and to build trading relationships with many of the city-states located around the Aegean Sea. Its increasing wealth and love of high culture also led its government to become a patron to many great works of architecture and art. Its poets and philosophers, like Sophocles, Plato, and Socrates, are still some of the most renowned today.

Nevertheless, it was not these internal differences that Thucydides believed caused the war between Athens and Sparta, but the *changing distribution of power* between them. Sparta, with its powerful army, had traditionally led the Hellenic system, as it had when the Greeks fought the Persians at the battle of Thermopylae in 480 b.c.e. After this battle, however, the Athenians continued to grow in power, as Athens' navy expanded along with its trading relationships. It eventually broke away from its alliance with the Spartans and created its own alliance, the **Delian League**. Sparta, although still leader of the **Peloponnesian League**, was economically static. It remained the same agrarian, slave-holding city-state it had always been.

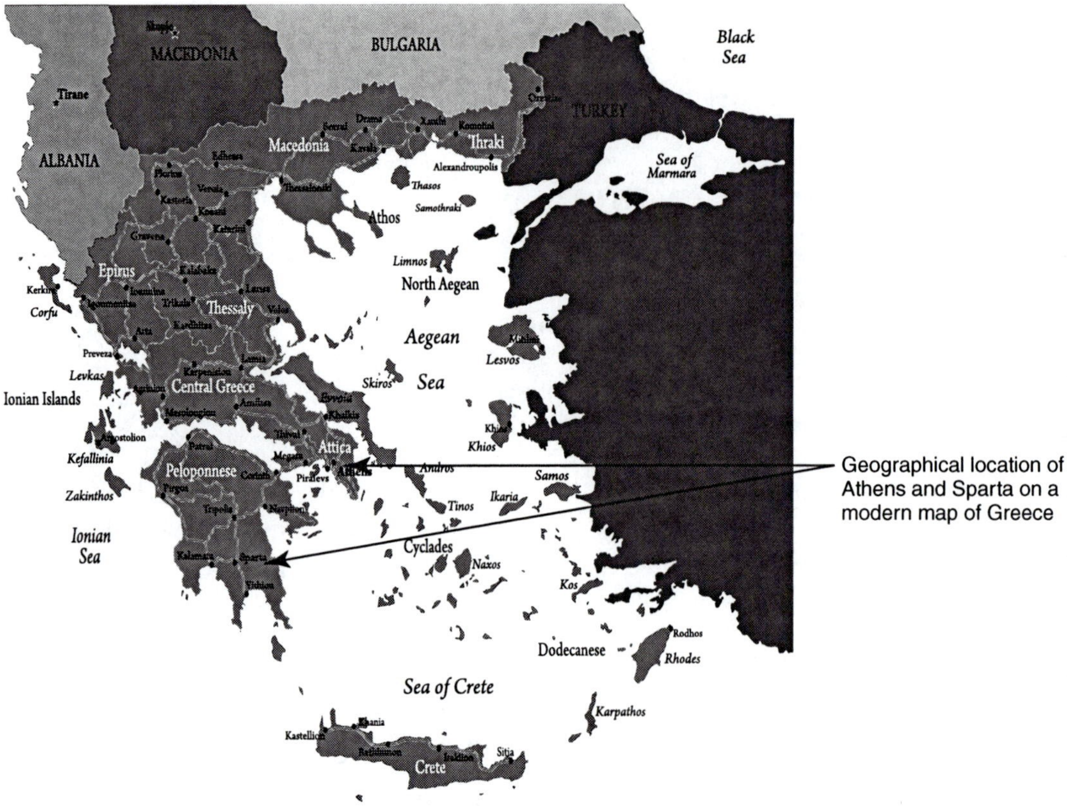

Geographical location of Athens and Sparta on a modern map of Greece

Image © Serban Bogdan, 2013. Used under license from Shutterstock, Inc.

Figure 2.2.

This meant that while Sparta had not actually lost any power, it was nevertheless still losing power in relation to Athens. In other words, although Sparta's **absolute** amount of power remained the same, its power **relative** to that of Athens was diminishing. As the **balance of power** changed increasingly in favor of the Athenians, Sparta became more and more concerned that Athens might attack it. Rather than wait for the Athenians to attack, Sparta thus decided to attack first, which it did in 431 B.C.E. Of course, it could have waited to ascertain if the Athenians had peaceful intentions, but with its very survival at stake, how could it take the risk? Who would protect the Spartans if Athens attacked? Hellas was an **anarchic** city-state system, so there was no central authority or world government that could come to its rescue. As a **rational** state, Sparta therefore had little choice. It launched what we would call today a **preemptive war**.

So, what are the truths about the behavior of states that Thucydides unearthed in this account that Realists believe are still relevant today? Essentially, Thucydides had highlighted the effects of fear and the importance of power in world politics. For Realists his account conveys the timeless lesson that states in an anarchic system cannot be sure of the intentions of other states and therefore have to be constantly concerned with the balance of power. This condition is today called a **security dilemma**. The effect of the security dilemma is that even when states seek power only to protect themselves, their growth in power generates fear in other states. It is this fear of a change in the balance of power, or a potential change, that leads states like Sparta to start wars.

How did Thucydides believe state leaders should behave in such a world? As power is the principal arbiter of conflict in an anarchic system, state leaders have to be guided by pragmatism rather than idealism. One can hope that the world they live in is different; that states will respect rules and seek negotiated compromise, but that is simply being unrealistic.

Thucydides conveys this message most explicitly in his infamous account of the interaction that took place between the Athenians and the city-state of Melos in 416 B.C.E. Now referred to as the

Melian Dialogue, Thucydides' account places the Athenian navy on the shores of Melos, a small, seemingly inconsequential, island state located in the middle of the Aegean Sea. Melos had stayed neutral in the Peloponnesian War, having refused to join either the Delian or Peloponnesian Leagues, but the Athenians were not content with this. With their great navy stationed off the island's coast, the Athenian delegates warned the Melian leaders that they could not afford for them to stay neutral because the Spartans would perceive this as Athenian weakness. If the great Athenian empire could not force Melos to capitulate, maybe it was not as powerful as the Spartans had thought! So they gave the Melians an ultimatum; join our Delian League and be left alone, or refuse and be destroyed.

What should they do? Idealism tells us that they should stand up to the Athenians and demand to be left alone; to insist on their right to independence; and to argue that the Athenians have no right to threaten them or compel them to join their alliance. This is what the Melians actually did. The result was an Athenian assault that ended with the slaughter of all the Melian males and the sale of all the Melian women and children into slavery. Athens even transplanted 500 of its own colonists to inhabit the island. The Melian state and people had been obliterated!

Thucydides' lesson is evident. Only power can protect you in an anarchic system. Do not be idealistic when you are responsible for the lives of your citizens. Do not put your trust in "laws" or "rights," because states will disregard them when convenient. In the words of the Athenian delegates to Melos, in an anarchic system, "the strong do what they can and the weak suffer what they want." The Melian leaders ignored this reality and all of Melos paid the price!

Niccolo Machiavelli (1469–1527) is another pioneer of Realist thought. When he wrote his most famous text, *The Prince* (1532), he was a former statesman of Florence, a powerful city-state in the Italian city-state system. *The Prince* is essentially a guidebook for effective leadership that Machiavelli hoped the ruling family of Florence, the Medici, would adopt. Believing that the world was like a jungle, in which only the strongest and wisest states could survive, Machiavelli encouraged the Medici to act like "both the lion and the fox." This meant that state leaders needed to "be like lions" and acquire as much power as possible, in order to be strong enough to defend their state. They also needed to be cunning "like the fox," not only to avoid traps that might be laid by other states, but also to lay traps of their own. States, he argued, could never fully trust one another, even if they claimed to be allies. States are self-interested; they only have their own interests in mind.

Machiavelli's account of world politics and the recommendations he made for good leadership were highly controversial, even in his own time. It shocked the moral conscience of many Florentines to be told that good leadership involved acquiring and maintaining power and that any actions to that purpose were appropriate. Even today, to be called Machiavellian is to be accused of expediency and having no ethical boundaries.

Figure 2.3. Niccolo Machiavelli.

However, Realists argue that Machiavelli has been misunderstood. Machiavelli was not without moral and ethical concerns. He simply believed that the most important moral duty of state leaders was to protect their citizens—it was their **civic duty**. Sometimes this would require them to act in ways that might appear abhorrent. To attack a state before it had attacked you; to pay mercenaries to fight; to assassinate leaders of other states. Nevertheless, for Machiavelli, state leaders are bound by the responsibilities of their office to do whatever is required to protect their state in a dangerous world. This is called **situational ethics**, meaning that the definition of what constitutes ethical or moral behavior depends on the responsibilities of the individual.

Machiavelli, like all Realists, would prefer not to have to make such recommendations, but what choice is there? In fact, the most immoral behavior would be for state leaders not to act in the way he suggests, for that would lead inevitably to the destruction of the state for which they were responsible. They would be failing in their civic duty. In this way Machiavelli echoes the lessons of Thucydides' Melian Dialogue.

Figure 2.4. Thomas Hobbes.

A third pioneer of Realism is **Thomas Hobbes** (1588–1679), an English political philosopher who wrote *The Leviathan* (1651). Like his Realist predecessors, Hobbes lived during tumultuous times, having lived through the English Civil War (1642–1651). In 1628 he produced the first English translation of Thucydides' *History* from its original Greek.

In *The Leviathan*, Hobbes imagines what life would be like if the state no longer had a sovereign to maintain law and order. This situation he called the "**state of nature**." His conclusion was that life for every individual would be *"solitary, poor, nasty, brutish and short."* Why was this so? Hobbes believed that human nature was selfish and egotistical. Without the constraints of government, human nature would be free to express itself in violence. Even the most powerful individual would be terribly scared in the state of nature because at some point he would need to sleep. It is this fear that compels individuals to sacrifice their freedoms in return for the imposition of order and security by a powerful central government—a Leviathan.

However, if every group of individuals creates its own Leviathan to escape the state of nature, this produces a world of Leviathans without a central government to instill order and security amongst them. In other words, if we extrapolate Hobbes' "domestic state of nature" to world politics, we can see that our anarchic international system resembles an "international state of nature."

So why isn't life for states in our modern anarchic international system "solitary, poor, nasty brutish and short"? Why doesn't the fear of living in an "international state of nature" propel states to create a world Leviathan, or one-world government, just as individuals in the domestic state of nature are propelled to create a domestic Leviathan? The answer lies in the ability of states to protect themselves. States are not as vulnerable as individuals. They do not sleep! If states feel sufficiently secure, they will not relinquish their sovereignty in order to escape international anarchy.

Hobbes thus makes explicit the philosophical underpinnings of modern Realist theory. Human nature is selfish, egotistical, and power-hungry. If states are simply collections of individuals, then the nature of states will reflect human nature. States will also be selfish, egotistical, and power-hungry. However, as there is insufficient fear to compel them to create a world Leviathan, they will continue to exist in an anarchic international system. This consigns them to live in a perpetual security dilemma, in which all states must be concerned with the balance of power.

The most important Realist of the 20th century was **Hans J. Morgenthau** (1904–1980). In his seminal text, ***Politics Among Nations*** (1948) Morgenthau became the first scholar to generate a true Realist theory of world politics. International politics, he believed, was governed by objective, universal laws, based on "the concept of [national] interest defined in terms of power" (Morgenthau 1965, Politics Among Nations: The Struggle for Power and Peace 1965).

The foundation of Morgenthau's theory was his answer to two questions. The first was, Why do states want power? The second was, How much do they want? His answer to the first question was twofold. First, he agreed with his Realist predecessors that states were power-hungry because their nature was a reflection of human nature. However, he also

Figure 2.5. Hans J. Morgenthau.

recognized that they were compelled to seek power to ensure their survival in an anarchic international system. His answer to the second question was that states would seek as much power as possible. How could states be sure they had sufficient power to defeat an opponent in the present? Equally importantly, how could they ever know whether they had enough power to defeat a future opponent? In such uncertainty, states are compelled to acquire as much power as possible—they must therefore be **power-maximizers**.

If states are power-maximizers, then they will naturally all seek to become the **hegemon** (dominant power) of the international system. Of course, while every state might aspire to this, each must also fear that another will achieve it before them. Thus, while trying to achieve hegemony themselves, every state must work to ensure that hegemony is not achieved by another. This, Morgenthau argued, is accomplished in the international system through "a configuration that is called the balance of power" (Morgenthau 1985, Politics Among Nations: The Struggle for Power and Peace 1985). Put simply, the desire of each state to prevent another from achieving hegemony leads ineluctably to a balance of power.

Morgenthau also described the ways in which states could maintain the balance of power. The principal ways were to either build up their own power—known as **internal balancing**—or create an alliance with other states—known as **external balancing**. Because states could not fully trust other states, Morgenthau expected them to "shun alliances" (Morgenthau 1985, Politics Among Nations: The Struggle for Power and Peace 1985) if they believed they were strong enough to maintain the balance of power alone.

2.4.3 Realism

We can now appreciate how Realism has developed into a modern theory of world politics. Its development began at least 2,500 years ago with the Greek historian, Thucydides, and it has since been influenced by many other important scholars, some of whom have been covered here.

Realism is a **state-centric** theory, which means it concerns itself only with the behavior of the most powerful actors in world politics—states. Realism treats states as **unitary** and **rational** actors. In other words, states act like rational individuals applying a cost-benefit analysis to the different options available to them in world politics. Realists thus assume that states will choose the option that provides them with the greatest amount of power at the least cost.

The most powerful states are referred to as **Great Powers**, and at any one time the international system contains one or more of them. A system with a single Great Power is called a **unipolar system**. A system with two Great Powers is called a **bipolar system**. A system containing three or more Great Powers is called a **multipolar system**.

Realists believe states are power-maximizers because they have an innate desire for power. However, they also believe that the pursuit of power is a rational reaction to the dangers of living in an anarchic international system. If states are rational, want to survive, and exist in a security dilemma, then they will all be driven to acquire power and constantly concerned with maintaining a **relative power** advantage over others.

If a state is not able to be the most powerful state in the system, it will at least try to balance the power of the most powerful state or states. This can be achieved through internal and/or external balancing. States with equal power are deterred from attacking one another because they cannot be assured of winning a subsequent war. Realists thus believe the international system is most **stable**, meaning war between the Great Powers is least likely to occur when a balance of power exists. How the balance of power will be configured obviously depends on whether a unipolar, bipolar, or multipolar system exists. It should be obvious from the above outline that (relative) power and the balance of power are very important concepts in Realism. For this reason Realism is also known as **Power Politics**.

2.4.4 Realism and Levels of Analysis

As noted in the introduction to the concept of levels of analysis (Section 2.2), theories of world politics tend to operate on more than one level of analysis; and Realism is no exception. Through the contributions of the prominent Realists that we have covered in this text, we can see that Realism actually operates on all three.

All the principal contributors to the development of Realist theory, including Thucydides, Machiavelli, Hobbes, and Morgenthau, possessed a pessimistic view of human nature. Realism could be identified, therefore, as a first (individual)-level theory. However, Realists believe that the state (as a collection of individuals) is a reflection of human nature, and that the nature of the state is also selfish and prone to aggression. Because Realists believe the state is the most important actor in world politics, it is therefore more appropriate to identify it as a second (state)-level theory.

Despite being primarily a second-level theory, Realism also operates on the third (systemic) level of analysis. While Thucydides held a pessimistic view of human nature, he believed the principal cause of the Peloponnesian War was the changing balance of power between two states, Athens and Sparta. Hobbes also held a pessimistic view of human nature, but argued that an anarchic system was necessary before conflict would result. Morgenthau argued that states are power-maximizers because they reflect human nature, but he believed the balance of power could reduce the likelihood of war.

Perhaps you can now see how Realism operates on all three levels of analysis and how the three levels interact to produce a more complete theory of world politics. The state is selfish and power-hungry because it reflects human nature, but phenomena like wars and peace can only be explained by combining this understanding with assumptions at the international level of analysis.

2.5 Introduction to Liberalism

Liberalism has developed as the primary theoretical competitor to Realism. Its philosophical roots spouted during the Enlightenment period of the 17th and 18th centuries, in the writings of such luminaries as John Locke and Immanuel Kant. Although Liberalism (like Realism) is today a broad theoretical school, with many scholars having spawned competing branches of the theory, its adherents all agree that there exists much greater potential for progress in world politics than Realists believe. What prevents such progress from being achieved? How can these impediments to progress be overcome? These are the central questions of Liberalism, and this section will explain how some of the most eminent Liberal scholars have tried to answer them.

2.5.1 Basic Assumptions of Liberalism

1. Human nature is not innately selfish.
2. States and non-state actors are important in world politics.
3. States do not act according to the unitary-rational actor model.
4. Although states exist in an anarchic system, peaceful relations can abound.
5. Peaceful relations are produced by democracy, international institutions, and economic interdependence.

2.5.2 The Evolution of Liberalism

Perhaps the most significant historical figure in the development of Liberalism is the German philosopher, **Immanuel Kant** (1724–1804). In his essay, *Perpetual Peace* (1795), Kant argued that the state of nature described by Hobbes was not inescapable. Rather, through reason, mankind could generate a just political and legal solution to the problems inherent in both domestic and international anarchy. Kant's own suggestions were for states to adopt republican political constitutions and for these states to then form an international federation of republics that could operate under the rule of law. This arrangement, he believed, would constitute a "pacific union."

The first element of Kant's argument today provides the theoretical foundation for the **Democratic Peace Thesis** (DPT). The DPT states that liberal democracies do not (or are very unlikely to) go to war with one another. Kant originally argued that republics would be more peaceful toward one another. To be considered a republic, a state had to have both a representative government and a system of checks and balances—what we would today call a liberal democracy. Kant believed this was the most effective political arrangement for the protection of individual political and economic freedoms and that it would also have certain repercussions for the behavior of these states toward one another.

Figure 2.6. Immanuel Kant.

As Michael Doyle explains, there are three pillars to Kant's argument (Doyle 2005). The first is a constitutional pillar. Kant argued that if the consent of the citizen was required for a republic to go to war, then this would cause the state to hesitate. The reason for this caution is that the ordinary citizen is averse to suffering the consequences of war, which include

> having to fight, having to pay the cost of war from their own resources, having painfully to repair the devastation war leaves behind, and, to fill up the measure of evils, load themselves with a heavy national debt that would embitter peace itself . . . ' (Doyle 1983, 229)

States that were not republican, on the other hand, could go to war at the whim of their unaccountable leaders for whom a "declaration of war [was] the easiest thing in the world to decide upon" (Doyle 1983, 229).

The second pillar of Kant's argument is a normative one. As republics are founded on principles of transparency, accountability, and individual freedom, they perceive each other as being just and legitimate. They therefore act toward one another with the same degree of respect and accommodation that they inherently provide to their citizens. However, non-republics, with their illiberal and undemocratic governments, are perceived as being in a "state of aggression" with their own people. This causes republics to treat them with suspicion (Doyle 2005, 464).

Finally, the third pillar is an economic one. Kant's republics have free markets that act according to Liberal economic theory. This suggests that liberal democracies will become ever greater trading partners and thus increasingly economically **interdependent**. As liberal governments play a limited role in the marketplace, the majority of these economic interactions will be transnational in nature. This will generate a lobby of transnational economic actors whose concern for continued prosperity will compel them to pressure for mutual accommodation and peaceful conflict resolution during times of tension. On the other hand, in their economic relations with non-liberal states, liberal states will always fear potential state manipulation of trade and an unwillingness to enforce the rule of law (Doyle 2005, 465).

Interdependence: Although usually implied to mean "mutual dependence," interdependence can mean simply that the decisions of states significantly affect one another. For example, if the United States decided to stop importing foreign-made goods, this would dramatically affect the economies of many states around the world. Liberals argue that interdependence encourages states to perceive their own security and prosperity to be dependent on the security and prosperity of others. Interdependence will therefore discourage states from behaving aggressively, or from making decisions that may engender retaliation from states on which they are dependent. Realists, on the other hand, argue that most so-called "interdependent" relationships do not consist of symmetric power relations, but actually are asymmetric. This means that rather than being "mutually dependent," one state tends to be more dependent than another. The state that is most dependent is therefore most vulnerable. For example, as the trading relationship between China and the United States grows, Liberals tend to see greater interdependence, while Realists argue that the growing U.S. trade deficit with China is leaving it increasingly vulnerable.

Significantly, these three pillars, when combined, explain not only why liberal democracies do not go to war with one another, but also why they are prone to war and imperialism with non-liberal states (Doyle 2005, 464). For contemporary Democratic Peace theorists, therefore, it is no surprise to find that statistical studies show that democracies go to war just as often as authoritarian states. However, despite going to war just as often as non-democracies, they do not go to war with one another.

Perhaps the most famous 20th-century Liberal scholar and politician is former U.S. president **Woodrow Wilson** (1856–1924). Wilson played an integral role in putting the second element of Kant's ideas into practice—that of a "federation" of states that could maintain world order.

Although he initially sought to keep the United States out of World War I, he eventually concluded that U.S. leadership would be essential in the post-war era if the world was to avoid a reoccurrence of the tragedy. In January 1918 he therefore delivered his "14 points" to Congress, in which he outlined the basis for a Liberal post-war international order. His principal concerns were first, to protect the sovereignty of nations; second, to provide the right of **self-determination** to ethnic groups that had historically been subjugated by the European colonial powers; and third, he expressed a desire to expand free trade. Finally, he called for the creation of an "association of nations" that could protect "strong and weak nations alike." This association was included in the **Treaty of Versailles** (which ended World War I) and was called the **League of Nations**.

Figure 2.7. Woodrow Wilson.

The League thus became the first global **collective security** organization. Collective security is essentially a Liberal alternative to Realist balance of power politics. As explained in the previous section, Realists believe that states need to pursue power in order to protect themselves. They also need to join alliances to maintain the balance of power. Such alliances are called **collective defense** organizations. The principal commitment in such organizations is to protect fellow members from an attack that originates from outside of the organization. For example, the **North Atlantic Treaty Organization (NATO)** is a modern collective defense organization that was initially created in 1949 in order to defend against a Soviet attack.

NATO: a collective defense organization created in 1949 to defend against a potential Soviet attack. It was initially composed of 12 members, including the United States and Canada. Since the end of the Cold War and the collapse of the Soviet Union, NATO has conducted three 'rounds of enlargement'. It is now composed of 29 countries. Montenegro was the last to join in 2017. Article 5 of its founding document, the Washington Treaty, commits all its members to defend one another against attack from outside of the organization. As it no longer faces a major military threat like the Soviet Union, NATO continues to reassess its role in the post-Cold War era. Website: www.nato.int

UN: a collective security organization created in 1945 as a successor to the League of Nations. It was initially composed of 51 states. As of 2017, it has 193 members. All members commit themselves to defend victims against aggression. Chapter VII of the UN Charter empowers its most powerful body, the Security Council, to mandate its members to use any means necessary to maintain international peace and security. Website: www.un.org

Wilson believed that World War I had started because European leaders had followed the dictates of Realism. They had created collective defense organizations like the **Triple Entente** and **Triple Alliance**. They had also conquered and subjugated weaker nations across the globe in the pursuit of power. When Germany attacked France and Russia in 1914, it had done so because of its fear of encirclement by members of an opposing alliance. Thus, by acting on Realist prescriptions, European leaders had actually created the kind of world that Realism suggests always exists. In essence, Realism had become a **self-fulfilling prophecy**.

Triple Alliance: An alliance composed of Germany, Austria and Italy formed before World War I.

Triple Entente: An alliance composed of Russia, France and the UK formed before World War I.

Self-fulfilling prophecy: A prediction that directly or indirectly causes itself to come true.

First Persian Gulf War: After the invasion of Kuwait by Iraq in August 1990, the UN Security Council passed a number of resolutions that called for an immediate Iraqi withdrawal and imposed a range of sanctions on Iraq in order to encourage it to comply. On 29 November 1990 the Security Council passed Res. 678 , which imposed a deadline of 15 January 1991 for an Iraqi withdrawal and authorized the use of 'all necessary means' by the international community to restore Kuwaiti sovereignty if it had not complied by that date.

For Liberals, the key to post-war peace was thus to convince national leaders to eschew Realism in favor of a new Liberal approach that included the concept of collective security. Instead of joining exclusive alliances that inevitably made non-member states feel more insecure, all states would be encouraged to join a universal collective security organization. As all states are members, none of them could be identified as enemies. So, rather than committing themselves to defend each other from attack by a state from outside of the organization, states in a collective security organization commit themselves to defend any state that is a victim of aggression. Once aggression occurs, they are required to join together in order to protect the victim, regardless of whether the aggressor is a member of the organization itself. For example, in the case of the **First Persian Gulf War** in 1990–1991, the United States led an international coalition of states to restore the sovereignty of Kuwait, which had been invaded by Iraqi forces. All of the states involved, including the aggressor, were members of the **United Nations**, which is the successor collective security organization to the League of Nations.

As Wilson himself stated, by protecting sovereignty, extending the right to self-determination, expanding free trade, and creating a collective security organization, he hoped to make the world "safe for democracy." Of course, as a Liberal, Wilson believed that the spread of democracy, economic interdependence, and international organizations was the key to world peace.

Robert O. Keohane is one the most prominent contemporary Liberal theorists. He published an extremely influential text with his co-author Joseph S. Nye, entitled *Power and Interdependence*:

World Politics in Transition (1977), in which they argued that world politics was being fundamentally transformed into a condition best described as "**complex interdependence**."

They believed that Realism, with its emphasis on states and the use of military force, was too simplistic to capture this growing phenomenon and had therefore become anachronistic. They argued that in a world of complex interdependence, the use of military force was becoming less and less effective (for example, states could no longer threaten one another to open up their markets to foreign goods). They also highlighted the growing number of non-state actors that were already conducting influential transnational relations (including government bureaucracies and NGOs). Finally, contrary to Realist assumptions, they suggested that many states no longer held a clear hierarchy of interests (economic security had become just as important as military security).

However, it is for his later work on the role of **international institutions** in generating international **cooperation** that Keohane has become particularly renowned. International institutions are composed of principles, norms, and rules shared by a community (regimes) and can include formal organizations. For example, the norms and rules of free trade make up the international "free trade regime," and in 1995 the World Trade Organization (WTO) was created to help enforce it. However, other regimes remain much more informal, such as the norm against slavery.

In *After Hegemony: Cooperation and Discord in the World Political Economy* (1984), Keohane acknowledged that international institutions tended to be created by hegemonic states. For example, the free trade regime cited above was established immediately after World War II when the United States was the hegemon of the international system. This is in accord with Realist expectations, as Realists believe international institutions are simply a vehicle through which the most powerful States can impose their wishes and achieve their goals. However, Keohane argued that once established, such international institutions would continue to exist even after the power of the hegemon had declined. Keohane thus argued that even if the basic assumptions of Realism were accepted, such as states being the most important actors, the system being anarchic, and that States are unitary and rational actors, international institutions could still generate and maintain greater cooperation than Realists expected (see section below for an explanation of how international institutions help achieve this).

2.5.3 Liberalism

For Liberals there exists much greater potential for progress in world politics than Realists believe. For example, over the past 60 years there has been a significant decline in both the number and severity of violent conflicts between states, especially since the end of the Cold War (Russett 2010, 11). Liberals argue that Realists are unable to account for this trend because they ignore the transformative effects of three relatively new phenomena in world politics: democracy, economic interdependence, and international institutions. These three phenomena compose the **Kantian triangle** of Liberalism (Russett 2010, 15).

The first is the effect of democracy. Liberals propose that the declining trend in conflict is primarily explained by the Democratic Peace Thesis, first elucidated by Immanuel Kant (see section 2.5.2). This thesis proposes that democracies do not/will not go to war with one another. The decline in conflict is thus inversely proportional to the spread of democracy in the international system. For Liberals, therefore, the most portentous trend witnessed in world politics is that over the past 70 years democracies that were once a minority in the international system have now become a significant majority (Russett 2010, 13).

Democracy

International Institutions   Economic Interdependence

Figure 2.8. Kantian Triangle.

The second is the effect of economic interdependence. Liberals believe that increased commerce, just like democracy, generates peaceful relations between states. The more states trade with each other, the more they become invested in maintaining peaceful relations, as any disruption will significantly affect their economic prosperity. Economic interdependence is thus also inversely proportional to the declining trend in conflict.

The third is the effect of international institutions. As mentioned in the previous section, International institutions are composed of principles, norms, and rules shared by a community (regimes) and can include formal organizations. To show how such international institutions can help states cooperate in an anarchic international environment, Liberals often use **Game Theory**. This is a branch of mathematics that illustrates or models strategic interactions. One such model is the **Prisoner's Dilemma (PD)**. Imagine that two criminals have been imprisoned for committing a murder and each is brought before the prison governor. The governor has insufficient evidence to convict them, but hopes to tempt one of them to incriminate the other. He thus offers each of them a deal: "Confess to the murder before the other prisoner does and I will give you your freedom and a reward. I will then hang your accomplice. However, if he confesses before you, I will give him his freedom and reward and hang you." "So what if neither of us confess?" each prisoner asks. "Then, I will imprison both of you for 10 years each," the governor replies. Finally, each prisoner asks: "What if we both confess at the same time?" The governor replies: ``Then I will set you both free, but without a reward." Having made his offer, the governor sends each prisoner to solitary confinement.

The options available to each prisoner are thus:

Options	Rewards	Drawbacks
Confess before other prisoner	Freedom and Reward	None
Confess at the same time	None	10 years imprisonment
Neither confess	Freedom	No reward
Confess after other prisoner	None	Death

As rational individuals, each prisoner would prefer to confess before the other. However, if each tries to confess before the other, the result will be that they will both confess at the same time. This will mean that they will each receive 10 years imprisonment. This is still better than allowing the other prisoner to confess first, as that would result in death. So what should each prisoner do? There is the option of neither confessing, but how could each prisoner trust that the other would not take advantage and confess first? In solitary confinement there is no way to communicate a decision, and even if there was, how could each be sure that the other would fulfill his side of the bargain?

For Realists, the PD accurately illustrates the dilemma in which states find themselves in world politics. They may realize that there is an opportunity to cooperate in order to achieve a better outcome for all, but the lack of trust in the anarchic international system prevents them from achieving it. This is where Liberals diverge from Realist analysis. Instead, they argue that international institutions can help states overcome the lack of trust in world politics so that they can cooperate for mutual gain. They do this in four ways. First, they establish standards of behavior. Second, they help ensure (or verify) compliance with those standards. Third, they can help resolve disputes. Finally, they reduce the costs of joint decision making (Frieden 2010). Once these institutions are established, states will not want to lose the benefits they provide.

In the case of the PD, one can imagine that if the prisoners were each given a telephone and a closed-circuit television system that enabled each to monitor the other prisoner, their behavior would change. Instead of trying to confess as soon as possible, they could establish a standard of behavior that neither of them should confess. They could then verify compliance with that standard through the closed-circuit television system. Thus, because of the introduction of international institutions into the PD, the prisoners are now able to achieve a level of cooperation that was otherwise improbable.

THEORY IN ACTION!

International Institutions, the Prisoner's Dilemma, and the Nuclear Non-Proliferation Regime

The Prisoner's Dilemma is evident in the international community's attempts to prevent the proliferation of nuclear weapons. Every state can try to build a nuclear weapon and then try to build more powerful weapons than their adversaries, but this will only result in nuclear proliferation and arms races. This is the same as each prisoner trying to confess before the other, only to end up with 10 years imprisonment. States could negotiate a treaty to limit the proliferation of nuclear weapons, but how could they trust other states not to take advantage of them by **cheating** on the agreement?

To highlight the role of international institutions in achieving cooperation in this area, Liberals point to the international nuclear nonproliferation regime. The Non-Proliferation Treaty (NPT) of 1968 established the **standards of behavior** among its signatories, committing most states not to acquire nuclear weapons and five recognized nuclear states to work toward complete disarmament. **Compliance** with the standards of the NPT is **verified** by an independent IGO, the International Atomic Energy Agency (IAEA). An NPT conference is held every five years so that its now 189 signatories can discuss and decide upon issues affecting the nonproliferation regime, thus **reducing the costs** of joint decision making. **Disputes** can also be **resolved** through negotiation at these conferences.

So, for Liberals, the inability of Realism to explain the declining trend witnessed in the number and severity of military conflicts around the world can be explained by its failure to acknowledge the transformative effects of the Kantian triangle: democracy, economic interdependence, and international institutions. Today, Liberals point to areas of the world like Europe and the Americas, where these three factors have become most consolidated, to show that states in anarchy can achieve levels of cooperation unthought-of by Realists.

2.5.4 Liberalism and Levels of Analysis

Unlike Realism, Liberalism does not propose that human nature is prone to either good or bad behavior. However, Liberalism does agree with Realism that the decisions of state leaders can be crucial in explaining events and other phenomena in world politics. To some extent then, Liberalism operates on the first level of analysis.

Nevertheless, Liberalism focuses perhaps to its greatest extent on the second level of analysis. If the main reason that states do, or do not, go to war is the nature of their political and/or economic systems, then this suggests that good people who lead dictatorships may be more aggressive in their foreign policy behavior than bad people who lead democracies. Thus, it is the political and economic systems in which decision makers operate that has the greatest influence on how the state behaves, which makes it primarily a second-level theory.

Like Realism, Liberalism also accepts that the international system is anarchic and that states thus exist in an insecure environment. However, they do not believe that states act in the same way because they share the same nature. Rather, for Liberals, there are two principal factors that affect the likelihood of conflict in anarchy. The first is the second-level factor of democracy, explained above. The second is whether international institutions are present. The greater the extent of international institutions in world politics, the greater likelihood of cooperation there will be. This explanation for cooperation in world politics operates on the third (international or systemic) level of analysis.

Once again, therefore, you can see how a theory can operate on more than one level of analysis. Liberalism operates predominantly on the second and third levels. Only by appreciating how the causes of conflict and cooperation that exists on both levels of analysis operate and interact, can we fully understand how Liberalism explains world politics.

2.6 Introduction to the Radical Approach

Since the mid-19th century, a third group of theories has emerged that can be categorized as forming a "radical approach" to world politics. Here, *radical* refers to the critical approach these theories take to the "mainstream" theories of world politics (like Realism and Liberalism) and dominant political and economic systems (like capitalism and democracy). For this reason, they are also commonly referred to as "critical" theories. Although the theorists within this approach disagree on many issues, they generally share a concern with issues of exploitation, class struggle, and imperialism.

2.6.1 Basic Assumptions of the Radical Approaches

1. Human nature is cooperative.
2. Conflict is generated by economic and political systems that encourage competition and exploitation.
3. The state is often used to help powerful groups exploit the weak.
4. Emancipation from a world of conflict and exploitation cannot be achieved within the current global capitalist economic system.

2.6.2 The Evolution of the Radical Approach

It is testimony to the continuing influence of the 19th-century German political philosopher, **Karl Marx** (1818–1883), that most contemporary Radical theories are considered to be Neo-Marxist. Marx, himself, sought a scientific explanation for the continuing evolution of the economic and political systems of states. By the early 19th century, these systems had already taken a number of forms, including primitive communism, feudalism, and capitalism. Marx argued that each of these systems (or **modes of production**) produced "classes" in society that would be in conflict with one another. For example, the capitalist system produces two classes, a ruling class that own the means of production (**bourgeoisie**)

Figure 2.9. Karl Marx.

and a subordinate class that labors to produce the goods (**proletariat**). It is the intensifying conflict between these classes that drives the evolution of the mode of production. At the heart of this conflict is the insatiable desire of the bourgeoisie, generated by the capitalist system, to exploit the labor of the proletariat in order to increase their profits.

Marx argued that this conflict would only end when a proletariat revolution had produced a new mode of production, communism, in which the means of production were owned collectively (a deeper analysis of this process is provided in Chapter 5 on international political economy).

Because capitalism was primarily a national phenomenon at the time of Marx, he focused the majority of his analysis on how exploitation generated conflict within states. The leader of the Russian revolution of 1917, **V. I. Lenin** (1870–1924), however, gave Marxism a

Figure 2.10. V. I. Lenin.

strong international dimension. In *Imperialism: The Highest Stage of Capitalism* (1917), Lenin argued that the crisis of capitalism (and subsequent revolutions) that Marx had predicted had not yet occurred because the bourgeoisie of the industrial countries had expanded the pool of workers that they could exploit through **imperialism**. This process, however, was resulting in two significant effects. The first was that the poorer, underdeveloped countries of the world were now being exploited by the rich capitalist countries, just like the proletariat continued to be exploited domestically.

The second product of imperialism for Lenin was international conflict. Because they were in constant competition with one another, he believed, the rich countries would continue to "divide up the colonial world in accordance with their relative strengths" until there were no more peoples to colonize. Once this point had been reached, the rich capitalist countries would then be drawn into conflict with one another. Conflict would also occur when the relative strengths of the rich countries changed over time, thus convincing the growing power(s) to demand a redistribution of the spoils of colonization. Thus for Lenin, World War I was not caused by a failure to balance power (as Realists suggest) or the aggressiveness of authoritarian states (as Liberals suggest), but as the inevitable consequence of the global expansion of capitalism and colonialism.

As one of **Andre Gunder Frank**'s (1929–2005) obituaries noted after his death, "few economists have inspired so many radical intellectuals in the Third World" as he (Andre Gunder Frank 2005). Frank was a pioneering advocate of what is today called **dependency theory**. This theory argues that the dependency of **Lesser Developed Countries (LDCs)** on the rich, industrial states of the global economy is the primary cause of their underdevelopment. The origins of this dependency can be traced back to the beginning of European colonization in the 16th century. Since then, he argued, the rich countries that make up the "**core**" of the global economy have continued to exploit the poor countries in its "periphery." Originally this was achieved through direct imperial control of states in the periphery. Since the end of colonialism in the mid-20th century, however, the core countries have continued to exploit the periphery through neo-imperialism, evidenced by their maintenance of unfair trading relationships; their control and manipulation of international organizations; their use of military interventions; and their collusion with corrupt elites within the governments and economies of modern LDCs (see Chapter 5 for greater explanation).

2.6.3 The Radical Approach

As one can see from its evolution, the Radical approach has been heavily influenced by Marxist analysis. In this sense, all the theories within it seek to highlight how existing economic and political systems help perpetuate inequalities by allowing and even encouraging exploitation. Although they differ on how change can be achieved, they also all agree that emancipation from this exploitation cannot be achieved within today's global capitalist system.

Theories within the Radical approach are also highly critical of the mainstream or dominant theories within the study of world politics. This is because they believe theories like Realism and Liberalism are used by the most powerful actors to legitimate their positions of power and excuse their exploitative behavior (regardless of whether they are conscious of it). For example, the wealthiest states in contemporary world politics all advocate the spread of capitalism. They all argue, on the basis of Liberal theory, that the spread of global trade and "interdependence" will make everyone wealthier. However, dependency theorists argue that the global spread of capitalism has not helped poor states or regions develop. Instead, it has locked them into a relationship of dependency in which they are perpetually exploited. For these theorists, therefore, capitalism is not the cure for underdevelopment, but rather the cause (Chapter 5 will discuss this point further).

Realism is also criticized because it advocates competition between states for power, thus encouraging relationships of domination and exploitation. Nor do theories in the Radical approach accept the Realist premise that the state is always a provider of security to its citizens. Rather, the state can be a source of insecurity, as it is constantly used by powerful groups in society to maintain their dominant positions. The large security apparatuses that states maintain are thus not only concerned with protecting the state from enemies from without, but also with protecting the existing economic and political systems (and their inherent inequalities) from "revolutionaries" within. Thus, in the Radical approach there is no such thing as the "national interest," because this is no more than a euphemism used by economic and political elites to convince the exploited masses to support policies that are contrary to their own interests.

2.6.4 The Radical Approach and Levels of Analysis

As with Realism and Liberalism, you have maybe already recognized that the Radical approach operates on all three levels of analysis. Radical theorists have a much more optimistic view of human nature than Realists. Like Liberals, they believe that the type of behavior that individuals will exhibit is determined less by innate tendencies and more by the political, economic, and social environment in which they are found.

As explained in the previous section, Radical theorists are primarily concerned with how the mode of production produces conflict between economic classes. These classes are, therefore, the specific level of analysis on which the Radical approach operates. However, it is the mode of production at the state level that is the principal determinant of how the state will behave. Capitalist states are therefore expected to behave more imperially than socialist states. Radical theories can thus be said to operate to a great extent at the second (state) level of analysis.

Similarly, in an anarchic international system, the dominant international mode of production is expected to determine the relations between states. For Radical theorists, "globalization" (discussed in more detail in Chapter 5) is simply a synonym for the global spread of capitalism, with which has come greater economic exploitation, poverty, and an increased likelihood of international conflict. Radical theories thus also operate to a significant degree on the third (systemic) level of analysis.

2.7 Case Study: The Second Persian Gulf War

The purpose of this case study is to apply the three theoretical perspectives explained in this chapter. Each of them purports to explain events in world politics the best. Which one do you think explains the U.S. decision to go to war in 2003?

Background

On 20 March 2003, an international coalition composed almost entirely of U.S. and British forces crossed the southern border from Kuwait into Iraq. By early April they had entered its capital city, Baghdad, and by the end of the year its president, Saddam Hussein, had been arrested. The George W. Bush administration claimed that this action was necessary because Hussein had refused to allow United Nations (UN) and International Atomic Energy Agency (IAEA) weapons inspectors to verify that his government had destroyed all of its chemical, biological, and nuclear weapons capabilities (as the UN had demanded after the First Persian Gulf War of 1990–1991). The administration claimed that the "irrational" Iraqi dictator might use these Weapons of Mass Destruction (WMD) against the United States, or that he might pass them to terrorists, a threat deemed more real after the attacks of September 11, 2001.

Much of the international community remained skeptical of the need to use military force. France, Russia, and China, all of whom are permanent members of the UN Security Council, and Germany, argued that weapons inspections needed to be given more time to achieve their objective. Thus, with no hope of being able to pass a UN Security Council Chapter VII resolution that would legally mandate the use of force to ensure Iraqi disarmament, the Bush administration claimed instead that previous UN resolutions (in particular UNSC Resolution 678, which authorized the use of force to remove
Iraqi forces from Kuwait and demanded that Iraq comply with UN demands for disarmament) had provided a sufficient legal foundation.

Investigations following the invasion concluded that Iraq had ended its WMD programs in 1991. The early years of the U.S.-led occupation were also marred by extreme levels of violence, both against coalition forces and between members of the Sunni and Shia Muslim communities in Iraq. By the end of the Bush administration's tenure in 2009, over 4,000 American soldiers had died in combat, and tens of thousands more had been seriously injured. As a result, some economists were predicting the entire cost of the war could reach $2 trillion. Estimates of Iraqi deaths have reached into the hundreds of thousands. Two million Iraqis had also become refugees, and 2.5 million more were internally displaced.

Despite this high cost in both lives and finance, the Bush administration continued to claim that the intervention was justified because it had removed a potential security threat to the United States and international community; it had helped end Iraqi human rights abuses; it had helped spread democracy to Iraq; and it had ended Iraqi support for Palestinian terrorists.

2.7.1 The Realist Perspective

Although Realist scholars can explain why the United States went to war, most of them did not agree with the decision to do so. Just like Sparta and Athens in the 5th century B.C.E., the United States and Iraq were caught in a security dilemma that eventually prompted the United States to launch a preemptive/preventive war. Realists note that the United States went to war without a UN Chapter VII resolution, confirming Thucydides' lesson of the Melian Dialogue that international law cannot and will not stop the more powerful state from attacking its adversary. Realists also argue that the Bush administration was driven by Wilsonian Liberal notions of making the world safe for democracy. By removing the Iraqi regime and replacing it with a liberal democracy, the administration had hoped to instigate a wave of democratic reform across the Middle East.

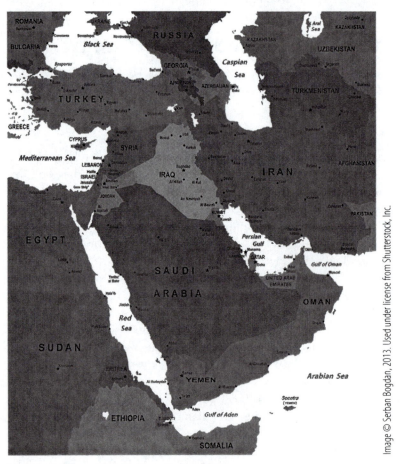

Image © Serban Bogdan, 2013. Used under license from Shutterstock, Inc.

Figure 2.11. Middle East Political Map.

For Realists the war was not only unnecessary, but actually counterproductive. Although they recognized the security dilemma that existed, they did not believe that a preventive war was the best solution. Rather, they argued that the United States could continue to contain Iraq through the existing policy of sanctions, weapons inspections, and no-fly zones at a much lower cost in both lives and expenditure. As two of the most prominent Realist scholars wrote a month before the war began, "Saddam Hussein needs to remain in his box—but we don't need a war to keep him there" (Mearsheimer 2003). Realists also argued that going to war risked destabilizing the Middle East; that U.S. forces would find themselves bogged down in a war of occupation and that the resentment generated would fuel greater radical Islamic terrorism (Layne 2007).

Realists also criticized the Bush administration's characterization of Saddam Hussein as irrational. Only an irrational leader would use WMD against the United States or pass them on to terrorists that might do so, when they knew that the United States would retaliate with the world's most deadly conventional and nuclear forces. Realists argued that there was no evidence in Hussein's history of behavior that suggested he was capable of such irrationality.

Finally, Realists criticized the Bush administration for acting on the idealist notion that it could transform the Middle East into a zone of democracy through the use of force. For Realists, the strongest ideology in world politics is not liberal democracy, but nationalism. For this reason they argued that rather than being met as liberators, U.S. forces would be perceived as occupiers. It was the failure to recognize this that led the United States to intervene and fail in Vietnam, and history seemed to be repeating itself in Iraq. The high death toll and spiraling costs in the early years of the occupation appeared to vindicate this Realist assumption.

2.7.2 The Liberal Perspective

Many Liberals felt torn on whether to support the war against Iraq. On the one hand, they could appreciate the threat that Saddam Hussein posed both to his own people and the international community. He was a brutal dictator who had already attacked two of Iraq's neighboring countries in the previous two decades—Iran and Kuwait. He was also continuing to defy the international community by refusing to allow UN and IAEA weapons inspectors unfettered access to sites of interest. Nor had the Iraqi authorities fully accounted for the destruction of all the WMD found after the First Persian Gulf War. Removing the Iraqi regime was thus an opportunity to end a serious threat to international peace and security and liberate the Iraqi people from an odious violator of human rights. They also hoped that spreading democracy to Iraq might encourage other authoritarian regimes in the Middle East to reform.

On the other hand, Liberals remained unconvinced by the Bush administration's argument that war was necessary. Although weapons inspectors had not been allowed everywhere they wanted to go and had not been given all the information they wanted, they had not found any evidence to suggest that the Iraqi government had reconstituted its WMD programs after 1991. Many Liberals thus argued that weapons inspections needed to be given more time to succeed.

Liberals were also uneasy about the manner in which the Bush administration dealt with the UN. The use of force by any state (except in self-defense) is illegal without having first acquired a UN Chapter VII resolution. Although the Bush administration argued that the numerous Security Council resolutions that had been passed since 1991 provided it with a sufficient legal basis for using force, most of the international community disagreed. For many Liberals, therefore, the U.S. decision to go to war threatened to undermine international law, and subsequently, international security by encouraging other countries to flout the law in a similar fashion whenever they felt it was in their interest to do so.

2.7.3 The Radical Perspective

It will probably come as little surprise that the Radical perspective is the most cynical when it came to understanding American motivations for going to war. For Realists, the U.S. decision to go to war was unnecessary, but still understandable, given the insecure nature of world politics. For Liberals, the desire to liberate Iraq and spread democracy was laudable, even if the manner in which the Bush administration went about it was unfortunate. However, for Radical theorists, the U.S. decision to go to war was motivated neither by security concerns or altruism. Instead, it was simply another manifestation of U.S. imperialism.

What was the true goal of U.S. policy? To gain control of Iraq's vast oil resources. Second only to those of Saudi Arabia, Iraq's oil fields promised immense wealth for U.S. corporations. By controlling Iraqi oil, the United States could also gain significant influence in the Middle East region. And in a world of depleting oil reserves, such control could allow the United States to manipulate the political economies of many countries around the world. Radical theorists thus believed that Iran would be next on the list for U.S. intervention.

Radical theorists were also skeptical about the Bush administration's ostensible concern for the plight of the Iraqi people. They noted that the United States was primarily responsible for economic sanctions imposed during the 1990s that contributed to the premature deaths of hundreds of thousands of Iraqis. They also noted that the United States had been a major supporter of the Saddam Hussein regime when it was at war with Iran in the 1980s, even to the point of preventing UN condemnation for its use of chemical weapons against Iranian soldiers and its own citizens. Finally, they cited the lack of adequate pre-war planning that led to the breakdown of law and order in Iraq following the initial intervention. This contributed significantly to the large death toll and immense hardship suffered by the Iraqi population.

For Radical theorists the Iraq war was thus simply another step in the consolidation of the American empire. The United States is compelled by the global capitalist system to spread its hegemony and punish those who oppose it. Radical theorists, therefore, believe that the decision to go to war was made long before 2003.

2.8 Foreign Policy Approaches

Now that we have debated which theory best explains world politics (and perhaps you have chosen one!), we can now look to see what foreign policy advice each theory proposes. As mentioned at the beginning of this chapter, the theory you prefer will act as the foundation of your foreign policy proposals.

Imagine, therefore, that you are visiting the doctor for chest pains, and she tells you that she has never studied the heart and circulatory system, has no idea what is causing your problem, but that she would recommend triple-bypass surgery. Would you have it? It is obvious that your doctor's prescription will only be logical (and successful) if it is founded on an accurate understanding of how the body works. So too with world politics! Each of the three theories we have debated so far provides a different prescription (or foreign policy approach) for the challenges the United States faces in world politics. To decide which foreign policy approach the United States should take, you must first conclude which theory is correct.

This section is thus designed to allow you appreciate the implications of your theoretical choice. If you believe Realists are correct, then what foreign policy advice should you give? What if you are a Liberal? Or support a Radical Approach? At the end of this section you will be encouraged to apply your policy choice to a major challenge to the United States in world politics, the rise of China. Are you happy to give the advice your theoretical choice demands?

2.8.1 Realist Off-Shore Balancing

Each of the three theories of world politics we have debated so far can support a number of different foreign policy approaches For example, some Realists argue that the United States should adopt a policy of nonintervention in world politics, more commonly known as **Isolationism**. Others may support a policy of **Primacy**, which advocates U.S. global leadership. However, the majority of Realists support another approach, that of **Off-shore balancing**.

Realists argue that because the United States is currently the only Great Power in its geographical region, it doesn't have to worry about competition and security threats from other nearby Great Powers. This means the United States is a **regional hegemon**. The United States does, however, still have to worry about the potential rise of other regional hegemons around the world. This is because these hegemons might use their powerful positions to threaten or undermine U.S. security. The central goal of an American Off-shore balancing approach is thus to prevent the rise of other regional hegemons.

Why do most Realists reject both isolationism and primacy? Their fear is that in pursuing an Isolationist policy, the United States will not be involved enough in world politics to ensure its security. As the policy suggests, the United States must work to manage the balance of power and prevent the rise of other regional hegemons. On the other hand, most Realists also reject the policy of primacy because it threatens to overextend American resources and thereby diminish U.S. relative power. It also encourages other states to **counter-balance** against the United States because of the fear generated by an excessive use of U.S. power. Thus, for most Realists, isolationism is too little involvement in world politics, while primacy is too much.

So, how can the United States prevent the rise of competing regional hegemons? First, it can allow the Great Powers of other regions to compete with each other. Great Powers that are geographically close will feel a greater threat from one another. They will therefore concentrate on balancing each other. At this point, the United States can stand back and allow them to expend their own resources on maintaining a regional balance of power (a policy known as **buck-passing**). However, if one of these Great Powers appears to have the potential to become a regional hegemon, the United States must then become involved in helping **contain** that state. This can be done through the creation of **alliances** (external balancing), the provision of resources to neighboring Great Powers, or the United States can deploy its own troops and resources in the region. Of course, containment policies usually involve a combination of all three of these options.

2.8.2 Liberal Internationalism

Because Realists have ignored the transformative effects of the Kantian triangle in world politics, it should come as little surprise that the foreign policy it advocates does not incorporate them either. Thus, for Liberals, the theoretical foundations of the Realist Off-shore balancing approach are fundamentally flawed. Rather than helping the United States avoid future conflicts, advocating that the United States must always worry about relative power and that it must therefore contain the rising power of future competitors, will only make them more likely. For Liberals, the best way to avoid future conflict is not to compete for power, but to promote greater cooperation in world politics.

Again, at this point there should be little surprise at what might constitute a foreign-policy approach of Liberal Internationalism. Its principal elements are that the United States should promote the spread of democracy and economic interdependence and help create and utilize international institutions. These three elements are mutually reinforcing. The more successful the United States is at promoting each of the three legs of this Kantian triangle, the more peaceful world politics will be and therefore the more secure the United States will be.

Nevertheless, the question remains of how the United States should seek to promote each of these three elements. As explained in the previous chapter, Joseph Nye argues that the answer lies in the use of the correct balance of hard and soft power. By relying too much on hard power and ignoring the role of international institutions, a Realist approach of off-shore balancing tends to undermine international cooperation on many issues of critical importance to U.S. security. For example, if the United States wishes to combat the threats of terrorism, drug trafficking, and global warming, it will not be able to do so alone (unilaterally) or with the help of only a few other Great Powers. Instead, it will need to engender cooperation among a much more diffuse group of actors, including a great number of large and small states, MNCs, and NGOs. This can only be achieved through a greater use of soft power than Realism suggests. International institutions can thus play a fundamental role in helping to formulate, coordinate, and execute **multilaterally** agreed policies on these issues. Whereas the use of hard power by the United States tends to frighten other states into colluding against it (or simply ignoring its calls for help), using soft power in order to attract states to cooperate will have a much greater long-term beneficial effect.

Of course, this does not mean that Liberals believe that the use of hard power is never required. Collective security (the Liberal alternative to Realist balance of power politics), as recognized by its greatest advocate, Woodrow Wilson, ultimately relies on the threat of economic and military force to protect victims from acts of aggression. However, when seeking to use hard power, Liberals argue that the United States should seek to legitimate its actions by working through multilateral institutions like the UN. In this way the United States embeds the use of force in a legal framework that encourages cooperation and minimizes international resentment.

2.8.3 Radical Anti-Imperialism

The Radical approach argues that capitalism, both domestically and globally, encourages exploitation. In world politics, this exploitation is manifest in the imperial policies of the world's most powerful states; and beause the United States is the most powerful of them all, it naturally receives the greatest criticism for being the most imperial. Of course, this implies that the United States has an empire—a charge that may seem nonsensical, given that the United States does not directly control other countries. However, although the United States lacks a territorial empire, it still controls foreign territories just as effectively as the Romans did in antiquity or the British did with their colonial empire in the 18th and 19th centuries. In fact, U.S. hegemony is much more efficient than the old imperial methods of military conquest and occupation. For the most part, the modern American empire is actually self-enforcing, because the global capitalist system on which it is based compels other countries to obey its rules.

One example of this is how the United States pressures the elites of LDCs to open up their markets to foreign competition, based on the premise that "free trade" will produce prosperity for everyone. Instead, as dependency theorists would expect, rather than receiving the developmental benefits of "globalization" the United States continuously promises, these states find themselves locked into a relationship of dependency and poverty. They could try to break free of the system by refusing to sell or buy any products and try to produce everything themselves, but that is a recipe for economic disaster (see Chapter 5). The United States also ensures obedience by persuading (through diplomacy and bribery) that the economic and political elites of LDCs see that their interests lie in continuing to cooperate with the demands of the capitalist system. These elites then police their own societies to ensure compliance from their exploited workers. The LDCs thus become prisoners in an American constructed self-regulating economic prison.

Despite this self-enforcing aspect to the modern American empire, the United States is still required to do some old-fashioned policing to protect its hegemony. Since the United States became a Great Power at the beginning of the 20th century, it has used a variety of methods to suppress dissent and maintain compliant governments in states around the world. These include support for governments, political parties, and other groups that the United States has perceived as being favorable to its interests, even if they have terrorized their own populations. It has also included covert operations to overthrow democratically elected governments, like those of Chile, Guatemala, and Iran during the 1950s. And when all else fails, it has even required military interventions, like those in Panama (1989), Afghanistan (2002), and Iraq (2003), to depose unfavorable governments and extend American control.

It may not come as a surprise, therefore, to find out that the foreign policy approach of Radical Anti-Imperialism:

> . . . does not prescribe what the United States should do in the world so much as it prescribes what it should stop doing: manipulating international relations and intervening in the internal affairs of other countries in order to maintain an empire that exploits the world's poor for the benefit of economic elites. (Callahan 2004, 128)

However, it is also apparent that it is impossible for the United States to stop its imperialistic behavior while its economic and political systems are dominated by its own self-interested elites. Thus, the adoption of a Radical Anti-Imperialist foreign policy approach will only occur after a fundamental transformation of America's political and economic systems. In the meantime, supporters of Radical Anti-Imperialism must seek to build a "coalition of forces opposed to imperialism . . . as a requisite step toward the long-run goal of affecting the fundamental social change needed to end" it completely (Callahan 2004, 115).

DISCUSSION BOX

Which Foreign Policy Approach Should the United States Adopt toward the Rise of China?

The Chinese economy has grown at a rate of 10% per year for the past 30 years. Today (2017) the Gross Domestic Product (GDP) of the Chinese economy is around $12 trillion, while that of the United States is $18.5 trillion. According to the Stockholm International Peace Research Institute (SIPRI), China's military budget has also increased by 175% since 2003. Although its current budget of around $160 billion is still dwarfed by that of the United States, which spent $600 billion in 2016, at current rates the Chinese military budget will overtake U.S. spending by 2022 (Wall 2013).

The Chinese argue that they are conducting a "peaceful rise" and that they are strengthening their military for the same reasons that every other major power does so: to catch up with other powers, to construct a more modern military with which it can better assert its territorial and maritime claims, and to secure its development on its own terms (Erickson 2013).

Do you believe these Chinese proclamations? Which of the foreign policy approaches do you think the United States should adopt toward China? What would this policy look like in practice? What theoretical reasoning would you provide to justify your policy choice? Why do you believe the other foreign policy choices would be less successful in achieving your foreign policy goals?

Key Terms

alliances
anarchy
anarchic international system
Andre Gunder Frank
authoritarian state
balance of power
bipolar system
bourgeoisie
Buck-passing
civic duty
collective defense
collective security
Complex interdependence
compliance
contain
cooperation
counterfactuals
Delian League

democratic state
Democratic Peace Thesis
dependency theory
external balancing
First Persian Gulf War
Game Theory
Great Powers
Hans Morgenthau
hegemon
Immanuel Kant
imperialism
interdependent
internal balancing
international institutions
Isolationism
Kantian triangle
Karl Marx
League of Nations

Lesser Developed Countries (LDCs)
Levels of analysis
liberalism
mode of production
multilateralism
multipolar system
Niccolo Machiavelli
North Atlantic Treaty Organization (NATO)
Occam's Razor
Off-shore-balancing
parsimony
Peloponnesian League
periphery
power maximizers
Power Politics
power, absolute
power, relative
preemptive war
Primacy
Prisoner's Dilemma
proletariat
Radical Approaches
rational
rational actors
Realism

regional hegemon
relative power
Robert Keohane
security dilemma
self-determination
self-fulfilling prophecy
situational ethics
standards of behavior
state of nature
state-centric theory
theory
theory, accuracy
theory, predict
theory, range
Thomas Hobbes
Thucydides
Treaty of Versailles
Triple Alliance
Triple Entente
uni-polar system
unitary actors
United Nations (UN)
Woodrow Wilson
Y. I. Lenin

CHAPTER 3

Security, Conflict, and War

Image © Elenarts, 2013. Used under license from Shutterstock, Inc.

CHAPTER OUTLINE

3.0 What Are Security, Conflict, and War?

In very simple terms, *security* means being free from risk or danger. Traditional "security studies" within the field of world politics has thus concentrated on the question of how states might achieve this security within an anarchic international system. As we will see in this chapter, Realists, Liberals and Radical theorists all disagree on the questions of whether states can ever be completely secure and on what states should do in order to reduce their feelings of insecurity.

In recent years, some scholars have even questioned the state-centric nature of traditional security studies. These scholars have instead called for the discipline to replace its traditional emphasis on the military threats faced by states with the concept of **human security**, a concept first elaborated in a 1994 *Human Development Report* published by the United Nations Development Program. The report argued that the concept of security had "for too long been interpreted narrowly: as security of territory from external aggression, or as protection of national interest in foreign policy or as global security from the threat of nuclear holocaust." It thus proposed a new concept of human security that possessed "two main aspects. It means, first, safety from chronic threats as hunger, disease and repression. And second, it means protection from certain and hurtful disruptions in the patterns of daily life—whether in homes, in jobs or in communities" (Paris 2001, 89).

As you can tell from its composition, the concept of human security broadens and deepens the concept of security in world politics to include *non-military threats* to the security of the *individual*. Once again, as you will see in this chapter, whether you support this expansion of the nature of security studies will depend on your theoretical approach to world politics.

Definitions of *conflict* and *war* also vary in the field. At one end of the definitional spectrum for conflict there are simply two or more entities having a disagreement or dispute. We would have to be the world's greatest utopians to believe we could ever reach a point in world politics in which disputes would never occur! In this sense, most would recognize that conflict is always going to be part of human existence. The question then becomes whether we can achieve an international environment in which those disputes never reach the opposite end of the definitional spectrum of conflict and cross the point at which disputes escalate into *violent* conflict.

Traditionally, scholars of conflict have not been interested in all types of violent conflict. Instead, they have concentrated on violent conflicts that occur between sizable organized groups (states or sub-state groups) and involve significantly greater levels of violence than one would expect to see in relatively peaceful societies. Scholars tend to describe these types of conflicts as **armed conflicts**. For example, the Uppsala Conflict Data Program (UCDP) defines an armed conflict as "a contested incompatibility that concerns government and/or territory where the use of armed force between the two parties, of which one is the government of a state, results in at least 25 battle-related deaths in one year." Using this definition UCDP recorded 37 such conflicts occurring in 30 different locations during 2011 (Themner 2012).

War is yet another category of conflict. Just as armed conflict is distinguished from disputes by the number of battle-related deaths involved, so too is war. To be categorized as a war, an armed conflict must reach a scale of 1,000 battle–related deaths per year. The final distinction that can be made between disputes, armed conflicts, and wars is whether they occur between states or within them. When they occur between states they are called **international (or inter-state) conflicts**. When a dispute, armed conflict, or war occurs within a state, it is called a **civil (or intra-state) conflict**. Civil conflicts can also become **internationalized** when an outside state sends troops in order to help one or other of the protagonists.

Our goal in this chapter is thus to try to understand why conflicts occur and why they escalate from disputes to armed conflicts and wars. If we can understand these causes and processes, we can use our knowledge to help *resolve* conflicts (**conflict resolution**) and even *prevent* (**conflict prevention**) them from happening. The processes of conflict escalation and conflict resolution are depicted in Fig. 3.1.

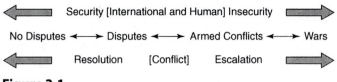

Figure 3.1.

3.1 Trends in Conflicts and Casualties

There are two principal trends in international conflict that scholars have identified in recent years. The first is that the vast majority of conflicts witnessed around the world today occur within states rather than between them. For example, of the 37 international conflicts identified by the UCDP in 2011, only one of them was occurring between states—a resumption of a decades-old dispute between Thailand and Cambodia over part of their shared border—while the remaining 36 were occurring within states. Of these civil conflicts, six had reached the level of civil wars, which were then being fought in Afghanistan, Pakistan, Libya, Somalia, Sudan, and Yemen (Themner 2012, 566).

The second trend is that violent conflict of all types, but especially international and civil wars, is in terminal decline. For example, the noted Harvard psychologist, Steven Pinker, has argued that all types of violence "from the waging of wars to the spanking of children" has declined over a number of millennia (Pinker 2011, i). However, most scholars have limited their assertions in this regard to the more easily documented decline in the number and severity of international and civil wars that has occurred over the past 60 to 100 years.

As Joshua S. Goldstein has noted, "the last decade has seen fewer war deaths than any decade in the past 100 years, based on data compiled by researchers . . . [at] . . . the Peace Research Institute, Oslo. Worldwide, deaths caused directly by war-related violence in the new century have averaged about 55,000 a year, just over half of what they were in the 1990s (100,000 a year), a third of what they were during the Cold War (180,000 a year from 1950 to 1989), and 100th of what they were in World War II" (Goldstein 2011). This decline has led one scholar to suggest that war has almost ceased to exist (Mueller 2009). (http://www.foreignpolicy.com/articles/2011/08/15/think_again_war)

Although the total number of international conflicts increased during 2011–2012, the general trends described above remain intact. For example, in 2011 the UCDP recorded an increase in the number of international conflicts from 31 to 37 from the previous year. As noted earlier, 36 of these were civil conflicts and despite their increase, the number was still significantly lower than the 50 armed conflicts recorded in the early 1990s (Themner 2012). So too, for those conflicts severe enough to be designated as wars. Despite an increase of two in this category to a total of 6 over 2011–2012, this number was also significantly lower than in previous decades—in fact 60% lower than the peak year of 1988 (Themner 2012, 566).

Although the first trend identified above remains uncontested, this is not the case for the second. For example, not all scholars accept the "classic" definitions of civil and international wars used by those who have documented their decline. Limiting the definition of armed conflicts to those that necessarily involve the government on one side, they argue, omits many conflicts in which only nongovernmental groups are in conflict (although the scholars above generally argue that these are in decline, too). As we will see in the theoretical discussion in section 4 of this chapter, some scholars argue that limiting our analysis to only classic definitions of international conflict also misses the wider violence suffered by individuals and societies in all states, but particularly in poor and weak ones. While a certain type of violence may therefore be diminishing, this does not necessarily mean that violence in general is doing so.

3.2 The Causes of Armed Conflicts and Wars

As explained in Chapter 2, the principal theories of world politics all disagree about the causes of insecurity, conflict, and war in our international system. To test our theories we must therefore collect as much empirical evidence (what we can observe) as we can about the conflicts that are occurring around the world so that we can ask whether our theories are correct in their explanations and predictions. When we collect this empirical evidence, we can normally identify the cause, or causes, of the conflict in question. In many cases the cause(s) may seem obvious—the combatants themselves might even explain why they are fighting to news reporters and others.

However, the *deeper* causes of the conflicts in question may not be apparent. For example, if you visit your doctor and complain about headaches, chest pain, and irregular heartbeat, she may diagnose you with hypertension (high blood pressure). You will thus assume that the cause of your problems is hypertension. The doctor will also give you medication to lower your blood pressure, and you will probably find that your symptoms will be reduced or even disappear, giving you an increased sense of security. However, if you stop taking the medication, you will find the symptoms returning. This is because your hypertension is not the true cause of your problems—it is rather whatever has caused your hypertension! As yet, the medical profession has not reached a consensus on what actually causes hypertension, although different theories are always being proposed and tested. So, too, with armed conflicts and wars in world politics. What might first appear to cause them may not be their actual cause. We must thus look to the theories of world politics to decide which one provides us with that.

Before we do look more closely at what each theory says about the deeper causes of conflict, we can first try to categorize the conflicts the world has witnessed according to the empirical evidence that has been collected about them. In this way, the majority of the world's armed conflicts and wars can be grouped into four categories, depending on their ostensible causes. However, as we will see when we look deeper into specific conflicts, most have a combination of these factors present.

3.2.1 Territory

The question of who controls territory is perhaps the most obvious issue that states fight over. Territory is important to states for many reasons, including establishing/protecting their sovereignty, controlling natural and human resources, and a sense of national pride. States therefore do not often lose territory easily and will often harbor intense desires to recapture any territory they believe they have unfairly lost—a goal called **irredentism**.

The territory states control actually extends beyond their territorial land to include their **territorial sea**, **contiguous zone**, and **airspace**. While for most of the history of our international system, territorial waters of states have stretched for only 3 nautical miles from their shoreline (the distance that a cannonball could fire), the need for clearer laws and international consensus led eventually to the signing of the UN Convention on the Law of the Sea (UNCLOS) in the 1980s. Although not all states have ratified UNCLOS, virtually every state has agreed to abide by it. This includes the establishment of sovereign territorial waters of 12 nautical miles from a state's shoreline. In addition to its territorial waters, a state may also claim a contiguous zone of up to 24 nautical miles from its shoreline, within which it may exercise the control necessary to prevent the infringement of its customs, fiscal, immigration, or sanitary laws and regulations.

In addition to territorial waters and a contiguous zone, UNCLOS also provides for an **Exclusive Economic Zone** (EEZ), which stretches for 200 nautical miles from a state's shoreline and within which states have exclusive fishing and mineral extraction rights. Nevertheless, international shipping can still pass through it without permission. The EEZ may be extended in those cases in which a state's continental shelf extends beyond 200 nautical miles from its shoreline. The airspace above a state's territory (including above its territorial waters) is also sovereign territory. Anything that flies through this airspace requires permission from the state concerned or risks being shot down. Flying (or firing a rocket) into the airspace of another state without its permission is a violation of that state's sovereignty and can thus be considered an act of war, just as sailing a ship into its territorial waters or driving a tank across its border can be. Space is considered to be international, in the same way that water beyond a state's territorial waters is considered to be international waters, or the **High Seas**. Airspace thus only stretches as high as the Earth's atmosphere.

The connection between territory and conflict is perhaps most evident in cases of shared borders. One study found that between 1815 and 1965, contiguous states were 35 times more likely to experience war than noncontiguous states (Gibler 2007, 510). However, improvements in technology, in particular, the development of Geographical Information Systems, has led to more nuanced studies of the nature of international borders and their relationship to conflict (Brochmann 2012). More recent studies utilizing GIS have found that certain types of shared borders may actually lead to more cooperative behavior (Starr 2006).

Conflicts over territory can also take place within states. Groups may wish to break away or **secede** from their state in order to form an independent state of their own or to join another. Prominent examples of the former include the Basques in Spain and the Kurds in Iraq and Turkey. In neither case have the groups been successful in persuading their current national governments to allow them to secede. Although it may be difficult to achieve, there are examples of successful secession in recent years. The Catalan regional government of Spain and the Iraqi Kurdish Regional Government both held referendums on secession from their respective states in 2017. Both countries' central governments have, expectedly, rejected the results of the referendum and have intervened to prevent secession. On the other hand, Kosovo declared its independence from Serbia in 2008 and has since gained recognition from over 100 members of the international community. Following its declaration of independence in July 2011, South Sudan became the latest state to secede (from Sudan) and join the United Nations.

As mentioned, secessionist groups may also want to join another state. This is a significant motivation for many Muslims in the northern Indian states of Jammu and Kashmir, a disputed region between India and Pakistan. Since their first war over the region in 1947–1948, India and Pakistan

Figure 3.2.   India map.

have each controlled portions of the territory and continue to face one another across a contested Line of Control. Despite the apparent willingness of India to accept the present Line of Control as a new international border, Pakistan refuses to do so and has instead continued to claim the whole of Kashmir for itself. While many in Jammu and Kashmir wish to join Pakistan, others wish to form their own independent state, and some wish to stay part of India. China also claims part of the region. Conflicts like this that appear very difficult to resolve are often called **intractable conflicts**.

3.2.2 Resources

Although fighting over resources has long been recognized as a major factor in the reason that states and non-state actors go to war, the connection has received increasing academic attention since the late 1990s. The reasons for this are threefold (Melvin 2011). The first is the growing fear of future international conflict over dwindling natural resources, such as oil, water, important minerals, gems, and timber. One of the earliest prophets of this concern was Michael T. Klare, who declared a "new geography of conflict," in which "the wars of the future will largely be fought over the possession and control of vital economic goods—especially resources needed for the functioning of modern industrial societies" (Klare, Resource Wars: The New Landscape Of Global Conflict 2001, 213). Areas of the world he thought were particularly prone to this type of conflict included the Caspian Sea basin and the South China Sea, both of which are believed to possess significant reserves of oil and natural gas and over which numerous states claim possession (see discussion box). Regions of the world he believed would be likely to see conflict over water included the Middle East and East Africa, because states in those regions compete over the water supplies from the Euphrates, Tigris, Jordan, and Nile rivers (Klare, Resource Wars: The New Landscape Of Global Conflict, 2001).

The second reason for the increase in academic attention to the potential for greater resource conflict is the fear that climate change will exacerbate this resource scarcity. Rising sea levels, increased desertification, and weather-related disasters will in the future threaten food, water, and energy supplies and make "internecine warfare over access to vital resources . . . a global phenomenon" (Klare, The Coming Resource Wars 2006). Even if states are lucky enough to escape direct involvement in these "resource wars," they will inevitably be drawn in through the need to react to the resulting humanitarian disasters and potentially massive "climate refugee" populations.

The third reason for the increase in academic attention to the connection between resources and conflict was the apparent role of resources in many of the civil wars that continued after, or emerged following, the end of the Cold War. Research into these conflicts highlighted several ways in which resources could influence conflict. First, in some cases armed groups were believed to have *initiated violence* in order to gain access to natural resources, such as oil, diamonds, and scarce minerals. Second, in some cases resource revenues provided the funds necessary for the violence to *continue*, thus making these conflicts more **protracted**. Civil wars motivated by disputes over the distribution of resources, as is often the case in secessionist wars, also appear more likely to restart than other types of civil wars (Rustad 2012).

Third, the heavy economic dependence of many of these states on natural resource exports appeared to lead to poor government policy choices and an ever-greater reliance on natural resource exports. For example, in the case of oil-dependent states, studies show that though they tend to be globalized economically (dependent on international trade, finance, and labor) they remain "strikingly *un*globalized" politically; they are less likely than other states to sign major treaties or join intergovernmental organizations and often defy global norms on human rights, the financing of foreign terrorism/rebellions and the expropriation of foreign companies (Ross, Unbalanced Globalization in the Oil Exporting States, 2011).

The cycle of ever-greater dependence on resources for export earnings is believed to be caused by the so-called "Dutch disease," named after the troubles that beset the Netherlands in the 1960s after it discovered natural gas in the North Sea. As rising resources exported push up the value of

DISCUSSION BOX

Will Asia Go to War over Territory and/or Resources?

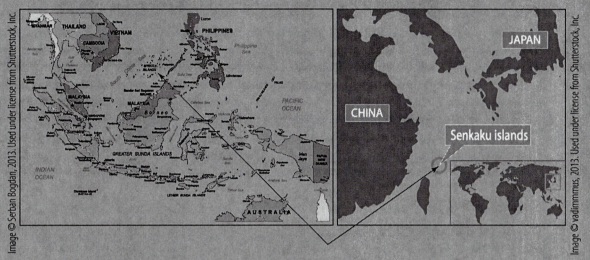

Over the past 30 years many of the countries of East Asia have witnessed extraordinary economic growth, which has required ever-greater supplies of energy. Although China became a net importer of oil in 1993, it is still able to obtain a majority of its petroleum and natural gas from domestic sources. Japan and South Korea, on the other hand, are almost completely dependent for oil on foreign sources, the overwhelming majority of which travels by ship through the South China Sea (Klare, Resource Wars: The New Landscape Of Global Conflict 2001).

As well as being one of the world's busiest trading routes, the South China Sea is also rich in resources. Some estimates suggest that it may hold as much as 11 billion barrels of oil and 190 trillion cubic feet of natural gas. Within the South China Sea there are also hundreds of small islands, rocks, and reefs, many of which are too small or too far submerged to be inhabitable. Three of the largest of these island chains are the Spratly, Parcel, and Senkaku islands (US Energy Information Administration 2013). Although the total land mass of these islands is very small, most of the states that border the South China Sea lay claim to part or all of them. These states include China, Japan, Vietnam, Taiwan, Brunei, Malaysia, and the Philippines. Although the last military confrontation over these islands took place between China and Vietnam in 1988, there have been numerous "incidents" in recent years that many (including the U.S. Secretary of Defense) fear may lead to a wider military conflict (BBC News 2012).

Why are these states claiming sovereignty over such small islands? Is their motivation primarily sovereign territory or resources? Do you think they will go to war? What role do you think the United States should play in the disputes/conflicts over their rival claims? Is the United States' objection to China for building artificial islands in the area driven by the same motivations as those of China's neighboring states?

its currency, the cost of its other exports (such as manufactured and agricultural goods) became more expensive. Export earnings on those products then declined, depriving the Netherlands of the benefits of a diverse and dynamic economy (Ross, Blood Barrels: Why Oil Wealth Fuels Conflict, 2008). For these reasons states with an abundance of natural resources tend to suffer from a **resource curse**; the paradoxical situation in which resource-rich countries tend to grow more slowly and achieve less development than resource-poor ones.

Resource dependence is thus perceived by many as contributing to the emergence of weak or failing states, with its associated higher risk of violent conflict (Melvin 2011, 41). Not all scholars, however, are convinced. For example, one study has found that resource dependence does not affect economic growth and that resource abundance positively affects economic growth and the quality of state institutions (Brunnschweiler 2008).

In his 2007 article entitled "What Resource Wars?" David G. Victor also dismisses the arguments concerning international wars over dwindling resources as "bunk." As he notes of the fear over water conflicts, "[despite] decades of warnings about water wars, what is striking is that water wars don't happen—usually because countries that share water resources have a lot more at stake and armed conflict rarely fixes the problem" (Victor 2007). Similarly, with regard to access to the Arctic's natural resources, despite initial bellicose statements and some provocative actions—including the planting of a Russian flag on the Arctic seabed by a science expedition in 2007—"there are [already] clear signs of international readiness to develop peaceful forms of competition and even cooperation based on international law, including the UN Convention on the Law of the Sea" (see above) (Melvin 2011, pg. 57).

3.2.3 Ideology

Ideology is defined as "a system of ideas and ideals, especially one that forms the basis of economic or political theory and policy" (Oxford Dictionaries n.d.). Common ideologies in American politics include conservatism, libertarianism, liberalism, and socialism, while ideologies believed to have been important in the history of world politics include liberal democracy, capitalism, communism, fascism, and Nazism.

Ideologies such as these are believed to cause or exacerbate international conflict because their believers, or "ideologues," become convinced that everyone should adopt it. They thus perceive alternative ideologies as barriers to the achievement of their own global "utopias." As will be discussed further in the next section, in this way ideology and religion have similar effects; they encourage what Martin Wight called **doctrinal wars**, which are "wars of righteousness and conviction based on doctrines that are not only right for us, they are right for everybody, everywhere. They are wars to bring one's religion or ideology to foreigners and ultimately all people around the world" (Jackson 2006, 274).

The power of ideology to foment international conflict was particularly apparent during the 20th century. It is common to split this period into three major events: World War I (1914–1918), World War II (1939–1945) and the Cold War (1945–1989). However, it might be more appropriate to see it as one long ideological struggle. Each of these wars, whether hot or cold, was a battle over ideology. The First World War pitted liberal democracy and capitalism against the absolutist monarchies of Central Europe. The Second World War pitted liberal democracy and capitalism against the axis powers, in particular Nazi Germany and fascist Italy. Finally, during the Cold War, liberal democratic and capitalist states in the West were opposed by communist states in the East.

DISCUSSION BOX

Have We Reached the "End of History"?

Perceiving the 20th century as a long battle over ideology has led some, like Francis Fukuyama, to conclude that the end of the Cold War represented not only the defeat of Communism, but also "the end of history as such: that is: the end point of mankind's ideological evolution and the universalization of Western liberal democracy as the final form of human government" (Fukuyama 1989).

Do you agree with Fukuyama that Western liberal democracy is the end point of mankind's ideological evolution? Do you think the United States should seek to spread democracy to other states around the world? Do you think the United States should use force in order to do so?

Although not everyone agrees that nationalism meets the definition of an ideology, it has continued to thrive in world politics, in many cases alongside other ideologies. The essence of nationalism is the belief that the world should be divided into nations and that ultimate political loyalty lies with the nation. Nationalism can thus be considered an ideology, but perhaps its greatest role in world politics is in providing an "identity" to groups who wish to form their own independent states and achieve other goals. Nationalism has continued to thrive, no doubt, because of its ability to complement other ideologies, or at least not compete with them. For example, Nazism and fascism are both inherently built on the notions of the nation and national superiority. Liberal democracy, on the other hand, has continued to spread across the world, despite the fact it is divided by national identities.

An interesting contemporary case of ideological evolution is occurring in China. Although still officially a communist state, China is currently undergoing a "national rejuvenation" in which Chinese nationalism is playing a fundamental role. What form of nationalism will this new communist/nationalist hybrid take? Will it be civic or ethnic? What will this mean for China's future international relations? At least one scholar has a pessimistic outlook. Based on her study of the origins of modern Chinese nationalism, Jacqueline Newmyer Deal concludes that the ethnic (Han Chinese) and collectivist nationalism now being forged in China,

> helps explain the recent flare-ups between China and its neighbors, as well as the United States and Europe, over issues that include fishing rights, territorial claims, intellectual-property theft and participation in international climate-change negotiations. . . . such clashes are likely to grow in intensity and frequency. Chinese nationalism will create turbulence for China abroad because its hierarchical, zero-sum perspective is fundamentally at odds with the principles underlying the current global order and because international engagement remains critical to the [Communist] party's economic growth strategy. (Deal 2013)

So, Deal is arguing that, on the one hand, the Chinese Communist Party is fostering an ethnic form of nationalism that is encouraging a sense of national superiority and historical grievance. On the other, China's economic growth requires that it engage with the world in a cooperative manner. Which of these forces do you think will win out?

China, however, is not the only state in the East Asian region with increasing nationalistic tendencies. There are growing fears that the Japanese government is also fostering a style of nationalism reminiscent of its old imperial age (The Economist 2013). The popularity of political right driven partly by appealing to populism and nationalism in Europe in places like Hungary, Poland, France, the Netherlands, and Germany also raises questions over the viability of liberalism in countering nationalism (Christina Pazzanese, 2017)[1]. Do you think we should therefore add nationalism to the explanations we have already provided for the growing tensions in the South China Sea? Which of the causes we have covered so far do believe is the principal cause of these tensions: territory, resources, or ideology?

3.2.4 Religion

As mentioned in the previous section, religion and ideology can both motivate their followers to conduct doctrinal wars. When justified by religion, doctrinal wars essentially become "holy wars," which are fought "to correct false religion and establish God's dominion on earth, as it is in heaven. Doctrinal wars are wars waged for nobler, higher, goals which cannot be compromised, or waged against false and menacing doctrines that cannot be tolerated. They are crusading wars against others whose beliefs and ways are regarded as a standing act of contempt for one's own values and convictions" (Jackson 2006, 287).

Historically, religion has not received as much attention in the study of world politics as one might expect. Only the terrorist attacks on September 11, 2001 were to change this. Nevertheless, you may have noticed that none of the theories of world politics that we have learned about in this text ascribe a significant role to religion in explaining individual and state behavior. For most of the 20th century, ideology was seen to be the most important force in world politics and the principal theories of the discipline reflect that. If religion was believed to be important, it was only in its contribution to the "identity" of ethnic and national groups, the role of which will be discussed in the next section. However, with some like the former British Prime Minister Tony Blair arguing that "religious faith will be of the same significance to the 21st century as political ideology was to the 20th century" (Heneghan 2008), religion is gaining increasing interdisciplinary attention (Snyder 2011).

Because this chapter is focused on explaining the causes of armed conflicts and wars, it may be easy to form the mistaken impression that all ideologies and religions are prone to violence and that the world is ablaze in ideological and religious conflict. In fact, the vast majority of the world's ideological and religious groups coexist peacefully. Our challenge, then, is to try to understand why, if so many people can live in relatively peaceful coexistence, some seem unable to do so.

Perhaps we can begin this challenge with categorizing the types of religious conflict that have been observed around the world. Rama Mani has divided religiously motivated violence into four forms (Mani 2012). The first is *interreligious violence* between distinct religions. Historic cases of such violence include the Crusades between the 11th and 13th centuries, while contemporary examples include violence occurring between Christians and Muslims in Nigeria, Iraq, Egypt, and Sudan, and between Hindus and Muslims in South Asia.

The second form of religiously motivated violence is *intrareligious*, or **sectarian** *violence*, that occurs between different sects or factions of the same religion. For example, the conflict that took place in Northern Ireland between 1969 and 1998 was fought principally between two sects of the Christian religion, Protestantism and Catholicism. Similarly, despite a historically peaceful coexistence, the majority of religiously motivated killing in the Middle East over the past decade has not been interreligious, but rather sectarian violence perpetrated by two sects of the **Islamic** religion against one another. These sects are the **Sunni** and **Shi'a** (or Shi'ite) branches of Islam.

Although a number of other smaller sects exist, the Sunni and Shi'a branches of Islam compose the vast majority of the world's Islamic community (or **Ummah**) of over 1.6 billion believers, with around 80–85% of the Ummah being Sunni and 15–20% Shi'a. While a majority of the Ummah lives in an arc stretching from North Africa through the Middle East into Asia (with Indonesia being the world's most populous Muslim country), the Shi'a community is concentrated in Iran, southern Iraq, Pakistan, Bahrain, and southern Lebanon.

The lethality of this Muslim sectarian conflict can be seen in the violence that erupted in Iraq following the U.S.–led invasion of 2003. Although the Iraqi population was 60% Shi'a and only 40% Sunni, with the latter being divided between Sunni Arabs (30%) and Sunni Kurds (10%), it was the Sunni Arabs who had held political power in the Saddam Hussein regime. When the Hussein regime collapsed, sectarian violence erupted between the Shi'a and Sunni Arabs, which between 2003 and 2013 is estimated to have cost over 100,000 lives. Although the worst of this violence occurred around 2006–2007, Iraq is still beset by sectarian killings, with an estimated 400 people killed in May 2013 alone. UN officials even expressed their fears that Iraq may soon "explode" into a full-scale sectarian civil war (Tawfeeq 2013). The simultaneous defeat of Daesh (aka, the Islamic State in Iraq and al-Sham (Syria), ISIS, or Islamic State in Iraq and the Levant, ISIL) in the closing months of 2017 promises a more stable Iraq ahead, although the Iraqi central government and the Kurdish Regional Government (KRG) remain at odds over the extent of Kurdish region autonomy and Kurdish leadership push for independence.

A third form of religiously inspired violence occurs between *believers and nonbelievers*. Christianity differentiates between those who do not believe in the religion at all (**infidels**) and those who have been baptized into the religion, but have since adopted beliefs and opinions thought to be at variance with traditional Christian dogma (**heretics**). The Crusades were thus fought against infidels, while the Spanish Inquisition sought to punish heretics. Islam also differentiates between "believers and unbelievers," with the latter commonly referred to as infidels. With no equivalent term for heresy, those who wish to criticize other sects within Islam tend also to refer to them as infidels. This is often done to justify violence that occurs between them, as in the case of the Shi'a and Sunni conflict described above.

A fourth form of religious conflict occurs between ***secular and religious institutions or individuals***. **Secular** governments and institutions are nonreligious. Theocracies, on the other hand, are states in which the government is run by clerics or by individuals claiming to be divinely guided. A current example of a **theocracy** is the Islamic Republic of Iran. Ultimate political authority in Iran lies with its Supreme Leader, presently Ayatollah Ali Khameini, who can ultimately make final decisions on all important political matters. An **Ayatollah** is a cleric within the Shi'a branch of Islam who is deemed to be an expert religious authority. Ayatollahs have large personal followings, and they are believed to guide the Shi'a com-

Figure 3.3. Ayatollah Ruhollah Khomenie. The first Supreme Leader of the Islamic Republic of Iran.

Image © Georgios Kollidas, 2013. Used under license from Shutterstock, Inc.

munity in the absence of the Mahdi, or 12th Imam, who disappeared in 873 c.e. (the Shi'a refer to this as "The Occultation") and who is expected to return as a messiah before the end of the world.

Sunni Muslims, on the other hand, do not have a formal clerical hierarchy, although the highest source of religious authority resides in a Mufti, who is a learned scholar of the Koran and Islamic jurisprudence. Sunnis also rely on members of the community who rise in expertise and authority to become **Imams**. Although generally chosen because of their superior knowledge of the Koran, they are not believed to receive divine guidance.

> **Religious Fundamentalism:** This essentially means that the individual or religious group in question believes in an interpretation of the religion that is closer to the original intent of its founder(s). Such groups thus tend to reject modern interpretations of their religious texts in favor of what they argue are unadulterated and thus more accurate interpretations.
>
> **Sharia Law:** Sharia law is Islamic law, and it differs from Western systems of law in two principal ways. First, the scope of Islamic law is much greater, meaning that it not only regulates the relationship of its subjects to one another and their government, but also personal matters of conscience. For example, ritual practices, such as fasting, daily prayers, and pilgrimage are integral to Sharia law. Second, the basis of Islamic law is divine will, meaning that the law does not emanate from society, but is expected to be obeyed by society as the will of God (Coulson n.d.). However, as one can tell from the description of the Islamic laws enforced in Iran and Saudi Arabia, the actual form that Sharia takes fluctuates from one society to the next, with some, like the Saudis, favoring draconian forms and most others opting for more enlightened versions.

Although members are elected to the Iranian Parliament, only those candidates deemed sufficiently Islamic are allowed to compete. In 2013 female members of the Iranian Parliament were also banned from competing in that year's elections for the Iranian presidency, on the basis that the country's constitution precludes women from running, although many argue that this is an incorrect interpretation of the text (Al Jazeera 2013).

Despite these constraints, Iranians living in a theocracy still enjoy much greater political and social freedoms than do their counterparts in Saudi Arabia. Although not technically a theocracy,

Saudi Arabia is run by a royal family who adhere to a **fundamentalist** interpretation of Sunni Islam, called **Wahhabism**, "that seeks to purify Islam of any innovations or practices that deviate from the 7th century teaching of the Prophet Muhammad and his companions" (Blanchard 2008). In Saudi Arabia women cannot vote, cannot drive, and cannot leave their own houses without being in the company of a male relative. The Saudi government in September 2017 granted women the right to drive, which will take effect in June 2018!

The fourth form of conflict also occurs when secular governments feel threatened by those who would seek to undermine the state's secular institutions. For example, the governments of Algeria, Turkey, and Pakistan are all currently grappling with Muslim groups who want to overturn the state's secular institutions and impose Islamic law (or **Sharia Law**). Such groups are often referred to as **Islamists**. Although most Islamist groups around the world are utilizing peaceful means to achieve their goals, such as seeking a mandate through democratic elections, and the type of Sharia law these groups wish to adopt varies widely between cases, state repression of such groups can lead to significant armed conflicts. In many cases the role of protecting the secular nature of the state has been assumed by the national armed forces, who may even conduct *coup d'etats* in order to prevent Islamists and other groups from assuming power.

Religion thus appears to play a role in armed conflict by helping convince believers that they need to conduct doctrinal wars in order to spread or defend their beliefs. As will see later in this chapter, the tactic of terrorism has also been utilized in all four forms of religious conflict that we have covered in this section. Terrorism does not therefore appear in this section, because it is not a *type* of religious conflict, but rather a *tactic* used in those conflicts, just as it is in ideological and other types of conflicts. Religion also appears to play a role in conflict by helping groups form around an "identity"—most commonly referred to as an "ethnic" identity—the discussion of which we turn to now.

3.2.5 Ethnicity

While conflict over ideology dominated most of the 20th century, the end of the Cold War and the collapse of the former Soviet Union appeared to open a Pandora's box of what quickly became labeled as "ethnic" conflict. Instead of heralding in a new peaceful age, the end of the Cold War appeared instead to unleash numerous conflicts in which groups appeared to be killing one another for no other reason than they were "different." By the mid-1990s these civil wars had reached a peak of around 50 across the globe and some analysts were talking of a "new world *dis*order" (Wimmer 2004, 2).

Ethnicity is a broad and malleable concept. A person's ethnic identity can be defined by any mixture of their lineage or ancestry, cultural traditions, language, or religious beliefs. **Ethnic groups** are thus formed around a common sense of ethnicity or **ethnic identity**. However, there is no way to determine which of the factors that make up ethnic identity will be most important for any particular group. For this reason, some of these ethnic conflicts are referred to as **ethnonationalist** or **ethno-religious**, depending on which factors appear to be most salient to outside observers. When conflicts appear to involve all of these elements of identity, they tend to be described generically as **ethnic conflicts**.

The terms *ethno-nationalist* and *ethno-religious* also help clarify for us how nationalism and religion, as we have discussed them above, contribute to ethnic conflict. If it is an ethno-nationalist conflict, then at least one of the ethnic groups fighting is assumed to have aspirations of forming an independent state based on ethnic criteria. Here we can see the connection between ethno-nationalist conflict and ethnic nationalism, as we discussed it in Chapter 1. If the conflict is ethno-religious, rather than simply religious, then at least one of the ethnic groups fighting identifies around a common religious belief.

Once again, however, we are left with the question of why the vast majority of the world's ethnic groups are able to coexist peacefully, while some are not. Scholars have suggested a number of reasons, and we can try to understand their reasoning by applying them to the case of the ethnic conflict that beset the former Yugoslavia between 1991 and 1995.

Before the end of the Cold War, Yugoslavia was considered to be one of the most developed communist states in Eastern Europe. Although it had existed as a monarchy since 1929, the Socialist Federal Republic of Yugoslavia was not created until the end of World War II. Translated into English, Yugoslavia means "land of the south Slavs," and it was so named because its inhabitants were nearly all ethnically **Slavic**. Despite this common ethnic identity, the Yugoslavs were still divided into six principal ethnic groups, the Slovenes, Croats, Bosniaks, Serbs, Montenegrins, and Macedonians. Eventually, a seventh ethnic group was recognized on the territory of the former Yugoslavia, the Albanian Kosovars.

Although the ethnic groups in Yugoslavia had lived in relative harmony since 1945, between 1991 and 1995 they fought a bloody civil war. The worst of this war occurred in the most ethnically diverse Yugoslav Republic of Bosnia and Herzegovina (Bosnia) between 1992 and 1995. Here the three ethnic groups, the Bosnian Croats (supported by Croats in the Yugoslav Republic of Croatia), the Bosniaks (referred to as Bosnian Muslims during the war), and the Bosnian Serbs (supported by Serbs in the Yugoslav Republic of Serbia) killed each other in a fashion that shocked the conscience of the world. By the end of the Bosnian civil war an estimated 100,000 people had died and over 2 million had been either **internally displaced** or had become **refugees**.

Refugees and Internally Displaced Persons (IDPs): Refugees are those people who have fled their homes and crossed an international border. IDPs are those who have also fled their homes, but have not crossed an international border.

The majority of refugees and IDPs are created as a result of the threat of violence, the direct and indirect effects of armed conflict, and natural/environmental disasters. In 2010 the UN High Commissioner for Refugees (UNHCR) estimated there to be 43.3 million forcibly displaced people worldwide—the highest number since the mid-1990s. Of these 27.1 million were IDPs, while 15.2 million were refugees (United Nations n.d.)

Slavic: The Slavs are the largest ethnic group in Europe. They are also concentrated in large numbers across northern Asia. States considered ethnically Slavic include Russia, Ukraine, Belarus, Poland, the Czech Republic, Slovakia, and all the new states formed from the former Yugoslavia, except Kosovo.

The Yugoslav civil war was also to witness some of the worst war crimes (see Chapter 4) of the post-War era. Most of the internally displaced and refugees of the war were forced to flee their homes because of **ethnic cleansing**. Ethnic cleansing is a process or policy of systematically removing or eliminating members of an ethnic group from a particular territory, whether through the use or threat of force. It is therefore usually committed in order to create a more homogenous ethnic population in the territory in question.

In 1995 Bosnia also suffered an internationally recognized case of **genocide** (see Chapter 4 for a full explanation of this crime and how it is being legally prosecuted). In July of that year Bosnian Serb forces overran the Bosnian town of Srebrenica (which had ironically been declared as a UN "Safe Area" and was thus under UN protection) and subsequently massacred some 8,000 Muslim men and boys. As a result of the policies of genocide and ethnic cleansing in Bosnia, tens of thousands of women also became the victims of mass

Figure 3.4. Map of Baltic Region. The seven recently formed independent states of the former Yugoslavia: Slovenia, Croatia, Bosnia and Herzegovina, Serbia, Montenegro, Macedonia, and Kosovo.

rape and sexual enslavement, both of which were recognized for the first time as crimes against humanity as a result of the prosecution of those who perpetrated them in the former Yugoslavia (Osborn 2001).

What then could have caused a multi-ethnic state like Yugoslavia that had lived in relative peace for so many decades to so quickly descend into such barbaric behavior? Contending explanations can be grouped into three broad categories. The first category is the **primordial** or "ancient hatreds" explanation. Here scholars argue that ancient hatreds that exist between ethnic groups can incite violence, especially when the central government cannot, or will not, prevent or stop it. In Yugoslavia, ethnic grievances and animosities dating back as far as the 14th century were believed to have erupted in violence as soon the Cold War ended and the Yugoslav state appeared weak. Primordial explanations help explain the roles of emotions and culture in conflict, although scholars disagree on whether the hatreds that exist between ethnic groups are truly primordial or are just relatively recently created and evolving "collective memories" (Blagojevic 2009).

The second explanation concentrates on the role played by so-called **political/ethnic entrepreneurs**. These political/ethnic entrepreneurs are political and ethnic leaders who seize opportunities to elevate themselves into positions of power (or stay in power) by inciting violence through the manipulation of the ethnic groups present in their societies. The politician accused most of inciting ethnic violence in Yugoslavia for his own ends was the former President of Serbia, Slobodon Milosevic. Milosevic rose to power by provoking an ethnic riot in the south Serbian region of Kosovo. As Stuart Kaufman describes it, once in power:

> [Milosevic's] ruling strategy centered around using the media to drum up Serbian nationalist passions [playing on the animosities that already existed between the ethnic groups], exaggerating the plight of ethnic Serbs in the mostly Muslim Albanian region of Kosovo, then denouncing Croats as equivalent to World War II era Ustasha fascists, blaming other nationalities for the economic problems facing Serbs and so on (Kaufman 2001, 5–6).

As you can tell from this description, ethnic conflict can be incited through a process of **ethnification** and the development of **ethnic intolerance** and **ethnocentrism**. Ethnification is the process of elevating ethnicity above other factors (such as national identity) in individual and group identities. Ethnic intolerance occurs when ethnic groups deny resources and rights to other ethnic groups (Blagojevic 2009, 4). This often occurs because of ethnocentrism, which is when an ethnic group perceives itself to be superior to others, or at least that another group is inferior. In extreme cases, ethnocentrism can lead to other ethnic groups being dehumanized, or treated as unworthy of basic human rights. Such dehumanization then excuses the awful treatment inflicted upon them, as the Nazis did to the Jews in the Holocaust or the Hutus did to the Tutsis in the Rwandan genocide of 1994.

John Mueller also argues that the violence in Yugoslavia was a product of political and ethnic entrepreneurs, but he does not believe they stoked ancient hatreds or ethnocentrism into becoming an "Hobbesian war of all against all and neighbor against neighbor" as the primordial explanation tends to characterize it. Rather, the violence was carried out mostly by "small bands of opportunistic thugs, criminals and soccer hooligans recruited for the purpose" and orchestrated by political/ethnic entrepreneurs and security services. For Mueller, therefore, ethnicity was *not* a motivating force in the violence, but simply a way to organize the armed groups and excuse their terrible behavior (Mueller n.d., The Banality of "Ethnic War": Yugoslavia and Rwanda n.d.).

The third category of explanations for the Yugoslav civil war focuses on the role of insecurity. This insecurity can be generated in a number of ways, but its effects are similar. For example, some scholars argue that the process of globalization and the modern pace of social change "makes people search for a secure homestead and produces an aggressive nationalism" (Wimmer 2004, 3). The majority of scholars in this category, however, concentrate on the effects on an impending sense of state weakness—or in the terminology we have begun to use in this text—a sense that the state is beginning to fail (see Chapter 1).

The first scholar to argue that state failure might explain much of the ethnic violence that was then occurring in the post-Cold War era was Barry Posen. In his 1993 article entitled "The Security Dilemma and Ethnic Conflict," Posen suggested that when governments became weak, states began to suffer from an "emerging anarchy" that was very similar to the international anarchy familiar to students of world politics. This meant that as the state began to fail (or was perceived as likely to fail) people and groups within the state could no longer rely on the central government to protect them and ensure their economic, political, and social rights. In these insecure conditions, it was natural for them to look for security in ethnic and other cultural groups.

Just like states in an anarchic international system, ethnic groups in emerging anarchy inevitably become responsible for their own protection. Once they do, they then have to ask "the following questions about any neighboring group: Is it a threat? How much of a threat? Will the threat grow or diminish over time? Is there anything that must be done immediately?" (Posen 1993, 27). Essentially, Posen had recognized that ethnic groups in emerging anarchy suffer from the very same security dilemma that states do in international anarchy (see Realism in Chapter 2). Ethnic groups thus begin to exhibit the same types of behavior as states; they worry about how much power they have relative to other ethnic groups; they arm themselves for defensive purposes, but in so doing are perceived by other groups as increasingly threatening; and they compete for, and fight over, economic and political resources in order to ensure their future survival. Ethnicity in this category of explanation is thus *not* a cause of conflict, but simply a way for people in insecure conditions to organize themselves for protection.

Perhaps the most important question in this discussion of the role of ethnicity in armed conflict is whether ethnicity causes violence, or whether is it simply a way to organize groups who are in conflict for other reasons. Because ethnic groups and historic animosities are usually present when conflict occurs, along with ethnic entrepreneurs and state failure, it is very hard to discern which is the most important factor and in what sequence they interact. Does the state fail, leading to ethnification, or does ethnification cause the state to fail? Do ethnic entrepreneurs incite violence that leads to state failure, or does state failure create the opportunity for ethnic entrepreneurs to incite ethnic violence? The answers to these questions are obviously still being debated, and this might be because each case is different. Building a single parsimonious explanation for the cause of all ethnic conflicts, or all conflicts in general, thus remains very difficult, if not impossible!

DISCUSSION BOX

The rise and fall of the Daesh (ISIL/ISIS) in Iraq and Syria between June 2014 and October 2017 intensified the seemingly sectarian conflict. Is the Sunni–Shi'a conflict in Iraq really over religious designation or a political conflict? To what extent the conflict is the result of political and religious leadership in each community? Still, to what extent the mal-distribution of socioeconomic resources and political power, instead of religious, ethnic, racial, or cultural characteristics, manifests itself in conflicts within and between different communities? Conflict, therefore, may be a result of **Bad "Governance,"** which is a manifestation of the failure of the state and agents of civil society to govern to ensure the presence of not only social harmony but also human security for the entire population. What do you think? (Abootalebi, 2015; Durac and Cavatorta, 2015)[2]

3.3 Theoretical Explanations for Armed Conflicts and Wars

So, what is the true cause of armed conflict and war in our international system? Is competition over territory and resources, as explained in the previous section, an actual cause of conflict? Or are they the result of deeper causes? Do religion, ideology, and ethnicity cause conflict? Or are they simply a means to organize groups that would fight anyway? To answer these questions we must move beyond an empirical study of actual cases and move toward a more abstract theoretical level.

As the analogy utilized at the beginning of section 3.2 suggests, hypertension may appear to be the cause of your headaches, erratic heartbeat, and chest pain. However, it is not hypertension that is the true cause of these symptoms, but whatever causes hypertension. Thus, we must find out what the cause(s) of hypertension is in order to be most effective in preventing or resolving it. So too, with armed conflict. If conflict over territory, resources, religion, ideology, and ethnicity are all symptoms, then what is their true cause? This section will explain what the three principal theories of world politics suggest is the answer.

3.3.1 Realism

Realists tend to despair at the idealism they see in those who extrapolate from relatively recent trends that our world may see the eradication of armed conflict and war. For Realists, this is the same type of idealism that was espoused during the 1920s, when the world was experiencing a similar bout of passivity. However, before the end of the following decade, much of the world was already engulfed in a war that by its end had cost over 50 million lives and had witnessed genocide on a previously incomprehensible scale.

Realists believe themselves to be more pragmatic than these "idealists" because they are not placing undue hope in relatively recent and inconsequential changes that have occurred in our international system. Rather, the true causes of armed conflict and war for Realists are just as present in our contemporary world as they were before World War I and World War II.

So, what are these true causes? As you may remember from our discussion in Chapter 2, Realism operates on all three levels of analysis (see section 2.3.4) in order to explain international and civil conflicts. On the first level (individual) Realists focus primarily on human nature. For Realists, human nature is unchanging. It is selfish, egotistical, and power-hungry. Humans will therefore always fight to ensure their own survival, but they will also do the same to enrich themselves and improve their power and status. International and civil wars over territory and resources are easily explained from this perspective. So too, is the barbarism that humans still appear persistently willing to inflict upon one another. Whether it is ethnic cleansing or genocide, mass rape and sexual enslavement, or the use of torture, the modern international system seems no less prone to such behavior. All that is needed to unleash the worst of human nature is to generate sufficient fear.

Realism, as we know, is a second-level theory because it is state-centric; it tries to explain the behavior of the most powerful actors in world politics, states. However, we also know that the behavior of states is explained to a large degree by the fact that they are reflections of individual human nature. States are little more than collections of individuals and their behavior will thus be similar. Trends in international conflicts and wars may thus fluctuate, but their underlying cause is ever present. For Realists, when peace exists, it is always precarious and does so only because something is preventing war from breaking out. This may be an international balance of power, the mutual possession of nuclear weapons, or the predominance of one state over all the others in the international system. It is certainly not because the nature of the state (or of the individual) has changed. States are rational actors and it is for this reason that Realism tends to dismiss the roles of religion and ideology in motivating state behavior.

However, there is one ideology that Realists believe is important in world politics—nationalism. As Stephen Walt, a prominent Realist scholar explains, nations can best achieve security by achieving statehood, while states can only survive if they have a population willing to fight and die to ensure their independence. Thus, in "the competitive world of international politics . . . nations have incentives to obtain their own state and states have incentives to foster a common national identity in their populations. Taken together, these twin dynamics create a long-term trend in the direction of more and more independent nation-states" (Walt 2011). In this way nationalism complements Realist theory and justifies its state-centric nature.

Although Realism was originally generated to explain the tendency of states to go to war, the work of Barry Posen (discussed in the previous section) also shows its relevance in explaining the tendency of sub-state groups to do the same. In conditions of emerging anarchy, ethnicity plays the same role as nationalism in international anarchy—it helps individuals and groups organize for protection. Although groundbreaking in its significance, Posen had simply applied the logic of Realism's third level of analysis to the question of civil conflict. On the third level of analysis, Realism argues that it is the anarchic international system that leaves states in a security dilemma and is thus the principal cause of war. When applied to civil wars, the failure of the state leaves sub-state groups suffering from the same security dilemma and prone to the same aggressive behavior. Ethnicity, religion, and ideology thus tend to play secondary roles in the Realist explanations for both international and civil conflict.

Once again, therefore, we can see how Realism operates on all three levels of analysis so as to explain international and civil armed conflict. While individuals and states are prone to aggressive behavior (to increase their power and security), they are usually deterred from doing so because of the presence of a law-enforcing central government in the case of the former and a configuration of the balance of power (unipolar or balance) that discourages international wars in the case of the latter. When the state begins to fail, sub-state groups begin to mimic states in the international system because they are now responsible for their own protection and become subject to the same security dilemma. These groups then fight for the same principal reasons that states do.

3.3.2 Liberalism

Just as Realism accuses Liberalism of being too idealistic about the prospects for international peace, Liberalism accuses Realism of being too pessimistic. For Liberalism, Realism fails to appreciate the tremendous changes that have taken place in the international system over the past century or so, changes that have significantly affected the behavior of states. Where Realists see only a temporary blip in the tendency of states not to go to war, Liberals have instead identified a growing trend—one that can be attributed to these very changes.

As explained in Chapter 2, the changes that Liberals argue makes states less likely to go to war rest on the second and third levels of analysis and are depicted in the Kantian triangle. The most transformative effects of the triangle are evident in the so-called democratic peace. As democracy has spread across our international system, so too has interstate peace. As Liberals would expect, the most peaceful regions of the world, like Europe and North America, are those in which the oldest and strongest democracies are to be found. On the other hand, those regions with the greatest tendency toward conflict, such as Asia and Africa, are those with the fewest and weakest democratic states within them. Liberals would also predict that the greatest threats to international peace and security would emanate from the world's least democratic states, like China, North Korea, Iran, and Saudi Arabia.

The second point on the Kantian triangle is economic interdependence. Just as democracy is spreading around the world, so too is economic interdependence. As interdependent states are dependent on one another for continued economic prosperity, they have powerful incentives to seek cooperation over conflict. This dynamic can be seen in the U.S.–China relationship, which despite being fraught with tensions and disagreements, continues to be cooperative. During the U.S.–China summit of June 2013, the recently appointed Chinese President, Xi Jinping (who has spent time in rural Iowa researching American agriculture and whose daughter is studying at Harvard University) openly declared that the "Chinese dream is about cooperation, development, peace and win-win . . . and it is connected to the American dream and the beautiful dreams people in other countries may have" (Rucker 2013). The proponents of economic interdependence also point to the growing evidence that shows that shared territorial borders may actually encourage greater cooperative behavior between states, rather than increase the risk of violence (see "Territory").

As with Realism, Liberalism has historically paid little attention to the effects of religion and ethnicity on the risk of international conflict. Ideology is obviously important because liberal democracy produces peace. Other ideologies and religions are only important in the sense that they reduce the degree of liberal democracy and thus make the state more prone to aggression, both against other states and its own citizens.

On the third level of analysis, the Kantian triangle points to the transformative effects of international institutions. By helping states overcome the prisoner's dilemma, states like the United States and China can cooperate to a degree thought impossible by Realists. Evidence of this can be seen even in the competing claims over natural resources and territory, two issues that have hitherto been especially prone to violence. As Melvin notes in our earlier discussion of resource conflicts, even in the face of the most provocative acts, states are utilizing international law (including the UN Convention on the Law of the Sea) to avoid violent conflict and ensure peaceful forms of competition and cooperation. Liberal scholars also highlight the contribution that international organizations like the UN make to the prevention, management, and resolution of international and civil conflicts, especially through their peacekeeping and post-conflict peace-building missions.

3.3.3 Radical Approach

Of the three theories of international relations discussed in this text, it is the Radical Approach that criticizes the state-centric nature of contemporary security studies the most. While Realism operates on a generally unquestioned assumption that the state is the principal provider of security to its citizens, Liberals tend at least to limit this assertion to liberal democracies. Radical theorists, on the other hand, fundamentally question the idea of the state as the *provider* of security and argue that in most cases, including in liberal democracies, the state is usually the *perpetrator* of the greatest violence against its own citizens.

It is because of this that Radical theorists tend to be the greatest proponents of replacing the state-centric nature of security studies with the human security approach introduced at the beginning of this chapter. For Radical theorists, focusing on armed conflict and war between states and organized groups within states serves only to mask the widespread violence, repression, and chronic insecurity suffered by the vast majority of the world's population at the hands of their own governments during times of "peace." For most Radical theorists the true cause of this violence, repression, and insecurity is the global capitalist system.

There is no better example of how capitalism operates in this regard than in the United States itself. While the United States continues to act in an imperial fashion abroad, demanding through the threat and use of violence that other states convert to its own ideology (doctrinal war), its own citizens are the victims of the very same systemic violence, repression, and insecurity that they are ostensibly trying to end in other societies. For example, the United States has the highest incarceration rate in the world (higher even than China, which has four times its population), 60% of which are nonviolent offenders. The vast majority of this prison population is, of course, drawn from the poorest sectors of American society. As an ironic sign of progress, the *New York Times* was able to report in 2013 that African American women were only 2.8 times more likely than white women to be imprisoned, rather than six times more likely, as they were in 2000. African American men were also only 6.4 times more likely to be imprisoned than white men, down from 7.7 times more likely in 2000 (Goode 2013).

Systemic insecurity in the United States is also evident in the high levels of gun ownership and gun violence, which also tend to disproportionately affect the poor. Between 2001 and 2010 4,519 people were killed by guns in Louisiana alone (1,000 more casualties than suffered by U.S. combat troops during the Iraq War), 75% of which were African American. For Radical theorists, U.S. military campaigns, incarceration rates, and gun violence are all products of the intertwining interests of the government, private industries, and the bourgeoise class within the capitalist system.

As Radical theorists would expect, the capitalist system is also producing ever-widening income and wealth inequalities, both in American society and globally. In 2011 the U.S. Census Bureau reported that 15% (46.2 million) of adult Americans were living in poverty, the largest number counted as poor in 53 years of its poverty measurements. Of American children, 22% were now living in poverty (National Center for Law and Economic Justice n.d.). At the same time, wealth inequality in America increased significantly with the richest 0.01% of Americans now enjoying an average yearly income of $27 million per household and the lowest 90% an average income of $31,244.

Internationally a similar dynamic is apparent. Despite the promised benefits of free markets and decades of American global leadership, 80% of the world's population still lives on less than $10 per day; 22,000 children die each day due to poverty; nearly 30% of those children who survive are estimated to be underweight or stunted; 1.1 billion of the world's poorest populations still have inadequate access to water (Shah 2013); and over 600,000 die from malaria (World Health Organization 2013). All of this, of course, takes place during times of "peace."

Economic exploitation within global capitalism is also rife. For example, on 24 April 2013 a building that housed a garment factory that primarily exported to Western markets collapsed in Dhaka, Bangladesh, killing over 1,000 workers. Although cracks had appeared in the walls of the factory over previous days, the workers were compelled by their supervisors to return to the building to complete their orders. The tragedy was symptomatic of the "unseen" plight of hundreds of millions of workers around the world, who toil all day everyday in terrible "sweatshop" conditions, with few or no rights, in order to supply wealthier countries with cheap clothes and other products. Bangladesh, one of the world's poorest countries, is the third largest garment exporter to the United States, after China and Vietnam. As the deaths and shortened life spans caused by such exploitation are never counted in official "armed conflict" statistics, this type of systemic violence goes unnoticed, thus giving a false sense of growing international peace and security.

For Radical theorists, therefore, focusing on organized armed conflicts between states and sub-substate groups leads scholars to miss the systemic violence that is inflicted on the poorest of the world's population because of the global capitalist system. However, Radical theorists also expect that the traditional forms of conflict will still return in a large scale too. States like China, the United States, and Japan are bound to come into conflict over their insatiable desire for natural resources, which is driven by the materialism and consumer culture of capitalist societies. These conflicts will only be exacerbated by the climate change that these very same rich countries have caused through their fossil-fuel-based economies. The world is thus caught in an inescapable (short of revolution) capitalist-driven conflict spiral.

3.4 Issues in International Security

As explained in Chapter 2, the three principal theories of world politics each have a different explanation for how the world works. This subsequently leads them to propose different approaches to managing international peace and security. Realists see an anarchic international system that leaves states in a security dilemma from which they cannot escape. The only means that to ensure state survival in this type of system is to manage the balance of power. Realists therefore propose U.S. foreign policies that seek to manipulate the balance of power in its favor, such as off-shore balancing (see Chapter 2).

Liberals, on the other hand, although they accept the anarchic nature of the international system, are not as pessimistic about the prospects for international peace and security as their Realist counterparts. Liberals remain hopeful that peace can be achieved, even in our anarchic system, mainly through the spread of democracy and economic interdependence. They also remain more optimistic about the ability of the world's most powerful states to maintain international peace and security through a collective security system (see Chapter 2). Liberal internationalism, the foreign policy favored by Liberals, thus seeks to combine all of these elements.

Finally, Radical theorists do not believe that international peace and security can be achieved in a world dominated by capitalism. Capitalism perpetuates domestic and global inequalities and encourages exploitation. While it is caught in this capitalist system, the United States will always seek to dominate and exploit weaker parts of the world. This means international peace and security can only be achieved through a revolution in the global economic system. For this reason, Radical theorists propose a Radical anti-imperialist foreign policy for the United States (see Chapter 2).

Although we can now appreciate the differences between the broad approaches briefly described here, it is still important to apply them to specific issues in international peace and security. By doing so, we can better assess whether the policies they propose will achieve the level of peace and security that they claim. Although there are a multitude of issues that could be discussed here, this text will take two of the most prominent challenges to international peace and security as examples. These are terrorism and the proliferation of weapons of mass destruction (WMD).

3.4.1 Terrorism

Although terrorism is often talked about as if it were a belief or ideology, it is in fact only a **tactic**—a means of achieving a larger goal. This confusion was particularly apparent in the U.S. declaration of a "war on terror" after the terrorist attacks of September 11, 2001. Declaring war on terrorism is thus equivalent to declaring war on bombing raids. How could the United States ever hope to win such a war? How could we even know when such a war had been won? Perhaps the most important questions to ask, then, are Who is using terrorism and for what purposes? Only after we have answered these questions can we begin to debate which **counterterrorism** strategies and policies the United States and other states should adopt.

As with so many of the terms we use in world politics, no universally accepted definition of terrorism exists. Nevertheless, we can identify it essentially as "politically motivated violence perpetrated against noncombatant targets by sub-state groups or clandestine agents, usually intended to influence an audience" (Atran 2003, 1534). The goals of terrorism are normally twofold: to coerce an identified enemy into changing its policies and/or behavior and to attract supporters to the terrorist's cause. Terrorism is not, therefore, irrational behavior, but rather a tactic used to achieve a larger, strategic goal. And although it may appear to be a relatively recent development, terrorism has in fact been around for thousands of years, with recorded accounts dating back to biblical times.

The non-state groups that have utilized terrorism vary significantly in their motivations for doing so. For example, as of 2012 the U.S. State Department lists around 50 foreign terrorist organizations operating around the world. Some of these groups are motivated principally by religion (al Qaeda and al Qaeda in the Arabian Peninsula); some by ideology and nationalism (Real Irish Republican Army and Basque Fatherland and Liberty). Others are accused of being little more than criminal organizations seeking power and financial gain (the Revolutionary Armed Forces of Columbia or FARC are often referred to as **narcoterrorists** because they are accused of conducting terrorism simply to protect their illegal narcotics trafficking). Of course, many of the terrorist organizations listed by the State Department have some combination of all three motivations.

When most Americans think of terrorism, they naturally think of the terrorist attacks conducted by al Qaeda on September 11, 2001 (see Figure 3.5). The psychological impact of these attacks was obviously significantly greater than any before or since. There are two reasons for

Image © Ken Tannenbaum, 2013. Used under license from Shutterstock, Inc.

Figure 3.5. Smoke billows from the Twin Towers due to impact damage from airliners on September 11, 2001, in New York.

this, both of which reflect the changing nature of terrorism in the modern era. The first is the tendency toward **mass casualty terrorism**. As terrorists have historically focused on generating fear and anxiety in their target audience, the actual numbers killed in their attacks tended not to matter. In fact, in many cases, killing too many people (or sometimes any people at all) risked undermining the terrorist's cause by alienating those who might otherwise have been sympathetic towards them.

With the emergence of al Qaeda, however, the United States was faced with a new form of terrorism, one in which the terrorists appeared to desire the death of as many civilians as possible. Having killed nearly 3000 on September 11, 2001, al Qaeda and its leader, Osama Bin Laden, continued to declare their intentions to perpetrate even greater attacks. The world thus became fearful that al Qaeda and its affiliates might actually acquire weapons of mass destruction, such as chemical, biological, or even nuclear weapons—a fear that justified much of the actions taken in the George W. Bush administration's subsequent "war on terror," including the invasions of Afghanistan and Iraq. The United States also created the Department of Homeland Security in reaction to the perceived threats from this more destructive form of terrorism.

DISCUSSION BOX

Democracy and Counterterrorism: Freedom versus Security

In early June 2013 a British newspaper, *The Guardian*, broke a controversial story concerning the collection and analysis of American telephone and Internet data by the U.S. National Security Agency (NSA). The uproar that followed the disclosure reignited the age-old debate of how much personal privacy and freedom must be sacrificed in order to ensure national security—in this case, to defend against potential terrorist attacks. Although the American public appeared surprised by the disclosure, the legal justification for the collection and "mining" of such data was included in the PATRIOT Act, which was passed 45 days after the attacks of September 11, 2001. The Protect America Act of 2007 further expanded the NSA's surveillance powers to include the collection of such data within the United States itself.

President Obama reacted to the controversy by defending the collection of phone and Internet data of millions of Americans as a modest encroachment on privacy and as something that is both lawful and justified in order to identify terrorists plotting to attack the United States (Finn 2013). Do you agree? Do you believe the former NSA contractor who leaked information about the program to *The Guardian* is a hero or a traitor? If you had been the president, would you have announced the NSA's work and debated its merits in public? Or would you have tried to keep it secret in order to foil future terrorist plots?

The second trend reflected in the attacks of September 11, 2001 was the increasing use of **suicide terrorism**. Suicide terrorism is conducted by terrorists who either kill themselves during an attack or at least expect to be killed in order for the attack to succeed. Since the early 1980s the number of suicide terrorist attacks has grown significantly, and they account for an ever-greater proportion of the victims of terrorism in general. Between 1980 and 2009 there were nearly 2,200 suicide attacks, increasing from 50 per year between 2000 and 2003 to 300 per year between 2003 and 2009. Although suicide terrorism may appear irrational and usually motivated by religious fanaticism, the most comprehensive studies of the phenomena prove that virtually all suicide attacks have the same strategic goal: to compel a democratic state to withdraw its armed forces from territory that the terrorists prize. And despite being associated in popular opinion with extremist Islamic terrorist organizations, the organizations that have conducted the most suicide attacks have been nationalist/ideological and secular in orientation, like the now defunct Tamil Tigers of Sri Lanka (Pape 2010).

The combination of mass casualty terrorism and suicide terrorism present in the September 11, 2001, attacks thus had a dramatic psychological effect on American society, one that was deliberately sought by its perpetrators. Americans had hitherto felt protected by their geographic distance from regions of conflict. Although terrorist attacks had occurred on American soil before (including an attempt to bring down the World Trade Center in 1993, which left six dead and over a thousand injured), none of them had been suicide attacks. And when suicide attacks had targeted Americans, like those against the U.S. military barracks in Beirut in 1983 and the USS *Cole* in 2000, they had occurred on foreign soil and had been directed at military personnel. After September 11, 2001, Americans were therefore understandably gripped by an intense fear of the massive death and destruction that might be inflicted by terrorists who appeared to be irrational and thus undeterrable (how do you stop someone who is willing to die in an attack?), a fear which continues to resonate through American society today.

Coordinating international action against terrorism is hindered by several important factors. First, terrorist organizations are non-state actors, but they are at times utilized and supported by **state-sponsors of terrorism**. These are states that are accused of supporting terrorist organizations that operate on foreign territory. The U.S. State Department lists four such states as of 2013: Cuba, Iran, Sudan, and Syria.

DISCUSSION BOX

Drones and Counterterrorism

Since taking office in 2009 President Obama has made the use of Unmanned Arial Vehicles (UAVs) or "drones," the centerpiece of his administration's counterterrorism policy. Within four years of taking office he had ordered six times as many drone strikes as his predecessor. Estimates of the number of people killed in "target killings" conducted with drones in Afghanistan and Yemen since 2002 range between 3,000 and 4,000.

On 23 May 2013 President Obama gave a speech on U.S. counterterrorism policy and the use of drone strikes to the National Defense University. In the speech he made a number of claims about the effectiveness, legality, and proportionality of drone strikes conducted on foreign territory. First, he claimed that "dozens of highly skilled al Qaeda commanders, trainers, bomb makers and operatives [had] been taken off the battlefield . . . and plots had been disrupted." Second, he argued that drone strikes were legal, both in domestic and international law based on the Authorization for Use of Military Force Against Terrorist s resolution, which was passed by Congress on 14 September 2001, and because the United States is still "at war with an organization" that is seeking to "kill as many Americans as they could if we did not stop them first." Last, the alternative to drone strikes, large conventional military operations, would inevitably lead to even greater civilian casualties than those inflicted by drones. Thus, the president concluded that "this is a just war—a war waged proportionally, in last resort, and in self-defense" (Obama 2013).

Despite the president's protestations, concerns about the use of drones as a counterterrorism tool continue to be expressed. The greatest fear is that drone strikes may actually undermine long-term counterterrorism goals by antagonizing and alienating the populations in which they take place. This is especially the case in Yemen, "where there appears to be a strong correlation between increased targeted killings . . . and heightened anger toward the US and sympathy or allegiance to al Qaeda in the Arabian Peninsula" (Zenko 2013, 11)

Do you think drones are an effective counterterrorism measure? Who should/should not be targeted by these strikes? Do you support their continued use, even if they violate the sovereignty of the states in which they are used? What alternatives exist to the use of drones?

The second complicating factor in implementing a counterterrorism strategy is evident in the list of state sponsors above. What is considered by the United States to be a terrorist organization is considered by these states to be a freedom-fighting organization and vice versa. For example, the United States considers the Lebanese-based political party Hezbollah (Party of God) and the Gaza-based political party Hamas (Islamic Resistance Movement) as foreign terrorist organizations. Iran and Syria, however, argue that these groups are fighting for their freedom against illegal Israeli occupation and persecution (both Hamas and Hezbollah also participate in electoral politics and claim to legitimately represent the Palestinian and Lebanese people). Similarly, the Syrian government considers many of the Sunni groups currently fighting against it to be extremist Islamic terrorists. The United States and other Western countries, on the other hand, tend to perceive them as fighting against authoritarianism. In the words of the old adage, one man's terrorist is another man's freedom fighter.

So, what kind of counterterrorism strategy should the United States adopt? Should it conduct a "war on terrorism" or concentrate only on those terrorist organizations that seek to attack U.S. citizens? Should it deploy military forces abroad in an attempt to eradicate these organizations? As we will soon see, each of the three theories of world politics that we have studied so far propose different approaches to the threat of terrorism, just as they do to the challenge of WMD proliferation-to which we now turn.

3.4.2 Weapons of Mass Destruction (WMD)

There exist three general types of Weapons of Mass Destruction (WMD): nuclear, chemical, and biological. This type of weapon is distinguished from more **conventional weapons** by the scale of their potential destructive capacity. In other words, they can cause much greater levels of death and destruction.

Nuclear weapons are currently the most destructive weapons in the arsenals of states. There are essentially two types, **fusion** nuclear weapons and **fission** nuclear weapons. Fission weapons work through the release of enormous amounts of energy when an atom is split in the **nuclear warhead**. Two forms of **fissionable material** are used to conduct this reaction: The first is developed from uranium and the second is plutonium. Obtaining this fissionable material and making it suitable for use in a nuclear warhead is perhaps the most difficult aspect of building a nuclear weapon.

Although uranium is found underground and is mined in a number of countries around the world, including Canada and United States, to be used in nuclear weapons it must first be processed into fissionable material through a process called **isotopic enrichment**. Through this process the fissionable isotope of uranium, uranium-235 (U-235) is separated from the nonfissionable isotope of uranium, uranium-238 (U238). Naturally occurring uranium is composed of less than 1% U-235, with the rest being U-238. The most common method of isotopic enrichment is the use of cascades of highly sophisticated gas centrifuges, which spin at tremendous speeds in order to progressively separate out the desired U-235, although this can also be achieved also through the use of lasers and electromagnets.

Uranium composed of more than 20% U-235 is classed as **highly enriched uranium (HEU)**. To be used in a nuclear weapon, the fissionable material must be composed of around 90% U-235, which is referred to as **weapons-grade uranium**. Uranium for a civilian nuclear power station, on the other hand, need only be 4 to 6% U-235. As we will see later, evidence of the production of HEU is thus often treated as the greatest proof of the intention of building a nuclear weapon.

Plutonium is not a naturally occurring element, but the byproduct of the reaction that occurs in a nuclear reactor. Thus plutonium is actually easier to produce than HEU. However, as well as requiring a specific type of nuclear reactor (fast breeder reactor) that is able to produce the appropriate type of plutonium, the separation of the plutonium from the other waste products that are produced also requires a **plutonium reprocessing plant**. The presence of such a plant, as with the presence of weapons grade HEU, is yet another indicator of weapons research and production.

Also, because plutonium bombs are more difficult to build than uranium bombs, states have tended to begin their nuclear weapons production by building the latter first.

Fusion nuclear weapons (also known as **thermonuclear weapons** or **hydrogen bombs**) have much greater destructive power than fission weapons (a 100 times or more), but are also much more expensive and technically demanding to build. They are, in fact, a combination of fission and fusion weapons, as the bomb works by using a fission explosion in the warhead to set off a fusion reaction. **Neutron bombs** are fusion nuclear weapons that produce a relatively small explosion, but a much greater level of radioactivity. These have the potential to kill people, while leaving infrastructure relatively unharmed.

Like nuclear weapons, chemical and biological weapons also have the potential to be WMD. **Chemical weapons** are any weapon that uses a manufactured chemical to kill or seriously harm its victims. They can range from chemicals designed to cause severe irritation, such as tear gas, to those that seriously interfere with the body's nervous system, breathing, circulation, and other functions. For example, the first recorded incident of lethal **chemical warfare** was the use of chlorine gas by the German army during World War I. Although chlorine is a common chemical found in many municipal water supplies and swimming baths, when inhaled in gaseous form it can cause damage to the nose, throat, and lungs and is potentially fatal. Other chemical agents that can be used in this way include Sarin and VX, both of which attack the nervous system and are therefore known as **nerve agents**.

Biological weapons use bacteria or a virus (and sometimes toxins derived from bacteria) to kill or seriously harm their victims. Fatal diseases that can be caused by viruses or bacteria released from biological weapons include anthrax (bacterium), smallpox (virus), and pneumonic plague (bacterium). Although they work in a very similar way to nuclear and chemical weapons, biological weapons have the potential to be even more destructive. Theoretically, one biological weapon could begin an epidemic across an entire population. However, a weapon of such potency would probably be equally as dangerous to the people that used it.

Delivery Systems

A **delivery system** is the method used to carry the WMD to its intended destination. The only two nuclear weapons ever to be used, which were both dropped by the United States on Japan in August 1945, were carried to their destination by a B-29 bomber or military aircraft. Modern nuclear arsenals, however, tend to rely on **ballistic missiles** as their principal delivery system. These ballistic missiles can be **strategic** (fired over thousands of miles; those with the longest range are known as Inter-Continental Ballistic Missiles), **intermediate** (fired over hundreds of miles), or **tactical** (fired within the battlefield or less than 200 miles).

Ballistic missiles are missiles that are guided only during the initial powered phase of their flight. Once past this stage, they rely on the laws of physics (classical mechanics) to accurately hit their targets. **Guided missiles**, such as the commonly known cruise missile, on the other hand, are guided and powered throughout their journey and can thus travel at very low altitudes. Ballistic missiles therefore tend to be launched from land based delivery systems (submarine-launched ballistic missiles being the principal exception), while guided missiles tend to be launched from airplanes, ships, and submarines. Both types of missile can carry conventional warheads, rather than WMD, making the guided missile the weapon of choice of most modern militaries, given their greater accuracy.

Compared to airplanes, ballistic and guided missiles are relatively small and fast. They are therefore much harder to defend against. During the Cold War both superpowers possessed thousands of Inter-Continental Ballistic Missiles (ICBMs) in order to ensure that they would overwhelm any defenses that their opponent might try to erect. However, now that the Cold War is over, the threat of a large-scale nuclear attack has receded. The principal threat facing the United States today appears to come from states that do not possess massive arsenals of these weapons, but might hope only to fire a small number of them at the United States or its allies.

These developments have led the United States in recent years to accelerate the research and development of **Anti-Ballistic Missile (ABM)** systems designed to shoot down a small number of ICBMs while their warheads are outside of the Earth's atmosphere. The world's militaries have also been busy developing or buying ever improving **surface-to-air missile (SAM)** systems designed to shoot down airplanes, as well as ballistic and guided missiles. The Patriot SAM system used by the U.S. Army became widely recognized after it was used in the First Persian Gulf War against Iraqi SCUD ballistic missiles.

(Non-)Proliferation of WMD and Their Delivery Systems

Proliferation technically means either an increase in the number of the weapons concerned, or their spread to more states in the international system. The first type is called **vertical proliferation**, while the second is called **horizontal proliferation**. Thus, vertical proliferation occurs when states increase their stockpiles of nuclear, chemical, biological, or other weapons. Horizontal proliferation occurs when more states in the international system buy or develop these weapons.

The first state to develop and use nuclear weapons was the United States in 1945. This was quickly followed by the Soviet Union, which tested its first nuclear device in 1949. By the mid-1970s, the two superpowers had been joined by the United Kingdom, France, China, Israel, and India. Over the past 20 years Pakistan and North Korea have also developed nuclear weapons, taking the current total of nuclear states to nine.

Recognizing the danger posed by the uncontrolled vertical and horizontal proliferation of conventional weapons and WMD, states have traditionally utilized two methods in order to contain them. The first is **arms control**, which imposes a limitation on the number and/or quality of certain types of weapon. The second is **disarmament**, which aims not only to reduce, but to eventually eliminate certain types, or even all weapons. Although, as we will see, they differ fundamentally in their approach, they both try to achieve the same objectives: to reduce the risk of war; to reduce the costs of preparing for war; and to limit the destruction that would be inflicted should war occur.

Despite sharing similar goals, arms control and disarmament represent two different approaches to maintaining international peace and security. Arms control rests on the premise that the best way to prevent war is to maintain stability. This can be best achieved by limiting the number and/or types of weapon that states possess, so as to maintain a balance between them. For example, the most recent arms control treaty signed between the United States and the Russian Federation in 2010, the New Strategic Arms Limitation Treaty (New START) calls for a reduction in the number of deployed strategic nuclear warheads to 1,550 each. Arms control thus strives for a reduction in the type or quality of weapons, but perceives full disarmament as being detrimental to the maintenance of peace and security.

Image © iurii, 2013. Used under license from Shutterstock, Inc.

Figure 3.6. Warship at sea launches a guided missile.

Disarmament, on the other hand, perceives the existence of weapons as increasing the threat of war and thus seeks to eliminate them. This is the approach that has been taking toward chemical and biological weapons. Despite maintaining large arsenals of chemical weapons during the Cold War, both the United States and Russia signed the 1992 Chemical Weapons Convention (CWC) along with most other states. The Convention prohibits the development, production, acquisition, stockpiling, transfer, and use of chemical weapons. The 1972 Biological Weapons Convention (BWC) does the same for biological weapons. Over 170 states have now ratified the BWC and nearly 190 have ratified the CWC.

The most important international disarmament agreement on nuclear weapons is the 1968 **Treaty on the Non-Proliferation of Nuclear Weapons (NPT)**. The NPT has now been ratified by 190 states, more than any other arms control or disarmament agreement. There are two groups of signatories. The first group is the nuclear-weapon states, consisting of the United States, the Russian Federation, China, France, and the United Kingdom. These states had all tested nuclear devices before 1 January 1967. All other signatories are classed as non-nuclear weapon states.

The central bargain of the NPT is that the non-nuclear weapons states commit themselves under Article 2 of the treaty not to acquire nuclear weapons, in return for a commitment from the nuclear weapons states under Article 6 "to pursue negotiations in good faith . . . [toward] nuclear disarmament." In addition, under Article 4 of the treaty, all the non-nuclear weapons states were promised help with the development of civilian nuclear energy production, if they so desired.

In order to ensure the fulfillment of the treaty's provisions, all the non-nuclear weapons states agreed to accept a **safeguard agreement** with the International Atomic Energy Agency (IAEA), an independent organization headquartered in Vienna, Austria. These safeguard agreements required the non-nuclear weapons states to provide the IAEA with information related to the acquisition or processing of fissionable material, or the development of nuclear facilities. At this point the IAEA was allowed to inspect all the officially declared materials and facilities.

In 1995, after a number of non-nuclear weapon states had appeared to have developed clandestine weapons programs, including North Korea, the IAEA sought to strengthen the safeguard program through the creation of an **Additional Protocol** to the NPT. The Additional Protocol requires much more detailed accounting of nuclear related activities: short notice "snap" inspections of both declared and undeclared sites; environmental sampling and remote monitoring; and automatic visa renewal for IAEA inspectors, to ensure speedy deployment. As of June 2013, 140 states have acceded to the Additional Protocol.

Of the nine known states to possess nuclear weapons in 2013, three have never signed the NPT, and one has signed and later withdrawn. The three that have never signed are India, Pakistan, and Israel. North Korea signed the NPT in 1983 and then withdrew from it in 2003, before testing its first nuclear device in 2006. It has since conducted two more and is believed to have developed a small nuclear arsenal. North Korea is also developing its ballistic missile capabilities, and as of 2013 did not have the capacity to fire a missile beyond its region. North Korea, however, tested 23 missiles in 16 tests between February and November 2017, and claimed to have successfully tested a new type of intercontinental ballistic missile, topped with a "super-large heavy warhead," capable of striking the US mainland. [CNN, Thu November 30, 2017.] http://www.cnn.com/2017/11/28/politics/north-korea-missile-launch/index.html

Dual-Use Technology

Identifying whether a state has broken its promises under one of the arms control or disarmament treaties is made especially difficult because of the **dual-use** nature of the technology involved. This means that the technology in question can be used for both civilian and military purposes. For example, chlorine is a common substance used worldwide to kill microorganisms and purify water supplies. However, as mentioned in the discussion of WMD above, it can also be used in gaseous form as a chemical weapon. Similarly, research into curing and defending against the spread of diseases can also be utilized in the building of a biological weapon.

Most nuclear technology is also dual-use. Nuclear reactors can be used to produce energy for civilian purposes, or they can be used to produce fissile material for a nuclear weapon. Even HEU is dual-use. Up to approximately 20% U-235 HEU is used in the production of medical isotopes utilized in the treatment and diagnosis of illnesses such as heart disease and cancer. As you will see in the case of Iran in the discussion box, a state under suspicion of enriching uranium for weapons production can claim that the uranium isotopic enrichment program it possesses, producing up to 20% HEU, is simply for medical purposes. Once a state has acquired the knowledge and technology to produce 20% HEU, it is but a short step to producing weapons-grade uranium.

Dual-use technology thus makes the identification of cheating on agreements much more difficult. It also complicates the options for punishing cheating when it is found. For example, the UN Security Council might impose sanctions against an offending state and perhaps ban its import of syringes, a technology essential to the production of WMD. However, as you will no doubt know from your own experiences, syringes are also essential in the provision of medical services, including vaccines for children. So, should the United States seek to ban the import of these dual-use products if a state is proven, or suspected, of trying to build a WMD?

DISCUSSION BOX

Iran and the NPT

Iran was one of the original signatories of the NPT in 1968. It then proceeded to develop a nuclear program, with help from the United States, until the Iranian Revolution of 1979. After the revolution, the new leader of the Islamic Republic of Iran, Ayatollah Khomeini, declared nuclear weapons anathema to Islam and ordered the program to be dismantled.[3]

In 2002, an Iranian dissident group based in London, believed to have been supplied with evidence from Israeli intelligence, revealed that Iran had been secretly working for years to build a 50,000-centrifuge uranium enrichment plant. Although, technically, Iran was not required to declare the site until six months before nuclear material was to be introduced, in 2004 the IAEA criticized Iran's "policy of concealment" and "many breaches" of its NPT Safeguard Agreement. This pattern of concealment continued when Iran failed to declare the building of a 3,000-centrifuge enrichment plant in the city of Qom until it was in "an advanced state of construction" in September 2009 (Peterson 2010).

Since the initial declaration by the IAEA of Iran's past concealment, negotiations led by the EU3 (the UK, France, and Germany) attempted to convince it to stop its uranium enrichment program. The UN Security Council demanded that Iran suspend its enrichment activities in 2006. However, Iran argues that it never violated its commitments under the NPT and that it had the right under Article 2 of the NPT to develop a civilian nuclear power program, as well as to enrich uranium to 20% HEU for medical purposes. Despite Iran's protestations, the United States continued to accuse it of trying to build a nuclear weapon, and the UN Security Council passed a number of resolutions imposing economic sanctions. Finally, after 20 months of negotiations, the P5+1 (the five permanent members of the United Nations plus Germany) and Iran and the European Union signed the Iran nuclear agreement, or the Joint Comprehensive Plan of Action, JCPOA, on July 14, 2015. Among the terms of the agreement, Iran agreed to eliminate its stockpile of medium-enriched uranium, cut its stockpile of low-enriched uranium by 98%, and reduce by about two-thirds the number of its gas centrifuges for 13 years. Iran further agreed to only enrich uranium up to 3.67% for the next 15 years.

So, do you believe the Iranians when they declare that they have no intention of building a nuclear weapon? Do you believe they have a fundamental right to enrich uranium, as stated in the NPT? Do you agree with the UN Security Council in its decisions to impose sanctions, despite the fact that the IAEA has never (after 2003) found evidence of a weapons program? Do you think the NPT should be renegotiated so as to prevent states from using the dual-use nature of uranium as a cover for research into a nuclear weapon? Does the case of Iran prove that the NPT regime works, or that it does not?

3.5 Theoretical Perspectives on Terrorism and WMD

3.5.1 Realism

As a state-centric theory of world politics, Realism concerns itself only with explaining the behavior of states. As a theory, therefore, it does not attempt to explain terrorism conducted by non-state actors. However, this does not mean that Realists do not form opinions on terrorism based on a Realist understanding of world politics.

For instance, Realists can understand why states may sponsor international terrorism when they are involved in **asymmetric conflicts**. These are conflicts in which there is a great imbalance of power between the conflicting parties. Weak states cannot hope to defeat a much more powerful adversary on the conventional battlefield. One need only remember how easily the United States defeated Iraq's armed forces in the Second Persian Gulf War to appreciate the futility of openly fighting a much better equipped opponent. Relatively weak states will thus seek other avenues to "level the playing field," and terrorism is one such option (so too is building WMD, as we will discuss later).

Realists also tend to emphasize the rationality of much of the terrorism seen around the world. Realists argue that terrorists do not hate the United States for what it *is*, but rather for what it *does*. In other words, U.S. foreign policy—much of it counterterrorism policy—plays a principal role in generating the terrorism aimed against it. Thus, despite the common conception of suicide terrorists as irrational religious fundamentalists, Robert Pape's extensive studies continue to prove that:

> what mainly motivate individuals to become suicide terrorists is . . . [a] . . . deep anger at the presence of foreign combat forces from territory they prize. This is the main reason why as American and allied forces have increasingly occupied Muslim countries from 2001 onward, the number of suicide attacks has skyrocketed. (Pape 2010, 29)

Pape's counterterrorism advice to the U.S. government is therefore to adopt a Realist foreign policy of offshore balancing (Pape 2010). By doing so, the United States can reduce the likelihood of future terrorist attacks by minimizing its deployment of combat forces in what local populations perceive as occupational roles.

Realists, as you might expect, also emphasize the rationality of states seeking to acquire WMD. As mentioned above, relatively weak states cannot defend themselves against much more powerful adversaries with conventional weapons. In such circumstances, it is rational for states to seek to acquire or develop the one type of weapon that will deter even a much more powerful state from attacking.

Deterrence is the act of threatening an adversary with unacceptable levels of punishment, in order to deter them from taking some form of action against you. **Nuclear deterrence** is specifically the use of the threat of nuclear attack to deter an adversary from attacking first. Far from seeing nuclear proliferation as a threat to international peace and security, Realists actually believe that limited proliferation can fundamentally enhance it. This is because states can deter attacks that would otherwise occur. For example, the United States has invaded Iraq and Libya and continues to threaten Iran with military action, because they are all relatively weak states. However, the United States has not threatened military action against North Korea, despite its mercurial leader and bellicose behavior, since it developed its own nuclear deterrent in the mid-2000s.

Realists also point to the stability achieved through nuclear deterrence during the Cold War. Although it was a period of very high tensions, war between the superpowers never broke out. Realists argue that the primary reason for this was the balance of power and the stability produced by both sides possessing large arsenals of nuclear weapons. This created a scenario of **Mutually Assured Destruction (MAD)**, in which both states knew that if they attacked first, they would also be destroyed by the response, or **nuclear retaliation**, of their adversary. MAD therefore required both states to have **second-strike capabilities**, which means the ability to absorb a

first strike and still respond with nuclear retaliation. Without these capabilities there would no deterrence, as it might be possible for one of the superpowers to launch a first strike and destroy all of their opponent's weapons.

Realists therefore see nuclear disarmament as potentially undermining stability and thus international peace and security. States that have acquired nuclear weapons outside of the NPT, like North Korea, Pakistan, India, and Israel have all continued to act rationally. In fact, Realists argue that the introduction of nuclear deterrence between India and Pakistan has actually reduced the likelihood of war between them. Based on this reasoning, rather than seeking to prevent Iran from acquiring nuclear weapons, Realists have argued that Iran's possession of nuclear weapons would actually improve stability in the Middle East by creating a balance of power between Iran and Israel (which already has nuclear weapons), as well as providing Iran with the deterrent it needs to feel secure against an American invasion (Walt 2012).

Realists are also skeptical of the willingness of states to fulfill their obligations in international treaties. States will not relinquish or deny themselves the benefits of weapons they believe are essential for national security. There is no hope, therefore, that the Great Powers, like the United States, Russia, and China will ever fully disarm as required in the NPT. However, these states are happy to place themselves in a privileged position of being classed as "nuclear weapon states" while using the treaty to prevent other states from acquiring them (the Great Powers are willing to fulfill to arms control agreements, but that is because they are designed to maintain a mutually advantageous balance of power).

This, of course, is true in the case of the U.S. goal of preventing Iran from acquiring a single nuclear weapon, even though it possesses thousands of its own. What may appear as gross hypocrisy is to Realists simply rational self-interested power politics. Nor do Realists believe that states like Iran and North Korea will forgo the benefits of nuclear deterrence simply because they signed up to an international agreement. National security will always trump moral obligation in world politics— especially when those states perceive the treaty as a tool of the Great Powers to keep them insecure.

3.5.2 Liberalism

Liberals remain much more optimistic than their Realist counterparts about the potential for international cooperation to reduce the threat of international terrorism and prevent the proliferation of WMD. Liberals argue that this cooperation can be achieved through collective security organizations and other international institutions.

Liberals remain skeptical of the notion that the United States might be able to prevent future terrorist attacks by withdrawing its combat forces from abroad as Realists suggest. American influence, through its diplomacy, trade, and cultural attraction, is a truly global phenomenon, and it is therefore always going to be a point of irritation for those who blame it for their society's ills. Withdrawing behind national borders and adopting a "fortress America" mentality can never succeed in the modern world.

Liberals argue that threats to international peace and security, like terrorism and WMD proliferation, cannot be dealt with by the United States alone, no matter how powerful it may be. Nor can the United States defeat these threats through the use of military power alone. The United States is simply incapable of policing every street in every state and to try to do so would only exacerbate the problem. The United States must therefore seek cooperation through international institutions. They thus point to the many international treaties that have been signed outlawing different forms of terrorism as the most effective means of combating it.

Rather than conducting a "war on terrorism," Liberals tend to prefer to treat terrorism as a crime that warrants prosecution in the criminal justice system. International law, as in the conventions against international terrorism mentioned above, can then be used to prosecute those involved in terrorist activities. This upholds the rule of law and encourages greater cooperation from states that might otherwise feel threatened and/or offended by the unilateral and aggressive behavior that a more militaristic approach entails. For example, many actions taken by the United States after

September 11, 2001, including secret renditions, torture, and imprisonment without trial, all led to the perception that the United States had placed itself above the rule of law.

In making these arguments, Liberals are once again emphasizing the role of soft power in world politics. International coalitions are much stronger if they are held together by a desire to cooperate, rather than the fear of punishment for not doing so. This is especially the case with issues like terrorism, in which simply looking the other way can lead to disastrous consequences. The United States can also use its soft power to encourage the spread of democracy, human rights, and economic and social justice, all of which will help reduce the sense of frustration and alienation felt by those who might otherwise become terrorists.

Liberals are also optimistic about the potential for nonproliferation and eventual disarmament of WMD. Rather than seeing the glass half empty, Liberals tend to see it as half full. They thus highlight the fact that there are still only nine states in the international system in possession of nuclear weapons, despite many predictions that that number would have reached 20 or 30 many years ago. Liberals tend to argue that the reason for this low number is the success of the nonproliferation regime that was established with the NPT in 1968.

As discussed in Chapter 2, whereas Realists remain pessimistic about the possibility for significant cooperation between states in an anarchic international system, Liberals believe that such cooperation can be achieved through the roles played by international institutions. These roles are establishing standards of behavior, ensuring compliance with those standards, resolving disputes, and reducing the cost of joint decision making. The NPT and the nonproliferation regime that it encapsulates is a model of this. The NPT establishes the standards of behavior among its signatories. Compliance with their commitments is verified by the IAEA through its intrusive information gathering and inspections regime, the details of which are included in its safeguard agreements and through the NPT's Additional Protocol. NPT conferences are also held every five years so as to allow for collective decision making and the resolution of disputes.

International institutions can thus help states overcome the prisoner's dilemma and achieve greater levels of cooperation than Realists would predict. Evidence for this is not only in the low number of nuclear weapons states in the international system, but also in the progress made by the nuclear weapons states toward complete nuclear disarmament. It is also evident in the success of the chemical and biological weapons conventions in achieving the disarmament of those weapons.

3.5.3 Radical Approaches

As with chronic insecurity, poverty, unemployment, and armed conflict, Radical theorists believe terrorism is just one more symptom of the global capitalist system. Although they might agree with Realists like Robert Pape when they conclude that terrorism is a product of military occupations, they disagree with them over the cause of those occupations. Whereas Realists see the deployment of U.S. combat forces as simply part of a misguided foreign policy, Radical theorists see it as the typical imperialistic behavior of a powerful state within the capitalist global economy.

For Radical theorists, terrorism is thus a form of resistance against oppression. Even terrorism seemingly motivated by religious radicalism can be seen in this light. Karl Marx called religion the "opium of the people" and argued that it was used by the bourgeoisie class to give false hope to the proletariat. Nevertheless, he still recognized it as a form of protest against the proletariat's terrible economic and social conditions. He would no doubt view religiously inspired terrorists today in the same way—as products of religions/ideologies intended to deflect the working class from recognizing the true cause of their suffering.

Like terrorism, the proliferation of WMD in the international system is another product of the insecurity produced by capitalism. Weak states are compelled to acquire such weapons because they exist in conditions of extreme insecurity. They are threatened by the imperial powers with occupation if they do not follow the rules that are established by the powerful to ensure their continued insecurity—including the NPT. If, like Iraq, you do not follow these rules and do not possess WMD, the imperial powers will invade at the behest of their political and corporate interests, occupy your streets, liberalize your economy for their own benefit—and call it "liberation."

Radical theorists, like Realists, thus expect the hypocrisy evident in the behavior of the world's most powerful states with regards to the NPT. International law and institutions are not means for states to overcome the prisoner's dilemma, but rather a means to cage weak states (and the world's poorest people) into a system of capitalist exploitation and domination.

Key Terms

Additional Protocol

airspace

Anti-Ballistic Missile (ABM)

armed conflicts

arms control

asymmetric conflict

Ayatollah

ballistic weapons

biological weapons

chemical warfare

chemical weapons

conflict prevention

conflict resolution

contiguous zone

conventional weapons

counterterrorism

delivery system

deterrence

disarmament

doctrinal wars

dual-use technology

ethnic cleansing

ethnic groups

ethnic identity

ethnic intolerance

ethnicity

ethnification

ethnocentrism

ethno-nationalist conflicts

ethno-religious conflicts

Exclusive Economic Zone (EEZ)

first strike capability

fission nuclear weapons

fissionable material

fundamentalism

fusion nuclear weapons

genocide

guided missiles

heretics

high sea

highly enriched uranium (HEU)

horizontal proliferation

human security

hydrogen bombs

Imams

infidels

Inter-Continental Ballistic Missiles (ICBMs)

intermediate or tactical weapons

Internally-dispersed people

internationalized conflicts

inter-state conflicts

intractable conflicts

intra-state conflicts

irredentism

Islam

Islamists

isotopic enrichment

mass casualty terrorism

Mutually Assured Destruction (MAD)

Narco-terrorists

nerve agents

Neutron bombs

nuclear deterrence

Nuclear Non-Proliferation Treaty (NPT)

nuclear retaliation

nuclear warheads

nuclear weapons

Plutonium reprocessing plant

political/ethnic entrepreneurs

primordial-ism

protracted conflicts

refugees

safeguard agreement

secession

second strike capability

sectarian violence

secular government

Shari'a Law

Shi'a Muslims

Slavs

state-sponsored terrorism

strategic weapons

suicide terrorism

Sunni Muslims

Surface-to-Air Missile (SAM)

territorial sea

terrorism

theocracy

thermonuclear weapons

Ummah

vertical proliferation

Wahhabism

war

Weapons of Mass Destruction (WMD)

weapons-grade uranium

End Notes

1. "In Europe, nationalism rising," Harvard Gazette, February 27, 2017) https://news.harvard.edu/gazette/story/2017/02/in-europe-nationalisms-rising/

2. Ali R. Abootalebi, "Nationalism, Power Politics, and Pluralism in Divided Societies," in Fonkem Achankeng, ed. *Nationalism and Intra-State Conflicts in the Postcolonial World*, Lexington Books, 2015, pp. 113–130; Vincent Durac and Francesco Cavatorta, *Politics and Governance in the Middle East* (New York, Palgrave, 2015).

3. Gareth Porter, "When the Ayatollah Said No to Nukes," foreign Policy, October 16, 2014. http://foreignpolicy.com/2014/10/16/when-the-ayatollah-said-no-to-nukes/

International Organizations and International Law

Image © Elenarts, 2013. Used under license from Shutterstock, Inc.

CHAPTER OUTLINE

4.0 Types of International Organizations

There exist two broad types of international organizations (IOs). The first is *inter-governmental organizations* (IGOs) and the second is *nongovernmental organizations* (NGOs). While IGOs number in the thousands and are composed of member-states, NGOs number in the tens of thousands and are principally composed of non-state groups and individuals.

IGOs can be further divided into two types. The first is *regional* IGOs. These are organizations composed of states located in a specific region. Examples include the European Union (EU) or the North Atlantic Treaty Organization (NATO). The second type is *global* IGOs, which are open to membership from states across the globe. Examples of these include the United Nations (UN) and the World Health Organization (WHO). Regional and global organizations can be further categorized by whether they have *general* or *specialized* functions. In the case of the examples given above, the EU is a regional IGO with general functions (member states cooperate across a range of issue areas, including trade, transport, security, and immigration policy), whereas NATO has a specific function (collective defense). Similarly, the UN is a general-purpose global IGO because it helps its members cooperate on a range of issues, from the management of international conflict and the protection of human rights to the economic development of poor countries. The WHO, on the other hand, is a specialized global IGO, as it works specifically in the area of public health. Table 4.1 shows the different types of IGOs.

NGOs can also be divided into two types. These are *substate* NGOs and *international* NGOs (INGOs). While substate NGOs are located and operate *within* state borders, INGOs operate *across* state borders. This latter type might therefore be better described as *transnational* NGOS (TNGOs). Based on the categorizations used by the World Bank, itself a specialized global IGO working on the economic development of the world's poorest countries, NGOs can be further categorized into two groups. The first is *operational* NGOs. These are NGOs whose principal function is to fund, design, or help provide services, programs, and projects to communities in need. Examples of these include *Doctors Without Borders*, *Oxfam*, *World Vision*, and *Catholic Relief*. The second category is *advocacy* NGOs. These are NGOs whose primary purpose is to promote and defend a specific cause and that seek to influence the policies and practices of governments and other organizations. This category includes NGOs like *Amnesty International* and *Human Rights Watch*, which both campaign for the protection and promotion of internationally recognized human rights. Another is *Greenpeace*, which operates and campaigns globally to preserve and protect the environment. However, as acknowledged by the World Bank itself, this is not a rigid distinction. Rather, the majority of NGOs actually fall somewhere between these two extremes. Table 4.2 shows types of NGOs.

Table 4.1　Types of IGOs

IGO	Regional or Global (R or G)	Specialized or General (S or G)
UN	G	G
WHO	G	S
EU	R	G
NATO	R	S

Table 4.2　Types of NGOs

NGO	Sub-state or Transnational (S or T)	Operational or Advocacy (O or A or O/A)
Oxfam	T	O/A
Human Rights Watch	T	A
Amnesty International	T	A
AARP (USA)	S	O/A

4.1 Global and Regional IGOs: United Nations and the European Union

In order for the reader to better understand the roles and effects of regional and global IGOs, this section will provide an overview of the workings of two of the most successful regional and global general-purpose IGOs in world politics: the UN and EU. As well as providing an evolutionary history and outline of each organization's structure, this section will also highlight some of the major issues confronting each of them.

4.1.1 United Nations: History, Structure, and Issues

The UN is the successor to the League of Nations, the world's first collective security organization. The League was formed in 1919, at the end of World War I, in the hope of preventing a similar disaster from recurring. Although U.S. President Woodrow Wilson had called for the creation of the League in his "14 points" speech to Congress in January 1918, the Congress refused to ratify the Covenant of the League of Nations following his return from Europe, where he had helped negotiate its creation. This left the embryonic League's membership devoid of the world's most powerful state and leading advocate.

The League's Covenant created three principal organs: an assembly, a council, and a secretariat. The League Assembly was the parliamentary body of the new organization. Its membership included all members of the League, which numbered around 60 at its foundation. The Assembly's principal role was to act as a forum for debate and discussion of political and economic issues affecting its members, although it also adopted an annual budget and elected new members. The Council was the executive body of the organization. Without the United States, it was originally composed of eight members, four of whom were permanent. The rest were elected to temporary positions from the Assembly. The size of the Council fluctuated throughout the League's existence, as members joined and withdrew from the organization. The Secretariat was the administrative (or bureaucratic) organ of the League and was headed by a Secretary-General.

Unfortunately, despite some notable successes during the 1920s (including arms control treaties and the outlawing of war in the Kellogg-Briand Pact of 1928), the League failed to fulfill its collective security mandate in the 1930s. The reasons for this failure are believed to be twofold. First, the League suffered from some institutional and legal weaknesses. For example, both the Assembly and Council could only make recommendations (nonbinding resolutions) and even these had to be adopted unanimously. This meant any member-state was free to reject its recommendations. The second reason was the lack of political will shown by the League's members to confront aggression, especially when it was committed by powerful states. The most infamous examples of this were the League's failure to confront Japan, Italy, and Germany when they invaded modern-day China (Manchuria 1931), Ethiopia (Abyssinia 1935), and the Czech Republic (Czechoslovakia 1938) respectively. Although the League was officially disbanded in 1946, it had thus become effectively defunct by the beginning of World War II in September 1939.

Although the League had failed in its principal mandate, the international community did not give up on the idea of collective security. Rather, the 51 states that met at the *United Nations Conference on International Organization* in San Francisco in 1945 hoped instead to build a new collective security organization, free of the deficiencies that had beset its predecessor. Expressed in its founding document, the **Charter** of the United Nations (UN), this new organization was given what its founders believed was an improved organizational structure and more effective powers and decision-making procedures.

Figure 4.1.   United Nations Headquarters during the 2008 General Assembly.

The UN, however, was also designed to be more than just a collective security organization. Rather than simply reacting to disputes and conflicts once they had occurred, its founders hoped this new organization would be more proactive in the maintenance of international peace and security. They thus charged it with promoting better relations between states and with promoting economic and social progress, including better living standards and human rights for individuals and societies across the globe. These additional goals helped shape the formal structure of the UN, which is composed of six main organs: the Security Council, the General Assembly, the Secretariat, the Economic and Social Council, the International Court of Justice, and the Trusteeship Council.

- ### *Trusteeship Council*

The Trusteeship Council was originally established to help eleven so-called "Trust Territories" to attain self-government or independence. The last of these territories, the Pacific island of Palau, became an independent state in 1994. The work of the Trusteeship Council has since been suspended.

- ### *International Court of Justice (ICJ)*

The ICJ is the main judicial body of the UN and is informally referred to as the World Court. Located in the Peace Palace in The Hague (Netherlands), it is the successor to the Permanent Court of International Justice, which despite having had a close working relationship with the League of Nations, was not an official part of that organization. The ICJ is composed of 15 judges elected by the General Assembly and the Security Council for nine-year terms. All its decisions are made by majority vote.

The Court has two principal roles. The first is to settle legal disputes voluntarily submitted to it by member-states (contentious cases). The second is to provide advisory opinions on legal questions submitted to it by UN organs and specialized agencies (advisory proceedings). Only UN member-states or states that have voluntarily submitted themselves to the ICJ's jurisdiction can bring cases before the Court. Under Article 36 of the ICJ's **Statute**, this can be done in one of three ways. First, member-states can agree to submit their dispute to the ICJ. Second, the ICJ can claim jurisdiction through a **compromissory clause** that may have been included in a treaty and that requires any future disagreement over an interpretation or implementation of its provisions to be submitted to the Court. Third, states can sign an **optional clause** submitting themselves to the compulsory jurisdiction of the Court. The position of the United States with regard to the optional clause remains controversial. In effect, under the optional clause, the United States decides on a case-by-case basis whether it will accept the Court's jurisdiction. Similarly, Egypt has accepted the jurisdiction of the ICJ only in matters related to the Suez Canal.

Although all the Court's decisions within its jurisdiction are legally binding on the parties concerned, there remains no formal mechanism of enforcement. The only recourse for an aggrieved state is for it to request the Security Council to take up the matter (Chapter 14 Article 94 of the Charter). This has led a number of states to ignore the Court's rulings. For example, Iran refused to release the American hostages held after the seizure of the U.S. Embassy in Tehran in 1979, despite an order of the Court to do so. Similarly, the United States ignored a ruling of the Court in 1984 that determined its mining of Nicaraguan harbors as a violation of international law. Similarly, Israel has ignored the Court's ruling on the illegality of building the separation wall in the Occupied Territories. Despite this weakness in the Court's powers, its decisions are still believed by many to be important because they continue to carry significant moral weight and help establish international legal jurisprudence.

- ### *Secretariat*

The Secretariat is the administrative body (or bureaucracy) of the UN. It contains approximately 16,000 international civil-service staff, around a third of which are located at the UN's headquarters in New York. The Secretariat June 30, 2016 report contains a demographic analysis of the global staff, which totalled 40,131.[1] It is headed by the UN Secretary-General, who is elected by the General Assembly (on the recommendation of the Security Council), for a five-year, once-renewable term. The present incumbent, António Guterres, is the former Portuguese prime minister, began his service at the UN in January 2017, and is the ninth Secretary-General to serve in office. Guterres succeeded Ban Ki-Moon of South Korea who was elected for his second term as the eighth Secretary-General in 2011.

The Secretary-General has at least three primary responsibilities inherent in the position. First, he or she must act as a bureaucratic manager and proponent for institutional reform. For example, the seventh Secretary-General, Kofi Annan of Ghana (1997–2006), significantly reduced the size of the UN's bureaucracy and instigated reforms such as the creation of a new Peacebuilding Commission and Human Rights Council. Continuing in this vein, the former incumbent, Ban Ki Moon, created a Change Management Team in May 2011, which he tasked with spearheading "efforts to implement a reform agenda aimed at streamlining and improving the efficiency" of the UN.

The second responsibility of the Secretary-General is to act as an international diplomat, representing both the UN organization and the international community. However, disagreement exists over the exact role of the Secretary-General in this regard, with some arguing that he should restrain himself to speaking only as the "chief executive" of the UN, while others argue that the Secretary-General has a responsibility to voice the concerns of the international community as a whole. For example, Kofi Annan was criticized by the United States for acting beyond his competency as Secretary-General when he declared the U.S. invasion of Iraq in 2003 to have been illegal under the UN Charter and thus, international law.

The Secretary-General's third responsibility is to help promote international peace and security. The greatest formal power of the Secretary-General is the power to bring matters to the attention of the Security Council (through Chapter 15 Article 99) that they feel may threaten international peace and security. This power has encouraged past incumbents to expand their roles to include the conduct of "fact-finding" missions and "preventive diplomacy." As international diplomats, past secretary-generals have also tended to define "international peace and security" in the broadest sense, thus allowing them to become involved in highlighting and finding solutions to a wide range of economic, social, and humanitarian problems. Finally, the Secretary-General can also provide "good offices." This means using personal prestige and institutional resources to help prevent and resolve disputes and conflicts. For example, the Secretary-General may personally mediate between conflicting parties or send a representative to do so. Alternatively, the Secretary-General may simply provide a safe place for conflicting parties to meet and negotiate among themselves.

• *General Assembly*

The General Assembly (GA) is the organization's parliamentary (or legislative) body. It is composed of delegations from all the UN's member-states, which by 2006 numbered 192 and increasing to 193 member states in July 2011 after South Sudan was admitted to the organization. The UN membership remains at 193 in 2017. It has four principal duties. First, it controls the budget of the organization, deciding on both how much each member state should contribute to the **UN's regular and peacekeeping budgets** and how that money should be spent. Second, it votes on a number of important institutional concerns, including the accession of new members, the election of the Secretary-General, and the election of judges to the ICJ (all in coordination with the Security Council). It also elects nonpermanent members to the Security Council and new members to the Economic and Social Council (ECOSOC). Third, it acts as a forum for the discussion of any topic within the scope of the Charter. Last, it coordinates the UN's programs and agencies through ECOSOC.

Figure 4.2. The General Assembly Hall is the largest room in the United Nations with seating capacity for over 1,800 people. March 30, 2011 in Manhattan, New York City.

It is in the GA that the UN's principal of sovereign legal equality is made manifest. All member-states possess one vote, regardless of their contributions to the UN budget or the relative size of their economies, populations, or territories. Thus Tuvalu, a small island in the South Pacific with a population of 11,000, has the same voting power as the United States, despite the latter having a population of over 320 million, the world's most powerful military, and a $18 trillion economy. The United States also pays 22% of the UN's regular budget, while Tuvalu donates only 0.001%.

Although the GA holds the "power of the purse" through its control of the UN budget and is a co-equal body of the UN within the spirit of the Charter, in practice it is a much less powerful body than the Security Council. Its resolutions (unlike the Security Council) are not legally binding. Nor can it pass resolutions under Chapter 7 of the Charter (explained below). Member states are thus effectively free to ignore GA resolutions they dislike. For example, in 2010 the GA passed its 19th consecutive resolution (one each year) by a vote of 187–2 urging the United States to end its economic embargo of Cuba. The attitude of the United States to this yearly tradition was perhaps most candidly expressed in 2005 by the then–U.S. ambassador to the UN, John Bolton, when he called the GA's 14th vote that year "an exercise in complete irrelevancy" (Associated Press 2005).

However, as GA resolutions on all important matters require a two-thirds majority to pass, many argue that they reflect the "will of the international community" or "world opinion" and thus possess significant moral authority. Perhaps not surprisingly, states tend to emphasize the importance of GA votes only when they are advocating the majority opinion. Thus, when Iran was comprehensively beaten by Japan in the GA's election for non-permanent seats to the Security Council in 2008, U.S. and UK diplomats argued that the vote clearly demonstrated that there was no support for the Iranians in the international community (Lynch 2008).

• *Economic and Social Council*

Under the authority of the General Assembly, the Economic and Council (ECOSOC) is responsible for coordinating the economic, social, and other related work undertaken within the UN system. It is principally composed of a number of functional and regional commissions, such as the Commission on Sustainable Development, the Commission on the Status of Women, the Economic Commission for Africa (ECA), and the Economic and Social Commission for Asia and the Pacific (ESCAP). ECOSOC holds four-week sessions each July, alternating between New York and Geneva. Its 54 members are elected by the GA

(18 each year for three-year terms), and seats are allotted based on regional geographical representation (Africa 14 seats, Asia 11 seats, Eastern Europe 6 seats, Latin America and the Caribbean 10 seats, and Western European and Others 13 seats).

ECOSOC's four principal responsibilities are to promote higher standards of living, full employment, and economic and social progress; identify solutions to international economic, social, and health problems; facilitate international cultural and educational cooperation; and to encourage universal respect for human rights and fundamental freedoms. Given this broad mandate, its purview extends to over 70% of the human and financial resources of the entire UN system (United Nations n.d.).

To achieve these goals, ECOSOC oversees the work of around a dozen UN Programs and Funds and 15 Specialized Agencies. The former group includes the United Nations Conference on Trade and Development (UNCTAD), the United Nations Children's Fund (UNICEF), the Office of the United Nations High Commissioner for Refugees (UNHCR), and the World Food Program (WFP). The latter group includes institutions such as the International Labor Organization (ILO), the World Health Organization (WHO), the International Monetary Fund (IMF), and the World Bank Group. ECOSOC also has a close working relationship with a number of independent "related organizations," such as the International Atomic Energy Agency (IAEA), the World Trade Organization (WTO), and the Organization for the Prohibition of Chemical Weapons (OPCW). Finally, ECOSOC consults with a wide range of civil society groups, including over 3000 NGOs. NGOs with "consultancy status" can participate in meetings of ECOSOC and its various subsidiary bodies, as well as propose new items for consideration on ECOSOC's agenda.

• *Security Council*

The functions and powers, composition, and voting procedures of the Security Council are outlined in Chapter 5 of the Charter. In order to avoid any confusion over the respective roles of the Security Council and General Assembly, Chapter 5 Article 24 of the Charter provides the Council with "*primary* responsibility for the maintenance of international peace and security." In order to fulfill this role, the founders endowed the Council with unprecedented powers. These powers reach their zenith in Chapter 7 Articles 39–42 of the Charter, which covers "action with respect to threats to the peace, breaches of the peace and acts of aggression." The Security Council is the only body of the UN that can pass Chapter 7 resolutions.

Under Chapter 7 Article 39 the Council can make the determination that a threat to international peace and security exists. Under Article 40 it can make any recommendations or determinations it believes might help resolve the problem peacefully. For example, it might recommend or decide that the parties to a dispute need to seek arbitration or judicial settlement, just two of the peaceful methods of dispute settlement contained in Chapter 6 (Pacific Settlement of Disputes) of the Charter. If, however, such peaceful methods are unsuccessful, under Chapter 7 Article 41 the Council can decide that greater action, short of the use of armed force, is necessary. Such action normally takes the form of economic sanctions, arms embargoes, or the freezing of personal or national assets. Finally, if these actions are deemed inadequate, under Article 42 the Council can "take such action by air, sea, or land forces as may be necessary to maintain or restore international peace and security." Chapter 7 resolutions that call for the use of military force usually authorize member-states to use "all necessary means" to fulfill the Council's mandate. In essence, with the powers of Chapter 7, the Security Council can thus become involved *anywhere*, at *any time*, and decide to do *anything* it feels necessary to restore international peace and security.

Chapter 5 Article 23 stipulates that the Security Council is composed of 15 states, five of which hold permanent seats. These are the United States, the United Kingdom, France, People's Republic of China, and the Russian Federation (informally called "the P-5"). The remaining

10 seats are non-permanent seats with two-year terms (not immediately renewable). Non-permanent members are elected by the General Assembly from informal regional groups (Africa 3 seats, Asia 2 seats, Eastern Europe 1 seat, Latin America and the Caribbean 2 seats, Western Europe and Others 2 seats). In accordance with Chapter 5 Article 27, resolutions on substantive matters require nine affirmative votes to pass, including the "concurrent" votes of its five permanent members. This form of qualified majority voting thus provides each of the permanent members with a veto over the Council's most important decisions. Since the early 1950s the convention has also developed that any permanent member not wishing to vote either yes or no (thus using its veto) on a resolution can instead abstain.

4.1.2 United Nations Debate: Are Economic Sanctions Effective?

We have already mentioned the UN sanctions imposed upon Iraq after the first Persian Gulf War in 1991. They were eventually lifted as a new Iraqi regime was established under the tutelage of the United States and UN in 2003. Although they caused extreme hardship for the Iraqi people, they nevertheless failed to force Saddam Hussein's regime to comply with the UN's demands for full cooperation on matters concerning the nonproliferation of nuclear, chemical, and biological weapons (or weapons of mass destruction (WMD)). With its oil industry under UN control, Iraq was unable to invest adequate resources in its infrastructure and imports of material for national development (other than food and medicine) remained scant. As UNICEF and other UN bodies and officials reported, the sanctions contributed to the premature deaths of nearly one million Iraqi civilians, up to half of whom are believed to have been children, primarily through starvation and disease, although this number remains contested.[2] The regime nevertheless outlasted the sanctions, and its leaders survived in relative comfort until the U.S. invasion of March 2003.

The Islamic Republic of Iran (IRI) had also been under U.S. and UN sanctions since 1979. This was the most prolonged experience with sanctions of any state, other than Cuba, which has been subject to U.S. sanctions since 1959, although President Obama's October 2016 directive loosened U.S. sanctions on Cuban cigars and rums. Since 1979 U.S. and UN sanctions (since 2006) had become increasingly intrusive and were strangling Iran's access to foreign credit, investment, banking, medicine, and equipment, including spare parts for its national airline industry and other vital products. Iran's oil sales had plummeted and its currency had dropped by over 100% in value. Many families of cancer patients and others needing imported medicine still blame the United States for their loved ones' premature deaths. The economic slowdown, high unemployment, and rampant inflation that Iran has suffered from in recent years are also blamed on the sanctions.

The goal of these sanctions has been to force Iran to stop its nuclear program, which Iran insists is peaceful and in compliance with its commitments in the Non-Proliferation Treaty (for a discussion of the NPT, see Chapter 3). However, the United States, together with a number of other UN members, continued to accuse it of secretly building a nuclear weapon. Yet, despite the heavy sanctions that have been imposed upon it, the Iranian government has remained steadfast in its determination to continue with its nuclear program. In fact, there is some evidence that sanctions may have actually encouraged it to accelerate its nuclear program. This has led at least one report to conclude that: "given the country's indigenous knowledge and expertise, the only long-term solution for assuring that Iran's nuclear program remains purely peaceful is to find a mutually agreeable diplomatic solution."[3] Ultimately, it took almost two years of diplomatic efforts and hard negotiations between Iran and P5+1 (the five permanent members of the UN Security Council and Germany) to reach an agreement. The Iran nuclear agreement, also known as JCPOA or Joint Comprehensive Plan of Action, signed on July 14, 2015, forced Iran to eliminate its stockpile of enriched uranium and to limit its nuclear activities under the supervision of the IAEA, the International Atomic Energy Agency, in return for the lifting of sanctions.[4]

So, what do you think about the effectiveness of sanctions? Do the examples above prove that sanctions don't work? Who do you think should have the authority to impose them, individual states or the UN Security Council?

4.1.3 United Nations Debate: Should the Security Council Be Reformed?

Although the UN's membership has almost quadrupled since 1945 (51 to 193 members), the Security Council has only been reformed once during that time. This occurred in 1965, when it was expanded from 11 to 15 members (with the inclusion of four new non-permanent seats distributed by informal agreement on a regional basis: 2 to Asia, 2 to Africa). Many thus accuse the Council of being anachronistic, because its membership has failed to evolve with the international community's changing power and values over the past half-century. As the president of the UN General Assembly stated in May 2011, the greatest threat to the future effectiveness of the Security Council is the loss of credibility and legitimacy that will occur if reform continues to stall. This, the president feared, would lead the UN to be marginalized and compel its member states to utilize "other forums and groupings which are perceived to be more efficient and more representative of the new realities of the day" (UN News Service 2011).

Unfortunately, despite 20 years or more of continuous discussion at the UN (both through an Open Ended Working Group and intergovernmental negotiations), there exists little consensus on how the Security Council should be reformed. Disagreement centers around two principal issues: membership and voting procedures. Although there appears to be a general consensus that the Council should be expanded to around 25 seats, the types of seats to be created and the question of which states should fill them remain hotly contested. So too, does the question of whether to provide new members with veto power.

These disagreements were perhaps best reflected in the 2004 report of the "High-Level Panel on Threats, Challenges and Change," which was established by former Secretary-General Kofi Annan. Composed of a number of experts and former politicians, the Panel was tasked with studying potential UN reform, including that of the Council. Significantly, the Panel was forced to acknowledge that it could not itself form a consensus on the issue. Rather, it suggested two models, which it labeled A and B respectively. Model A provided for six new permanent seats (2 for Africa, 2 for Asia and the Pacific, 1 for Europe, and 1 for the Americas) and three new two-year term non-permanent seats, divided among the regional groupings (4, 3, 2, 4 respectively). This arrangement thus provided for each regional group to have a total of six seats. Model B, on the other hand, provided for no new permanent seats, but instead created a new category of eight four-year renewable-term seats (2 provided to each regional grouping) and one new two-year nonpermanent (and non-renewable) seat, divided among the major regional groupings (4, 3, 1, 3, respectively). Thus, both models envisaged a total of six seats for each regional grouping, with a total membership of 24. Neither model proposed changing the current permanent membership or providing new members with a veto.

The models proposed by the Panel reflected the principal divisions among the UN's member states on the issue. While some states, like Germany, India, Brazil, and Japan (collectively known as the G4) continue to lobby for their own permanent seats, many others feel that creating a new set of permanent members will only consolidate the power inequalities that already exist in the UN and make the organization even less democratic. And even if there are new permanent seats created, could the regional groups ever reach a consensus on which states should fill them, especially when they know it might be another 65 years before they are changed again? Alternatively, although the creation of semi-permanent seats would appear to solve this problem, states like the G4 have so far been unwilling to accept seats that they may lose in a number of years, particularly when they know that states like the UK, France, and Russia will continue to sit on the Council (with veto power), despite possessing smaller populations and/or making far lower contributions to the UN budget.

The final and perhaps greatest hurdle to be overcome is the actual process through which the UN Charter is changed. Chapter 18 Article 108 of the UN Charter stipulates that any change requires a vote of two-thirds of the General Assembly and that two-thirds of the UN's membership must ratify that change in their own legislatures. This in itself is a significant hurdle. However, it is compounded by the requirement that all five permanent members must be included in those ratifications. This provides each of them with an effective veto over Security Council reform. It is because of this that neither model proposed by the High-Level Panel suggested either replacing current permanent members or weakening their veto power. It also explains why the Security Council has only been reformed once in its lifetime, as mentioned at the beginning of this section.

So, how do you think the Security Council should be reformed? How many members should it have? Should the current P-5 be changed? Should the veto power of the P-5 be abolished, amended, or extended to new members? Should the Council have new permanent members or should new temporary seats be created? If you wish to create new permanent members, which criteria should be used to determine who they should be? Should it be contributions to international peace and security or regional representation? Should it be size of contributions to the UN's budget or do relatively poor states deserve seats too? Should it be size of population or representation of the world's largest religions? Should different political and economic systems be represented or should they be awarded to those possessing the greatest degree of democracy and respect for human rights? And, finally, is your proposal feasible given the requirements of Article 108?

4.1.4 European Union: History, Structure, and Issues

The European Union (EU) is the world's most successful regional general-purpose IGO. It is composed principally of a single economic market between its now 27 member-states (28 members minus the departing United Kingdom upon the completion of separation negotiations, or commonly known as the Brexit). The EU's origins can be traced to the first major European organization created in the postwar era, the European Coal and Steel Community (ECSC). Created in 1951 and first proposed by French Foreign Minister Robert Schuman, the ECSC placed all French and German coal and steel production under a joint authority. Schuman's principal motivation in proposing the organization was to ensure that Germany could never again secretly mobilize for war. Along with France and Germany, the ECSC's founding members also included Belgium, Luxembourg, The Netherlands, and Italy.

Six years later, in 1957, the same six countries established the European Economic Community (EEC) and the European Atomic Energy Community (Euratom). The EEC, established by the Treaty of Rome, was the first attempt to create a common economic market (the EEC was thus generally referred to as "the common market") among its members, which was to include the free movement of people, services, and capital; the creation of a common agricultural market; and common policies in areas like transportation and competition. Euratom acted in the same manner as the ECSC, only this time in the area of nuclear energy.

By 1992 the original six members had been joined by Denmark, Ireland, and the UK (all joined in 1973), Greece (1981), Portugal and Spain (1986). In that year, the now 12 member-states met in Maastricht, The Netherlands, to sign the Treaty on European Union. Subsequently known as the Maastricht Treaty, this agreement contained three principal achievements. First, it committed its signatories to a closer political union. Second, it created a three-pillar organizational structure, for what was henceforth to be known as the European Union (EU). The first pillar was the European Community (EC). This pillar incorporated the previous treaties concerning the provisions for the common market. The second pillar concerned Justice and Homeland Affairs, while the third involved an attempt to create a Common Foreign and Security Policy (CFSP).

At this stage, while the **supranational** institutions of the EU were to assume authority over the EU's first pillar, the latter two were to be advanced principally through intergovernmental discussions and agreements. This separation of powers reflected the continuing sensitivity of member-states toward the loss of national control over policies concerning national defense and law and order, which were both perceived as bastions of the sovereign state.

The third major contribution of the Maastricht Treaty was its establishment of "convergence criteria" for the fiscal and monetary policies of the member states within the process of European

Economic and Monetary Union (EMU). The aim of the EMU process was the adoption of a single EU currency (which was achieved in 2002, see later).

Since the adoption of the Maastricht Treaty, the EU has undergone both a significant enlargement of its membership and a deepening of its political and economic integration. Austria, Finland, and Sweden joined in 1995. These countries were followed by Poland, the Czech Republic, Slovakia, Hungary, Slovenia, Latvia, Lithuania, Estonia, Malta, and Cyprus in 2004. With the ascension of Romania and Bulgaria in 2007 and Croatia in 2013, the EU's membership reached 28 (27, Brexit pending) states. It now incorporates 743 million people (2015) and has 23 official languages.

Since the Maastricht Treaty, the EU's member states have also signed three major treaties (Amsterdam Treaty, Nice Treaty, and Lisbon Treaty), which have all furthered the EU's political and economic integration. For example, the Amsterdam Treaty of 1997 created a position now called the High Representative of the Union for Foreign Affairs and Security Policy, informally referred to as the EU Foreign Minister. This was an attempt to forge further consensus on foreign policy positions among the EU's member states, to enhance the EU's ability to present unified positions and speak with a "common voice," and to provide a focal point for those seeking to know the "European position" on important issues.

The treaties of Nice (2001) and Lisbon (2007) continued the process of restructuring and streamlining the EU's institutional structure and voting procedures. Since its foundation in 1957 the EU's principal decision-making body, the Council of Ministers, had always worked on the principle of unanimity, but with the addition of so many new members, it was increasingly being threatened with gridlock. To avoid this, the Lisbon Treaty, which entered into force in December 2009, expanded the use of qualified majority voting (QMV) into a host of policy areas that had hitherto required unanimous voting. However, as the policy areas affected also included a number that had until this point been located within the second and third pillars of the EU (including defense policy and foreign and security policy), the Lisbon Treaty also represented an expansion of the EU's **pooled sovereignty**.

Other notable political elements of the Lisbon Treaty included its creation of the position of President of the European Council, who was to serve a two-and-a-half-year term (renewable once). It also increased the power of the European Parliament by requiring greater co-decision making with the Council of Ministers. Finally, it consolidated the three-pillar structure of the EU, created by the 1992 Maastricht Treaty into one single EU body, which was now endowed with **legal personality** (previously only the EC pillar had legal personality). The EU is now represented at the UN, WTO, G8, and G20.

It is, however, in its goal of economic integration that the EU has witnessed its greatest success. Since the organization's establishment in 1957, the integration process has passed through four principal developmental stages. The first was the establishment of a **free trade area** in which tariff barriers were eliminated between its member states. By the late 1960s it had evolved into a **customs union**, which in addition to eliminating tariffs between its members also applied common tariffs on imports from countries outside of the organization. This was completed by July 1, 1968. The third stage was the development by the early 1970s of a **common market**, which in addition to the previous measures allowed for the free movement of capital and labor across national boundaries. Finally, by the early-1990s, the EU had become an **economic union**, in which its member-states committed to plan jointly for monetary, fiscal, and social policies (Ray and Kaarbo 2008, 425).

As of 2016, the EU has a combined GDP of over $16.4 trillion (still smaller than the US ($18.5) trillion in 2016) and a labor force of around 228 million (2012 the United States has 144 million) (CIA n.d.). It has become the world's largest exporter and second-largest importer, accounting for approximately 16% in 2013 of global imports and exports (European Commission).[5] The process of EMU has also culminated in the creation of a single currency (the euro), in which 19 states now participate (informally referred to as the eurozone). A European Central Bank was created in 1998 to manage monetary policy, and the euro currency officially entered into circulation in January 2002.

Although the EU has thus evolved in very significant ways over the past 65 years, its organizational structure has remained essentially the same (apart from the addition of the European Central Bank in 1998). The most important bodies within the EU are:

- ### *Council of the European Union (formerly the Council of Ministers)*

  Together with the European Commission, the Council makes up the EU's executive branch. Each member-state is represented by one minister who represents his or her respective national government. Meetings are attended by whichever ministers have responsibility for the issues being discussed. For example, some meetings will be attended by the foreign ministers, others by ministers responsible for transport, immigration, agriculture, or the economy. The Council reviews and approves decisions made by the European Commission. Decisions require either unanimity or a qualified majority, depending on the issue being discussed.

- ### *European Commission*

  Together with the Council, the Commission acts as the EU's executive branch. It is composed of one Commissioner from each member state (nominated by the Council and approved by the European Parliament for five-year terms). However, as a "supranational" body, Commissioners are expected to act independently of any national allegiance they may have. Each Commissioner is assigned responsibility for a policy area by the president of the European Commission (who is also nominated by the Council and approved by the European Parliament). The Commission's functions are to initiate, oversee, and implement EU policies. It achieves this in four principal ways. First, through its "right of initiative" the Commission proposes new laws to the Parliament and Council. Second, it manages the EU's budget and allocates funding. Third, it enforces EU laws (together with the Court of Justice). Fourth and finally, it represents the EU internationally in international forums like the WTO and UN, and by negotiating agreements between the EU and other countries (European Union n.d.).

- ### *European Parliament*

  Although the Parliament began life as the EU's weakest body, it has steadily grown in power over recent decades and now acts as a co-legislator for nearly all EU law. Together with the Council, the Parliament can now adopt or amend proposals from the Commission. The Parliament also supervises the work of the Commission and adopts the EU's budget (European Union n.d.). It is composed of 750 members (European Parliament, 2017)[6],

Image © AND Inc, 2013. Used under license from Shutterstock, Inc.

Figure 4.3. The European Parliament building, in Strasbourg, France.

all of whom are directly elected to five-year terms (before 1979 they were selected by the parliaments of each member-state). As a prominent symbol of its supranational role, parties in the Parliament sit together, caucus and vote along ideological lines, rather than by traditional national allegiance. Working in such "political groups" also provides parties with greater political leverage than they would otherwise enjoy. For example, the Group of the Progressive Alliance of Socialists and Democrats (S&D) of the European Parliament is composed of members drawn from all 28 (27, Brexit pending) member-states. By joining together to create one overarching political group, the S&D controls 190 (2017) of the chamber's votes, thus enabling it to promote its ideology of social democracy much more effectively. This political group mechanism may allay the concern of smaller countries in the EU to some degree who have expressed dissatisfaction "with the weighted vote" scheme that rules in both the Parliament and the Council of Ministers. However, it is still the case that larger states, because of their larger population size, have more voting rights in both the Council of the European Union and the Parliament.

- ***European Court of Justice (ECJ)***

The ECJ is the EU's judicial body and is composed of one judge from each member state. Its principal roles are to adjudicate disputes over EU treaties and to ensure a uniform interpretation of EU laws. Significantly, unlike the UN's ICJ, the ECJ can hear cases brought not only by member states and other bodies of the organization, but also by corporations affected by EU treaty provisions and even individuals.

Given that its decisions are also legally binding, such extensive scope and powers make the ECJ a truly unique court in world politics.

- ***Court of Auditors***

As its name suggests, the Court of Auditors (established in 1975) has 28 (27, Brexit pending) members and audits all EU's revenues and expenditures to ensure accountability, efficiency, and transparency.

- ***European Central Bank (ECB)***

Located in Frankfurt, Germany, the ECB was created in 1998 in order to manage the EU's common monetary policy in the lead-up to the adoption of the euro in 2002. Its main task now is to maintain the euro's purchasing power and thus price stability in the euro area (European Central Bank n.d.).

Image © Carole Castelli, 2013. Used under license from Shutterstock, Inc.

Figure 4.4.　European institutions buildings: Court of Auditors, Court of Justice, European Investment Bank, and European Parliament–Luxembourg City.

DISCUSSION BOX

EU Ordinary Legislative Procedure (co-decision-making procedure)

The co-decision procedure was introduced by the Maastricht Treaty on European Union (1992), and extended and made more effective by the Amsterdam Treaty (1999). With the Lisbon Treaty that took effect on 1 December 2009, the renamed ordinary legislative procedure became the main legislative procedure of the EU's decision-making system.

Ordinary legislative procedure gives the same weight to the European Parliament and the Council of the European Union on a wide range of areas (for example, economic governance, immigration, energy, transport, the environment, and consumer protection). The vast majority of European laws are adopted jointly by the European Parliament and the Council.

1. The Commission sends its proposal to Parliament and the Council.
2. They consider it and discuss it on two successive occasions.
3. After two readings, if they cannot agree, the proposal is brought before a Conciliation Committee made up of an equal number of representatives of the Council and Parliament (Representatives of the Commission also attend the meetings of the Conciliation Committee and contribute to the discussions).
4. When the Committee has reached agreement, the text agreed upon is sent to Parliament and the Council for a third reading, so that they can finally adopt it as a legislative text. The final agreement of the two institutions is essential if the text is to be adopted as a law.
5. Even if a joint text is agreed to by the Conciliation Committee, Parliament can still reject the proposed law by a majority of the votes cast. (European Union n.d.)

4.1.5 EU Debate: IGO or United States of Europe?

Whether the EU should remain an IGO composed of sovereign states or unify into a "United States of Europe" has been a contentious question since its foundation in 1957. Those in favor of a federalist structure tend to argue that ever-greater economic and political integration will inevitably consolidate the unprecedented peace that has existed in Europe since the end of World War II. This theoretical assumption dates back to scholars such as Immanuel Kant and Jean-Jacques Rousseau (see Liberal theory in Chapter 2).

However, some scholars (generally referred to as **functionalists**) argue that rather than being the result of a grand design by political leaders, the process of European integration has actually been driven by the desire of states and other economic actors, who have all reaped the benefits of greater efficiency and "economies of scale" produced by earlier integration attempts, to expand integration into ever-more sectors of their economies. Thus, the economic benefits reaped through greater cooperation in coal and steel production in the 1950s has spurred an integration process that has culminated in similar cooperation across areas such as agriculture, transport, communications, and even a single currency. Such economic integration inevitably leads to calls for greater political integration, in order to make decision making over these economic policies more efficient, effective, and democratic.

Regardless of whether it is the result of a political grand design or simply the product of economic self-interest, federalists argue that a United States of Europe will prevent a return to the region's fractious past. It will also allow Europe to compete economically with other major countries and regions and allow it to assert itself politically. For example, a common European foreign and security policy will allow Europe to defend itself more effectively and promote its values and interests globally in a manner that would be simply impossible as independent states.

Those opposed to creating a United States of Europe do not generally argue against the economic benefits of greater cooperation. Usually, they are at least in favor of maintaining a regional free-trade area. However, they tend to argue in favor of the independence and flexibility provided by a Europe of sovereign states. They argue that there is plenty of evidence suggesting that the populations of many European states do not wish to sacrifice their sovereignty to the degree required by the federalist project. For example, when the EU's leaders produced a "European Constitutional Treaty" in 2004, it was rejected by French and Dutch voters the following year. When the Lisbon Treaty (which "reformed" the EU's previous treaties, rather than replacing them with a new "constitution") replaced it in 2007, it was also initially rejected, this time by Irish voters in a June 2008 referendum. However, in a manner many opponents argued was somewhat undemocratic, the Irish were convinced to hold the referendum again the following year, which passed.

The contending perspectives of these two approaches can be seen in the reaction of their respective supporters to the economic crisis that has afflicted the region since 2008, the "eurocrisis." On the basis that "[no] monetary union has ever succeeded without concurrent political union," supporters of further European integration are now suggesting that this could be the opportune time for the EU to become "the broader political union needed as the basis for a single currency" (McNamara 2010, 2). Germany has been the greatest proponent of this approach, with its Chancellor, Angela Merkel, arguing that the eurocrisis has shown that "step-by-step [EU members] must from now on give up more competences to Europe, and allow Europe more powers of control" (BBC 2012).

On the other hand, there are those who argue that the eurocrisis has been exacerbated by the very lack of flexibility that membership of the eurozone imposes. For example, eurozone members like Greece and Spain cannot depreciate their currencies in order to promote exports whenever they face a financial crisis. Having never joined the eurozone, the United Kingdom remains a major proponent of this approach. In response to Germany's calls for greater political union, the UK's Foreign Secretary, Lord Owen, suggested that the UK "remain part of a single market and let other countries develop a closer political union if they so wished" (BBC 2012). In a referendum held on Thursday June 23, 2016, to decide whether the United Kingdom should leave or remain in the European Union, the leave won by 51.9–48.1%. The referendum turnout was 71.8%, with more than 30 million people voting. The United Kingdom is scheduled to depart on March 29, 2019 (BBC News).[7]

So, do you think the EU should work to transform itself into a United States of Europe? If the United States has become the most powerful and prosperous nation in the world as a federalized system of 50 states, why might a similar political arrangement not be equally as successful for Europe? If you believe a federal European state is desirable, how large should it become? In other words, which states should be allowed to join? Which states should be excluded? What criteria would you use to decide whether a state could become a member?

Figure 4.5. European Union Map (EU)

4.2 Do NGOs Affect World Politics?

Along with IGOs, NGOs are playing an increasingly significant role in world politics. While sub-state NGOs can work to influence the policies of their respective governments, TNGOs generally help generate and ensure compliance with international regimes in areas such as human rights, the environment, arms control, and economic development. For example, TNGOs like *Amnesty International* and *Human Rights Watch* campaign for the protection and promotion of internationally recognized human rights. Another TNGO, *Greenpeace*, operates and campaigns globally to preserve and protect the environment. Many TNGOs also help distribute critical assistance to populations in need, including *Doctors Without Borders*, *Oxfam*, and *Catholic Relief*.

TNGOs can also be controversial, because their activities can be construed by political leaders as intrusive and as violations of their national sovereignty. This can be especially true if the TNGO in question relies significantly on financial resources from private businesses, corporations, or organizations that are perceived to be politically motivated (and not on contributions made by private citizens). NGOs are also sometimes accused of working for foreign political purposes. For example, the leader of the Russian Liberal Democratic Party and its State Duma faction, Vladimir Zhirinovsky, asked in April 2013 to close every Russian NGO with connections to foreigners, claiming that their goal was to instigate an "orange" revolution in Russia (Interfax 2013).⁸

4.3 International Law

International law is an international institution (see Liberalism in Chapter 2) utilized by states and other actors in world politics to achieve a diverse set of goals, including the maintenance of international peace and security and the promotion and defense of human rights. Due to the anarchic nature of the international system, international law is much more contentious than its domestic counterpart. At the state (or domestic) level, law is hierarchical. It is usually created by legislatures and executives with widespread political legitimacy and enforced by legal systems with the power to compel individuals and groups to obey it. This, of course, is not the case in our anarchic international system.

Despite these limitations, international law has grown tremendously since the end of World War II. This growth is evident in the creation of numerous international legal documents, including the United Nations Charter (1945), the Geneva Conventions (1949), and the Convention Against Torture (1984 and 1987), which are all commonly used to frame contemporary political debates (for example, in relation to how the United States has prosecuted its "war on terror").

Perhaps the most significant recent development in international law was the creation of the International Criminal Court in 2002 (discussed below). Unlike the UN's International Court of Justice, this court is an independent body with the power to prosecute individuals for criminal behavior. Nevertheless, as in the case of the International Court of Justice, there is still no international police force that can enforce its rulings.

So, is international law worth the paper it is written on? If not, why do states expend so much time and energy either promoting it or preventing it from being created? Once again, we will see that the answer to these questions depends on your theoretical approach. Realists, Liberals, and Radicals each have their own explanation for why international law is created and obeyed. However, before we investigate what they are, we must first become more familiar with the nature of international law and how it is created.

4.3.1 Sources of International Law

There are four principal sources of international law. The first is **treaties**. Treaties are essentially **codified** international law. For example, the UN Charter is the primary source of international law on questions of state sovereignty and the use of force. Similarly, the International Law of the Sea

Treaty (1982) is the primary source of international law for disputes over territorial waters and fishing and mineral rights. The general primacy of treaties in international law is due to the fact that they are the most explicit and widely accepted statements of the legal principles involved.

The second important source of international law is **custom**. Custom, in this context, is any generally accepted and expected behavior among states. Such customs can eventually reach the level of **customary international law**, but only if states are conscious of the need to abide by the relevant custom—it cannot be simply habitual behavior. Some customary international law may eventually be codified in a treaty. For example, the legal principle that states possess territorial waters became customary international law because states respected each other's territorial waters. However, for hundreds of years custom had only allowed for a three-mile extension from the shoreline, as that was the furthest distance that a cannonball could be fired. With the invention of more modern weaponry, the custom of three miles began to appear rather arbitrary. Thus, when states met to negotiate the International Law of the Sea Treaty in the 1980s and thereby codify the law, they decided to establish 12 nautical miles as territorial waters.

As customary international law is by definition uncodified, it tends to be subjected to greater legal challenges and suffer from greater ambiguity in its interpretation. As mentioned, it is because of this that treaties are generally treated as the primary source of international law. However, there are cases in which older treaties have been superseded by newer customs, resulting in the creation of newer customary international law. This means the question of which source of international law has primacy depends ultimately on the legal question/dispute being addressed.

The opinions of judicial bodies form a third source of international law. These bodies can be international and national courts. For example, the opinions of the International Court of Justice, International Criminal Court, or a national court like the U.S. Supreme Court, all contribute to the creation of international **jurisprudence**. The fourth principle source of international law is the writings and opinions of significant juridical scholars or **publicists**.

4.3.2 The Expansion of International Law

When international law was first established in our modern Westphalian system, its principal role was to prevent international conflict through the preservation of international order. It was for this reason that legal principles, such as sovereignty and non-intervention, were the first to be enshrined in international customary and treaty law. However, the 20th century witnessed a major expansion of the scope of international law, as it moved beyond the role of ensuring international and state security and began to concern itself with issues of justice and **human security**.

Although states remain the primary subjects of international law (only states can enact international law, and only state practice contributes to the development of customary international law), this broadening has led to non-state actors, such as corporations, NGOs, and individuals, being increasingly recognized as subjects of international law.[9] Non-state actors are also playing significant roles in the formation and promotion of international law. For example, they work to affect the normative environment in which states create international law; they lobby and advise national governments in support of specific international laws; and they even draft treaties and conventions for states to adopt.

The expanding scope of international law and the increased roles of non-state actors described above has perhaps been greatest in the interrelated areas of international human rights law, international humanitarian law (also known as the "laws of war" or the "laws of armed conflict") and international criminal law. International human rights law is the body of international law that is designed to promote and protect human rights. International humanitarian law is another subset of international law that seeks to limit, for humanitarian reasons, the effects of armed conflict. It protects persons who are not (or who are no longer) participating in hostilities and restricts the means and methods of warfare (ICRC 2004). Finally, international criminal law is a body of international law that seeks to prohibit certain types of atrocities and hold those responsible for committing them criminally accountable.

It is, perhaps, only in the past 60 years that the international community has made its greatest advances in promoting international law in all three of these areas. With the horrors of World War II acting as a catalyst, the preamble to the UN Charter affirmed the international community's faith in "fundamental human rights." However, the Charter failed to adequately define what those human rights were and thus the international community decided to complement it with another, more explicit, document; the **Universal Declaration of Human Rights** (UDHR). Adopted by the UN General Assembly in 1948, the UDHR is composed of 30 articles outlining the fundamental human rights and freedoms of all individuals, regardless of nationality, place of residence, gender, national or ethnic origin, color, religion, language, or any other status. It is now generally agreed to be the foundation of all international human rights law (United Nations n.d.).

The cornerstone treaties of international humanitarian law are the **Geneva Conventions** of 1949. The Geneva Conventions actually include four treaties (the First Geneva Convention for the Amelioration of the Condition of the Wounded and Sick in Armed Forces in the Field, 1864; the Second Geneva Convention for the Amelioration of the Condition of Wounded, Sick and Shipwrecked Members of Armed Forces at Sea, 1906; the Third Geneva Convention relative to the Treatment of Prisoners of War, 1929; and the Fourth Geneva Convention relative to the Protection of Civilian Persons in Time of War, 1949).

The Geneva Conventions have since been developed and supplemented by two further agreements: Additional Protocols I and II of 1977 relating to the protection of victims of armed conflicts (ICRC 2004). Together these treaties contain the essential rules protecting persons who are not, or who are no longer, taking a direct part in hostilities when they find themselves in the hands of an adversary: namely, the wounded and sick, the shipwrecked, prisoners of war, civilian internees, civilians living under occupation, and civilians in general. They also confirm and strengthen the role of the medical mission (for example, the neutrality of the ICRC) in hostilities (Dormann 2009).

Along with the protection of noncombatants during times of war, international humanitarian law also tries to prohibit the use of certain types of weapons and military tactics and protect certain categories of people and goods. For example, certain categories of weapons have been prohibited through conventions like the Biological Weapons Convention (1972), the Conventional Weapons Convention (1980), the Chemical Weapons Convention (1993), and the Ottawa Convention on Anti-Personnel Mines (1997). Certain categories of people and goods have been provided with specific protection through conventions like the Optional Protocol to the Convention on the Rights of the Child on the involvement of children in armed conflict (2000) and the Convention for the Protection of Cultural Property in the Event of Armed Conflict (1954) (ICRC 2004).

Since the adoption of the UDHR, a number of treaties and conventions have been adopted by the international community at both the international and regional levels, to further advance the protection of human rights. For example, at the international level, the Convention on the Prevention and Punishment of the Crime of Genocide (Genocide Convention) entered into force in January 1951. One example at the regional level is the **Council of Europe's** (an international organization created in 1949) adoption of the European Convention on Human Rights in 1950. This Convention also established a European Court of Human Rights (began operation in 1959), to rule on applications from states (that believed another contracting state had violated its obligations under the Convention), individuals, or other legal entities, such as companies or associations, who believed their rights under the Convention had been violated. By 2012 the Court had delivered more than 15,000 judgments, nearly half of which concerned violations of the Convention by the states of Turkey, Italy, Russia, and Poland (ECHR 2012). This ground-breaking European human rights regime has acted as a model for other regions, including for the Organization of American States, which adopted an American Convention on Human Rights in 1978 (Janis 1984, 69).

As one can see from the preceding account, individuals and non-state groups have become (if they were not already) recognized subjects of international law. In the case of the European Court of Human Rights described above, individuals from anywhere in the world can apply to hold a member-state of the Council of Europe accountable for violating their rights under the European

Convention on Human Rights. However, just as individuals have become increasingly protected under international law, they have also become more accountable. This is particularly the case under international criminal law, which seeks to prosecute those who commit grave human rights violations, regardless of whether they are committed during times of war.

This principle of individual accountability under international criminal law was particularly apparent during the Nuremberg and Tokyo war crimes trials following World War II. By trying and convicting thousands of individuals (and executing hundreds of them) the war crimes trials in Nuremberg and elsewhere "reestablished plainly and forcefully that the rules of international law should and do apply to individuals" (Janis 1984, 66). Following atrocities committed in Cambodia (1975–1979), the former Yugoslavia (1992–1995), Rwanda (1994), and Sierra Leone (from 1996), the United Nations created *ad hoc* courts to try those individuals believed responsible. Ad hoc courts are limited in that they are created to prosecute crimes that have been committed during a specific time period or on a specific territory, or both. For example, the International Criminal Tribunal for Rwanda was established to try crimes committed on Rwandan territory (or by Rwandans in neighboring states) between January and December 1994. Also, in all four of the cases above, former heads of state have been either indicted or prosecuted by their respective courts. For supporters of international justice, prosecutions such as these promise to end the "age of impunity" for leaders of countries that commit such egregious crimes. In the case of the International Criminal Tribunal for the Former Yugoslavia, the former president of Serbia, Slobodan Milosevic, died of a heart attack while in custody in 2006. In the case of the Special Court for Sierra Leone, the former president of Liberia, Charles Taylor, was convicted and sentenced to 50 years imprisonment in April 2012 for his support of rebels in Sierra Leone, who were responsible for perpetrating horrendous atrocities against their own people.

4.3.3 International Criminal Court

Although supporters of international justice have applauded all of the developments outlined above, many still felt that ad hoc courts were incapable of ensuring the effective enforcement of international human rights law. They therefore worked toward the establishment of the world's first permanent international criminal tribunal, which was achieved in 2002 with the creation of the International Criminal Court (ICC). Located in the Peace Palace in The Hague, The Netherlands, the ICC's founding document, the Rome Statute (which has been open for signature since 1998), has now been signed and ratified by over 120 countries. Just over 30 countries have signed, but not yet ratified the Statute, including the Russian Federation, Sudan, Israel, and the United States all withdrew their signatures after initially signing it. Some, including China, India, North Korea, Saudi Arabia, Pakistan, and Indonesia have never signed it. As of 3 December 2016, 124 states have ratified or acceded to the Rome Statute.

Image © jan kranendonk, 2013. Used under license from Shutterstock, Inc.

Figure 4.6. International Criminal Court in The Hague, The Netherlands

Several, mainly African, states have argued that, because of a perceived disproportionate focus of the Court on Africa, the ICC is a tool of Western imperialism. There are 34 members of the ICC from African states, but 9 out of the 10 situations, which the ICC has investigated, were in African countries.[10]

The organizational structure of the ICC is principally composed of an Assembly of State Parties, three judicial divisions (a pretrial division, a trial division, and an appeals division) with a total of 18 judges and an Office of the Prosecutor. The Prosecutor can initiate an investigation on the basis of a referral from any state party or from the United Nations Security Council (under Chapter 7 of the UN Charter). In addition, the Prosecutor can initiate investigations on the basis of information on crimes (within the jurisdiction of the Court) received from individuals or organizations, but only if they can persuade a Pre-Trial Chamber (usually composed of three judges) that a sufficient case exists.

The jurisdiction of the ICC covers four types of crimes: genocide, crimes against humanity, war crimes, and acts of aggression. All four of these types of crimes are defined in the Rome Statute. The crime of genocide is defined as an atrocity "committed with intent to destroy, in whole or in part, a national, ethnical, racial or religious group." The prosecution of this crime thus rests on the ability to prove the "intent" of the perpetrator. Contrary to popular understanding, genocide does not therefore require the massacre of large numbers of innocents. It does not even require killing at all. For instance, genocide includes "imposing measures intended to prevent births within the group" and "forcibly transferring children of the group to another group" (ICC 2011). As one can see, it is the *intent* of the perpetrator and not the scale of the crime that is the defining factor in the crime of genocide.

A crime against humanity is defined by the Rome Statute as one of a number of acts "committed as part of a widespread or systematic attack against any civilian population, with knowledge of the attack." As one can see, in this definition it is the manner or scale of the crime that is its defining feature. Acts that constitute a crime against humanity when conducted in this way include murder, enslavement, imprisonment, torture, and rape, among others. War crimes are crimes committed against international humanitarian law. They are thus defined in the Rome Statute as "grave breaches of the Geneva Conventions . . . in particular when committed as part of a plan or policy or as part of a large-scale commission of such crimes." These breaches of the Geneva Conventions include willful killing, torture, depriving prisoners of war over their legal rights, and the extensive destruction and appropriation of property, among others (ICC 2011).

Because the ICC's Assembly of State Parties was unable to agree on a definition for the crime of aggression by the time the Court began operation, it was left to subsequent review conferences to do so. This was eventually achieved in 2010, when the crime of aggression was defined as "the use of armed force by a State against the sovereignty, territorial integrity or political independence of another State" and "which, by its character, gravity and scale, constitutes a manifest violation" of the UN Charter. Consistent with the principle of individual accountability, the Court will not hold states responsible for acts of aggression, but rather any "person in a position effectively to exercise control over or to direct the political or military action of a State" believed to have committed aggression (ICC 2010).

However, in recognition of the sensitivity that many states still exhibit on this issue, the Court began exercise jurisdiction over this crime only beginning in January 2017 and only after 30 State parties have ratified the requisite amendment to the Statute. State parties still unwilling to accept the Court's jurisdiction over the crime of aggression may also opt out by lodging a declaration of "non-acceptance of jurisdiction" with the Court. Non-state parties have also been explicitly excluded from the Court's jurisdiction over aggression, whether committed by their nationals or on their territory. The UN Security Council has also been awarded greater powers to delay prosecutions under this crime than it possesses over the three other types of crimes within the Court's jurisdiction.

Notwithstanding these exceptions for the crime of aggression, the ICC's jurisdiction extends to any of the crimes described above when committed by a national of a State party, or when committed on the territory of a State party, or under any circumstances referred to the Court by the UN Security Council. The Court can only prosecute crimes committed after it was founded in 2002.

Also, under the principle of "complementarity," the ICC can only exercise its jurisdiction when a State party (of which the accused is a national) is unable or unwilling to prosecute. The ICC is thus a court of "last resort." The Rome Statute also provides the UN Security Council with the power to delay a prosecution for a period of 12 months through the normal voting procedures under Chapter 7 of the UN Charter.

DISCUSSION BOX

Should the United States Join the ICC?

As we know from the description above, the International Criminal Court (ICC) was officially established in 2002 in order to prosecute individuals for the grave offences of genocide, war crimes, and crimes against humanity. A majority of the states in our international system have joined it, including an overwhelming majority of the world's democracies. However, despite the fact that President Clinton signed the Rome Statute in 2000 (but did not present in to the Senate for ratification), his successor President George W. Bush "unsigned" it two years later. The United States is therefore not a State party to the Rome Statute, alongside states like China, Sudan, and Syria.

Opposition to the ICC in the United States has taken two principal forms (Kerr 2007, 66). The first is a general opposition to the United States participating in any international institution that might threaten its sovereignty and limit its freedom to act. The principal fears in this regard are that U.S. leaders will be prosecuted in politically motivated trials and that U.S. political and military leaders will be restrained in their foreign policy decisions by the fear of future prosecutions. To these critics, international institutions act like the Lilliputians, tying down Gulliver, so as to prevent it from doing what is in its own interests and in the interests of the rest of the world.

The second form of opposition is not necessarily motivated by a deep suspicion of international institutions per se, but is driven instead by the concern that the Rome Statute contains provisions that undermine the legal safeguards U.S. citizens enjoy in their own Constitution. These include the protection against double jeopardy, the right to trial by an impartial jury, and the right of the accused to confront the witnesses against him or her (Dempsey 1998).

The United States has argued that all prosecutions should first be sanctioned by the UN Security Council. This, of course, would allow it to prevent prosecutions it thought were inappropriate through the use of its veto. Although the United States abstained in the 2005 vote to refer Sudan to the ICC (so as to allow for the prosecution of those responsible for the genocide in Darfur), in 2011 it actually voted in favor of referring Libya to the ICC. For some, this is a reflection of the closer relationship the United States has developed with the ICC under the Obama administration (Kersten 2011).

Do you believe the U.S. refusal to join the ICC is warranted? How do the supporters of the ICC counter the arguments made above? What effect do you think the failure of the United States to join the ICC has on the success of the ICC in its role of preventing and prosecuting gross human rights violations?

4.4 Theoretical Perspectives on International Organizations and Law

So, why do states create international institutions, like international organizations and international law? Do these international institutions significantly affect state behavior? Will their creation bring about international peace and security? This section will explain how Realists, Liberals, and Radical theorists answer these questions. Which theory do you think is correct?

4.4.1 Realist Perspective

Realists do not believe that international institutions like international organizations and international law play a significant role in world politics. For Realists, international institutions "are basically a reflection of the distribution of power in the world. They are based on the self-interested calculations of the great powers, and they have no independent effect on state behavior." Realists, therefore, do not believe that International institutions are an important cause of peace; rather "they matter only on the margins" (Mearsheimer 1994/95, 7).

An analogy that might help explain this perspective on the effects of international institutions is the addition of protective padding to the equipment worn by American football players. The padding might change the interactions between the players by softening the blows they suffer whenever they come into contact, but they do not fundamentally change the nature of the game itself. Teams still want to win. The game remains zero-sum in the sense that a point for your rival team is a point lost. Teams thus continue to worry about relative scores. Larger players may also utilize the padding they are wearing to prevent rival players from scoring and even push their opponents around, especially if they feel stronger than them.

Similarly, despite the existence of international institutions in world politics, great powers continue to be self-interested and concerned with the relative balance of power. The nature of world politics does not change. Just as padding does not fundamentally change the behavior of football players, institutions do not significantly change the behavior of states. Rather, just as football players utilize safety equipment to help them win the game, states utilize institutions to achieve the same goals they have always pursued in the anarchic international system. As John Mearsheimer, a contemporary Realist scholar at the University of Chicago, explains, the "most powerful states in the system create and shape institutions so that they can maintain their share of world power, or even increase it. In this [Realist] view, institutions are essentially 'arenas for acting out power relationships'' (Mearsheimer 1994/95, 13).

A prominent example of one such arena is the UN Security Council. Although the Security Council was created to allow the great powers of the post-WWII era to cooperate in the provision of collective security, it quickly became deadlocked and remained so throughout the Cold War, as the superpowers pursued their own interests (and used their vetoes to prevent their rivals from gaining a geopolitical advantage). Even in 2012 the Security Council remains deadlocked over the crisis in Syria, as the great powers continue to protect their own interests and compete over relative power and influence (Nichols 2012). Indeed, the United States–Russian gridlock over Syria still remains in the closing months of 2017. Such behavior confirms for Realists that states are simply too selfish for collective security to ever work.

Realists are equally skeptical of international law. They note that powerful states like the United States can violate the UN Charter with effective impunity, as it did in 2003 when it attacked Iraq without a UN Chapter 7 resolution. They also note that the United States constantly requests the UN Security Council to pass resolutions condemning and sanctioning states it does not perceive as friendly, for human rights abuses (like Syria and Iran), yet ignores (and even protects) those like Saudi Arabia, Bahrain, and Israel, which are all accused of serious violations of international human rights law.

Finally, Realists do not believe the ICC will ever hold powerful leaders accountable. Realists point to the fact that all of the individuals indicted by the ICC so far herald from relatively weak African states. Powerful leaders from states like the United States, Russia, and China are even willing to vote for the Court to investigate and prosecute governmental leaders of weak states, whilst they refuse to subject themselves to the Court's jurisdiction. Thus, to paraphrase Thucydides' famous saying, "the powerful create and impose international laws, while the weak have to accept them."

4.4.2 Liberal Perspective

As explained in Chapter 1, along with democracy and economic interdependence, international institutions are one of the three components in the Kantian triangle of Liberalism. For Liberals, international institutions are capable of helping states overcome the inherent insecurity in the anarchic international system and thus enable them to achieve levels of cooperation thought impossible by Realists. Institutions do this by helping states establish standards of behavior; by helping to ensure compliance with those standards; by helping to resolve disputes; and by reducing the costs of joint decision making (see Chapter 2).

Perhaps the best example of how international institutions can transform world politics in this way is the process of European integration, described earlier in this chapter. Few could have predicted during the mid-20th century that a war-ravaged Europe, torn apart by nationalism and racial hatred, would be transformed into an exemplar of regional cooperation across a range of economic and political policy areas, including trade, monetary, social, environmental, justice, and even foreign and defense policies. As one scholar has noted "[it] is astounding that the states of Europe, so long used to dealing with each other with bayonets and tanks, are now tightly bound together within a series of interlocking laws and institutions. Rather than shooting at each other, they spend their time squabbling over the rules of long-haul truck transport and labeling of genetically modified organisms" (McNamara 2010, 1).

Although Liberals accept that international law is regularly flouted, they point to the example above and to the daily actions of states across the globe, to emphasize that adherence to the law is actually much more common. And in the words of the political scientist Louis Henkin:

> If one doubts the significance of this law, one need only imagine a world in which it were absent. . . . There would be no security of nations or stability of governments; property would not be respected; vessels could navigate only at their constant peril; property—within or without any given territory—would be subject to arbitrary seizure; persons would have no protection of law or diplomacy; agreements would not be made or observed; diplomatic relations would end; international trade would cease; international organizations and arrangements would disappear. (Mingst 2011, 220)

4.4.3 The Radical Approach Perspective

For Radical theorists, international institutions are created by the dominant social classes and states in the international system in order to serve their own interests. Radical theorists believe international institutions are the product of a specific time and historical process. For example, the birth of international law can be traced to the transformation from feudal to capitalist economies in the 17th century (Keach 2003). Since then, the different phases of the world capitalist economy have yielded corresponding international legal "superstructures" designed to facilitate these changes. Contemporary international institutions are thus today being transformed to facilitate the latest phase of capitalism: globalization (Chimni 1999, 338).

As capitalism is an inherently exploitative mode of production (see Chapters 2 and 5), the process of globalization is, in fact, simply encouraging and enabling exploitation on an ever greater scale. International law thus "reflects the domination of [the] bourgeoisie [from both rich and poor countries] which profits at the expense of working classes." However, as a tool of the most powerful states and social classes, international law not only reflects domination, but actually "creates and congeals inequalities in the international system" (Chimni 1999, 337).

Just like Realists, Radical theorists are dismissive of the power of international law to positively affect the behavior of powerful states. For example, in the case of the Geneva Conventions, powerful states will simply ignore them (as the United States did when it used cluster bombs in Afghanistan), or interpret them in a manner that allows them to contravene their basic principles (as the United States did when it labeled prisoners of war as "unlawful combatants" in order to deny them their basic human rights and legal protections). Powerful states can even create international law to justify their exploitative behavior. This is what happened when the European powers created concepts in international law, such as **Terra Nullius** (territory belonging to no one) and **Pescription** (occupation is justified if not objected to), to permit their own colonization of large parts of the world. The Berlin Conference of 1855 simply declared the whole of Africa as Terra Nullius on the basis that Africans could not govern themselves. Similar claims were made on Australia. Radical theorists thus dismiss the notion that the International Criminal Court will ever be "fair and effective" in bringing war criminals to justice because "it will never [be able to] enforce the same international laws against government officials in the US, or China or Britain" as it has against those of smaller countries (Keach 2003).

Similarly, international organizations are created to serve the interests of the most powerful states and social classes. Radical theorists note that the most prominent international trade and financial organizations, including the World Trade Organization, the International Monetary Fund, and the World Bank, all reflect the domination of these groups. These organizations also help powerful states consolidate their domination by perpetuating the illusion that capitalism is the "natural order" of things (Chimni 1999, 345). The powerful states then continually police the system, using international institutions (like the UN and NATO) to legitimate their interventions in the sovereignty of states through the imposition of sanctions and the use of force.

As international institutions, including international law, IGOs, and TNGOs, are all controlled by the "capitalist ruling class to serve their interests and to regulate or conceal their ceaseless rivalries," many Radical theorists thus argue that "[such] laws and institutions [can never] provide a substantial basis for resisting or preventing the wars and other miseries that are an inherent feature of global capitalism." The UN is no exception. To be realistic, one must no longer hold out for "an improved UN that can really enforce international rules fairly," but simply accept that "UN decisions only have teeth when US policy requires it." Therefore, to be successful, political resistance to this domination must be organized outside of these institutions (Keach 2003).

Key Terms

Charter of the UN
codified international law
Common market
Compromissory clause
Council of Europe
Council of Ministers
Council of the European Union
Court of Auditors
customary international law
customs
Customs Union
Economic and Social Council
economic union
European Central Bank
European Commission
European Court of Justice
European Parliament
European Union (EU)
free trade area
functionalists
General Assembly
Geneva Conventions

Global IGOs/NGOs
human security
ICJ Statute
International Court of Justice (ICJ)
International Criminal Court (ICC)
jurisprudence
Legal personality
Optional Clause
peacekeeping
pooled sovereignty
Prescription
Publicists
Regional IGOs/NGOs
Secretariat
Security Council
Supranational institutions
Terra Nullius
treaties
Trusteeship Council
UN regular and peacekeeping budget
United Nations (UN)
Universal Declaration of Human Rights (UDHR)

End Notes

1. http://www.un.org/ga/search/view_doc.asp?symbol=a/71/360

2. Matt Welch, "Iraqi death toll doesn't add up," *National Post*, 2002. http://mattwelch.com/NatPostSave/Sanctions.htm

3. Yeganeh Torbati, "Iran's nuclear program entails huge costs, few benefits: report," Reuters, Tuesday April 2, 2013.

4. For full detail on the Iran nuclear agreement, see the US State Department Website at https://www.state.gov/e/eb/tfs/spi/iran/jcpoa/

5. http://ec.europa.eu/trade/policy/eu-position-in-world-trade/

6. http://www.europarl.europa.eu/portal/en

7. http://www.bbc.com/news/uk-politics-32810887

8. Interfax, "Zhirinovsky suggests closing all NGOs connected to abroad." 14:16 April 10, 2013.

9. Some theorists of international law (referred to as Positivists) argue that only states are the subjects of international law. M. W. Janis, however, argues that individuals have always been the subjects of international law and that the actual practice of international law has never matched the positivists' narrow "subject-based" definition of it. See Janis (1984).

10. Africa and the International Criminal Court: A drag net that catches only small fish?, Nehanda Radio, By William Muchayi, September 24, 2013, http://nehandaradio.com/2013/09/24/africa-and-the-international-criminal-court-a-drag-net-that-catches-only-small-fish

International Political Economy (IPE)

Image © Elenarts, 2013. Used under license from Shutterstock, Inc.

CHAPTER OUTLINE

5.0 Introduction: Post-War IPE

The immediate post–WWII era saw the division of the world into two ideological, political, and economic camps: a capitalist camp led by the United States and a communist camp led by the Soviet Union. This polarization was further solidified by the creation of their respective collective defense organizations: the United States led **North Atlantic Treaty Organization (NATO)** in 1949 and the Soviets led **Warsaw Pact** in 1954.

However, the dissatisfaction of many newly independent developing countries with the increasingly tense bipolar system led many of them to establish a **nonaligned movement** by the late 1950s. Composed principally of **Lesser Developed Countries (LDCs)**, many of whom had come under intense pressure to side with one camp or the other, the nonaligned movement saw the polarization of world politics as detrimental not only to the national development of its members, but also to world peace in general. Nevertheless, the Cold War persisted until the early 1990s when the Soviet Union collapsed after years of relative economic decline.

Despite the growing tensions between East and West, the early post–WWII period still saw the rapid economic recovery of the major European and Japanese economies, much of which was achieved through major U.S. aid, investment, and trade. The international system also witnessed wars, political instability, as well as overt and covert intervention in the politics and economics of many LDCs by both sides in the Cold War, all of which had a devastating effect on their development. Despite these unstable conditions, the economic news was not all bad. Although the **absolute income gap** between the developed states and LDCs increased during the Cold War, millions of people were also lifted from relative poverty and some LDCs did experience improvements in general living standards (Seligson, 2008).

The demise of the Cold War did not result in the end of the post–WWII liberal IPE. On the contrary, the present IPE is still dominated by many of the same principles, institutions, and organizations that dominated the previous era, including the **United Nations (UN)**, the **General Agreements of Tariffs and Trade (GATT)**, the **World Bank (WB)**, and the **International Monetary Fund (IMF)**, all of which will be discussed later in this chapter.

Globalization is perhaps the most discussed topic in post-Cold War IPE. The definition of *globalization* is subject to much debate, but it is generally understood to incorporate economic, trade, and financial dimensions. The Merriam Webster Dictionary defines globalization as the "development of an increasingly integrated global economy, marked especially by free trade, free flow of capital, and the tapping of cheaper foreign labor markets." Similarly, the Business Dictionary defines it as the "worldwide movement toward economic, financial, trade, and communications integration."[1] These definitions portray globalization simply as a *process* of ever deepening integration of economic markets that began long before the end of the Cold War.

On the other hand, Thomas Freidman, the *New York Times* foreign correspondent, sees globalization as a fundamentally different economic system to that which existed before the Cold War's end. He believes the new global economy operates with its own rules and logic that "directly or indirectly [influences] the politics, environment, geopolitics and economics of virtually every country in the world." Friedman has a broader understanding of globalization than the definitions provided above. He believes globalization to be more than a continuing process of integration of economic markets, and instead proposes that globalization has six dimensions—politics, culture, technology, finance (and trade), national security, and ecology—the boundaries between which are quickly disappearing.[2]

There is no doubt that technological development since the early 1980s is helping to "shrink" the world in so many different ways. Geographical barriers and national boundaries have become much less significant as revolutions in information technology, communication, and transportation have enabled people and businesses to instantly connect with each other across the globe. In a globalized world, traditional national boundaries are becoming less and less important, which means globalization is running counter to nationalism in its message and agenda.

Although globalization is discussed as a global phenomenon, it does not affect all states equally, and in some ways it has complicated the national development of many of them. That is, the forces of globalization are touching the lives of people everywhere in different ways, creating both opportunities and hardships. Although globalization may have helped lift millions of people out of poverty worldwide, it has also intensified global competition over natural resources, raw materials, and cheap labor. It has also accelerated global demand for consumer products that have an adverse impact on the environment.

The evidence so far also suggests that globalization favors those states that are "prepared" for it—states with stable political systems (although not necessarily democratic) in which cheaper, semi-skilled, and skilled labor is in abundance. In the new global economy, China and India have led the way in attracting new foreign investment and finance and in increasing their worldwide exports. Although both states have created millions of export-driven jobs, they are still facing immense problems, including internal rural-to-urban migration, overcrowded cities, increasing income gaps, rural poverty (especially India), and terrible environmental degradation. States like Indonesia, Malaysia, and Singapore have done equally as well, as have the so-called BRICS (Brazil, Russia, India, China, and South Africa). In the Americas, Argentina, Brazil, Chile, and Uruguay (all members of the Mercosur trade group) have also "adapted" relatively well. However, others like Cambodia, Myanmar, Vietnam, Paraguay, and Colombia have not fared so well. Similarly, many sub-Saharan African states are yet to experience any real benefits from globalization. In this way the global economy is becoming increasingly marred by ever-widening disparities in wealth and power.

We will discuss these points in more detail later in this chapter, but first we need to have a brief discussion of the dominant theories in the study of IPE. These theories, as with the theories of world politics we have already studied, each attempt to explain how the current global economy works. We must, therefore, try to decide which theory is correct before we choose the economic and political policies we hope will resolve the problems we perceive. Thankfully, we do not have to "reinvent the wheel" in learning about these theories. Each of the three principal theories of IPE are founded on one of the theoretical approaches to world politics we are already familiar with. We are therefore about to explore what Realists, Liberals, and Radical theorists all think about IPE and the policies the United States should adopt within it.

The three principal theories of IPE are Mercantilism/Economic Nationalism, Economic Liberalism, and (neo-) Marxism. The following section will explain the development and approaches of each of these theories and show how they differ in their interpretation of the past and present state of IPE.

5.1 Theories of IPE

As already mentioned, the three theories of IPE we are about to discuss are grounded in the theories of world politics that we have already covered in earlier chapters. However, the primary focus of IPE theories is on the interplay between economics, politics, and society. Discussions of IPE theories can be lengthy and complicated, but our goal here is to explain them in a simple and systematic way so you can fully appreciate each of their contributions to our understanding of how IPE works.

5.1.1 Mercantilism/Economic Nationalism

Mercantilism holds the same basic assumptions as Realist theory. It argues that government intervention in (or control of) the state's economy and trade is essential in order to protect national security. It perceives the international system and economy as a **zero-sum** environment. It thus calls for extensive state regulation of the national economy to ensure both the safety of the state and to avoid the brutal "state of nature" that would emerge if individuals were allowed to pursue their self-interest without government-imposed constraints.

Mercantilism evolved simultaneously with the rise of the modern state and was readily embraced by state-building absolutist princes in Europe between the 16th and 19th centuries. During this period, national wealth and security depended on how much gold and silver the state could accumulate, for that was how it could pay for military defense and war. In the 19th century states began to abandon the search for rare metals and concentrated instead on **industrialization** as the means to accumulate wealth. By the late 20th century the most developed states had already begun to move beyond industrial economies and were beginning to embrace new service-, technological-, and information-based economies. For Mercantilists, all of this suggests that the means to ensure wealth may change, but that the ultimate goal of states' remains the same—to try to ensure national security through the accumulation of wealth and the management of the balance of power.

One of the most important means to ensure relative power advantages is the state's **balance of trade**. This is essentially the revenue earned through exports minus the cost of imports. Mercantilists advise states to run a **balance of trade surplus**, rather than a **balance of trade deficit**, in order to ensure the most beneficial relative wealth and power. Managing the balance of trade in this way requires states to enact policies that will protect their domestic producers from foreign competition, whether fair or unfair: policies thus referred to as **protectionism**.

Protectionist policies take two principal forms: **tariffs** and **non-tariff barriers (NTBs)**. Tariffs are taxes imposed on imports in order to increase their cost to domestic purchasers. Non-tariff barriers are any protectionist policies that are not taxes. All states use some combination of these in order to protect domestic producers from foreign competition or **predatory practices**. Many states see trade barriers as imperative to protect infant industries from international competition. For example, how could a start-up software company in South Africa compete with Microsoft in the free market? Protectionism might also be needed to provide time for a domestic producer to "reorganize" or "restructure," so as to be better able to compete in the international marketplace. Or businesses, unions, and other interest groups might pressure their governments to impose trade barriers to safeguard their profits, jobs, and other interests.

In these circumstances governments might impose tariffs and NTBs to protect domestic producers from what might even be considered fair competition. Whilet tariffs take only one form, NTBs take many, including quotas (a limitation on the number or value of an import over a reason), licensing fees, and safety regulations, as well as interest reduced loans and subsidies.

These protectionist policies can also be used against predatory practices, such as **dumping** and **price-fixing**. *Dumping* is selling products in international markets at prices below the cost of production in order to gain a greater market share. *Price-fixing* occurs when producers or consumers collude to set the price of a product. While Anti-Trust laws in the United States make this type of behavior illegal in the domestic economy, there are no such laws against it in the international economy. Thus **cartels** like the Organization of Petroleum Exporting Countries (OPEC) can meet openly and regularly to set their production quotas, so as to fix the price of petroleum on the international market.

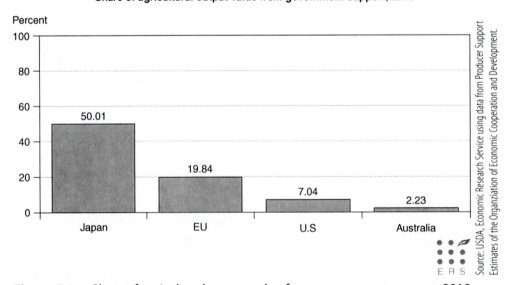

Figure 5.1. Share of agricultural output value from government support, 2010.

Image © vita pakhai, 2013. Used under license from Shutterstock, Inc.

Figure 5.2. Alexander Hamilton, Secretary of the Treasury, on ten-dollar bill.

Of the developed countries, Japan stands out as the one with the greatest protectionist policies. According to the **Organization for Economic Co-operation and Development (OECD)**, Japan's producer subsidy estimates (PSEs) showed over 45% of the value of its farm production in 2010 came from NTBs or domestic subsidies—a number that is very high by world standards.

Despite their concern with becoming too dependent on other states, Mercantilists do not believe that states should seek to reduce their reliance by trying to produce everything themselves—a policy known as **autarky**. Rather, they argue that states should trade for nonessential items and work to prevent dependency on foreign supplies of essential products, like food, oil, metals, and computer chips. When states have tried to become autarkic, as China and Albania have in the past, it has always had disastrous economic consequences.

Famous historical advocates of the Mercantilist approach include the U.S. founding father **Alexander Hamilton** (1755–1804) and the forefather of the German historical school of economics, **George Friedrich List** (1789–1846). For Hamilton, U.S. self-reliance in agriculture and industrial production was a matter of national security. Frederick List, in turn, believed that economic policy had to be adapted to the needs of specific nations. He argued, for example, that Germany should not try to compete with foreign producers until it had attained a greater degree of industrial growth.

Although Economic Nationalism is not the potent force it once was, it continues to have significant influence in the economic policies of many states. Fears of its revival are always present, especially in the insecure periods after major economic crises, such as the recent global recession. The fear is that in turbulent times the world will turn inwards and become more protectionist, just as it did after the U.S. stock market crash of 1929, thereby destroying world trade and turning an economic crisis into the Great Depression. Economic Nationalists, however, argue that "free trade" is undermining the U.S. economy and leaving it dependent on foreign, especially Chinese, investment and loans—developments that threaten not just the economic health of the United States, but its national security.

Economic Nationalists thus do not believe that free trade is an appropriate trade policy for all countries to adopt. They believe that free trade should be curtailed if it leads to persistent trade deficits and job losses and undermines the general economic well-being of the state. For example, political commentator and one-time presidential contender **Patrick Buchanan** has argued that the U.S. government must intervene in trade matters to "level the playing field" and remedy the "unfair" trade practices of China. The presidential candidate and later President Donald Trump also has complained about the United States' signing "terrible" trade agreements with other countries, such as the North American Free Trade Agreement (NAFTA) or the Trans-Pacific Partnership Agreement (TPP). The Trump administration insists on renegotiating NAFTA and TPP agreement as detrimental to the U.S. economy and national interest. In January 2017, United States withdrew from TPP. On the contrary, the liberal Obama administration viewed TPP as to "promote economic growth; support the creation and retention of jobs; enhance innovation, productivity and competitiveness; raise living standards; reduce poverty in the signatories' countries; and promote transparency, good governance, and enhanced labor and environmental protections."[3] Similarly, Economic Nationalists in **Newly Industrializing Countries (NICs)** and in many other developing countries continue to call for state intervention and management of their economies in order to promote their own economic development, sovereignty, and national interest.

Figure 5.3. Adam Smith (1723–1790) Monument on Edinburgh's Royal Mile. The Scottish Enlightenment philosopher's book *The Wealth of Nations* is considered a pioneering guide to economics and free market enterprise.

Image © Heartland, 2013. Used under license from Shutterstock, Inc.

5.1.2 Economic Liberalism

Adam Smith (1723–1790) is perhaps best known as the intellectual father of Economic Liberalism. In his book, ***The Wealth of Nations*** (1776), Smith argued that the best means to improve the wealth and power of the state was to improve the general productive capacity of its economy. The best way to achieve this, he argued, was to limit government interference in the economy to the greatest extent possible. Free of interference, the economy would be subject to certain market forces or "laws." These forces would act, he suggested, like an "**invisible hand**," naturally operating to ensure that the pursuit of self-interest by every individual ultimately led to the greatest public good.

Contrary to popular perception, Smith was not an advocate of unrestricted free trade. Smith realized that, without some constraints, free trade could actually harm the public good. He therefore argued that it should be managed or restricted in at least two ways. First, he believed that free trade should be phased in gradually and that protectionist policies should be adopted to help equalize competition between domestic and foreign producers. Second, he believed free trade had to be limited by the exigencies of national security. For example, Smith lauded the Navigation Acts of the mid-17th century, which sought to curtail colonial trade with the Netherlands, as "the wisest of all commercial regulations of England (Smith 2003, the Wealth of Nations, 2003)."[4]

In his 1817 book, ***Principles of Political Economy and Taxation,*** the English political economist **David Ricardo (1772–1823)** introduced the theory of **comparative advantage**, also called comparative cost theory. According to the theory of comparative advantage, organizing markets on the principle of the division of labor will maximize economic efficiency and thus prosperity. Essentially, the theory suggests that each state should specialize in what it is most efficient at producing and then trade with one another, rather than trying to become autarkic. This will maximize efficiency and produce greater profits, which the states can then invest in producing even more of the goods in which they have a comparative advantage. So, if a state is efficient in producing wheat and another is efficient in producing steel, they should each **specialize** in producing wheat and steel respectively. This is true even for states with an **absolute advantage**.

Bettmann Contributor/Bettmann/Getty Images

Figure 5.4. David Ricardo.

Liberals like Smith and Ricardo obviously saw the international economy as a **win-win** (positive-sum) environment and not as the **win-lose** (zero-sum) environment perceived by Mercantilists. They both saw free trade as a way, first, to counter the entrenched political interests that were subverting free market forces and, second, to spread global economic prosperity. As they saw it, if free trade was encouraged, the likelihood of international conflict and war would also diminish. Classical liberalism was thus the best means to produce a harmonious international community—unlike the international system based on competing national interests that Mercantilists envisioned.

Liberal theory is also optimistic about the potential for LDC development. Liberal theory envisions the eventual convergence of wages and prices at the global level (as LDCs experience economic development their average wages will increase, a middle class will emerge and general living standards will improve). This **convergence theory** assumes that all economies will eventually converge in terms of per capita income, since poor economies tend to grow at faster rates than richer economies. However, critics of convergence theory argue that LDCs are not all the same, and their success in development varies widely. These critics also point to the fact that rather than seeing a convergence of economic conditions, the post-war period has actually seen greater divergence, as states and/or people around the world have been divided into the haves and have-nots. We will discuss this issue further below.

Along with the emphasis placed on economic cooperation and peace produced by classical liberalism, modern liberals also place significant emphasis on the roles of international economic institutions like the **World Trade Organization (WTO)** in helping states improve their trading relationships. Other international institutions, like the UN and its affiliated organs and functional agencies, such as the World Bank, IMF, **World Health Organization (WHO), International Labor Organization (ILO), Food and Agricultural Organization (FAO)**, the **UN Economic and Social Council (UNESCO),** and the **International Criminal Court (ICC), the Kyoto Protocol** (although officially expired in 2012) and regional organizations like the **European Union (EU)** and the **Association of Southeast Asian Nations (ASEAN)** are also helping states cooperate on economic policies, coordinate and consolidate help for LDCs, as well as protect human rights and the environment.

John Maynard Keynes (1883–1946)[5] witnessed events in Europe unfolding as the Great Depression of the early 1930s led to the rise of fascism and Nazism in Italy and Germany and subsequently to World War II. His goal thus became to prevent the "boom and bust" tendencies he saw in the unmanaged global economy that had produced this economic and political disaster. To do so he challenged the classical liberal assumptions about markets inherently tending toward beneficial equilibrium and argued, instead, that when unemployment was relatively high, production and consumption would become imbalanced.

Figure 5.5.   John Maynard Keynes.

For Keynes, only state intervention in the economy to stimulate both employment and investment could overcome this imbalance. When demand in the economy was low, Keynes believed that states needed to act as a substitute for private demand by buying goods and paying for public works. In order to prepare for such times, Keynes also argued that states should save during times of economic prosperity.

Keynes believed that all rational states would seek to run a balance of trade surplus and thus recognized that international cooperation would be necessary to prevent conflict. He believed the creation of an **International Trade Organization (ITO)** would increase international trade and cooperation, but his idea did not materialize until the commencement of the World Trade Organization in 1995. He lobbied against the gold standard, which he believed caused domestic deflation (falling prices) and raised unemployment. Keynes views on gold standard is subject to debate. See, for example, Brian Domitrovic, "Against The Gold Standard? That's Not Quite Ivy League," Forbes, July 14, 2017 at https://www.forbes.com/sites/briandomitrovic/2017/07/14/against-the-goldstandard-thats-not-quite-ivy-league/#469e8f839d39. Retrieved October 17, 2017.

Keynesian economics was put into practice in the interwar period and especially after World War II in Europe and the United States, with a great deal of success. However, Keynesian policies eventually came under sustained attack by some policymakers and critics, like Milton Friedman, who were pessimistic about the government's ability to manage the economy through its **fiscal policies**—government policy dealing with revenues (e.g., taxes) and expenditures (e.g., defense, entitlements). Nevertheless, the advent of repeated economic crises in the post–Cold War era has led to a renaissance of Keynesian economics, in particular in the economic policies of the Obama administration. In 1999, *Time* magazine included Keynes in its list of the 100 most important and influential people of the 20th century. The Nobel Prize laureate economist Paul Krugman has been an advocate for the U.S. government who increased spending on infrastructure in the economy to stimulate growth and employment. Krugman's "Keynesian" approach sets him apart from classical economics approach where market with minimal government interference determines the state of the economy.[6]

5.1.3 Marxism and Other Radical Approaches

Karl Marx (1818–1883) did not believe that Individuals were rational egoists, as Mercantilists and Liberals did. Rather, for Marx, human motivations were shaped by their material environment. Marx saw history as driven by epochal changes in the **mode of production**, e.g., slavery, Feudalism, Capitalism, and Socialism. The way society is organized essentially conditions political activity, as well as individual consciousness.

In Marxist analysis, human history is a "history of class struggle," and only in the Communist utopia will class conflict come to an end through the achievement of a classless society. In this utopia there is no government, since governments are a product of capitalism. Governments are only required to represent the interests of the dominant class, the **bourgeoisie**, over the dominated class, the **proletariat** or the working class, so there is no reason for them to exist in communism.

Marx argued that the intrinsic contradictions (the growing inequality of the two classes) within capitalism eventually prod the working class to foment revolution and usher in a new mode of production, socialism. The growing inequality in capitalism is a product of the capitalists drive for more profit, which leads to more and more automation (replacing workers with machines). This process ends in chronic unemployment, **underconsumption** and **overproduction** and eventually to economic crises and revolution (Marx 1848).[7]

Vladimir Ilyich Lenin (1870–1924), the revolutionary and intellectual leader of the 1917 Russian Revolution, expanded upon Marx's analysis of capitalism and argued that capitalist development, in its advanced state, also results in **imperialism** (Lenin 1917).[8] He argued that to avoid capitalist breakdown and revolution, the capitalists in advanced countries were being forced to expand overseas in search of markets and raw materials. For Lenin this reinforced Marx's expectations that capitalism would spread to all corners of the world and that imperialism would lead LDCs to develop into capitalist economies. Lenin also believed that this process would lead eventually to an inter-imperialistic war.

In China, the victory of the communist movement in 1949 led to the adoption of **Maoism**, named after the former Chinese leader, Mao Tse Tung. Maoism argued that in a predominantly agrarian China, the peasants would be the backbone class of the communist revolution and not the industrial working class (as Marxism had argued). Chinese Communist Party leaders and experts thus encouraged the collectivization of agriculture, along with some small-scale industrialization, and later, a very costly Cultural Revolution.

The results of the Cultural Revolution in China were disastrous: Millions lost their lives due to famine. With the death of Mao in 1976 and the eventual economic opening of China to capitalism, the ideals of Maoism were abandoned in practice (Cheek 2002).[9] However, a brutal and "degenerative" brand of Maoism was imposed by the infamous Khmer Rouge in Cambodia between 1975 and 1979, which resulted in over a million more deaths. This episode was eventually memorialized in a Hollywood movie, *The Killing Fields*.

Figure 5.6. Mao Tse Tung.

Image © Hung Chung Chih, 2013. Used under license from Shutterstock, Inc.

Dependency and World System Theories

After WWII, the Marxist contention that imperialism would lead to the capitalist development of LDCs was heavily criticized. Many newly independent countries actually found development to be both difficult and daunting. The leading theory of development after World War II, **Modernization theory**, held that all societies would progress through similar stages of development as they moved away from traditionalism toward modernity. Modernization theory expected LDCs to modernize in a similar process to the already developed countries in the West, which would themselves help the cause of modernization in LDCs through foreign investment, foreign aid and technology transfer.

Dependency theory, on the other hand, suggested that LDCs would not develop in the global capitalist economy. Rather they believed that resources were actually flowing away from the poor states in the "periphery" of the global economy, toward a "core" of wealthy states. **Paul Baran** (1957)[10] was the first to recognize that the interaction of foreign capital with social groups and forces within LDCs (the economic and political elites of LDCs) did not always result in the development of a capitalist mode of production. Instead, because the surplus was being expropriated from poor and underdeveloped areas by the advanced capitalist states, the result was not capitalist development, but rather underdevelopment. Andre Gunder Frank (1967)[11] also argued that capitalism was causing underdevelopment—a position that provoked a great deal of criticism from both Marxists and Liberals alike (see Chapter 2).

As noted earlier, the argument that capitalism was causing underdevelopment was a challenge to orthodox Marxism and its analysis of capitalist development. The economic growth rates of **Newly Industrializing Countries (NICs)** in the 1960s were impressive (e.g., Taiwan, South Korea, Singapore, among others), but Dependency theorists dismissed these cases as exceptions to the rule. Some Dependency theorists have tried to explain away these exceptions. **Fernando Cardoso** (1979), for example, has argued that Industrialization takes place in historically specific instances of mutually advantageous interrelationship between foreign capital, domestic capital, and the indigenous state. He called this **"Associated dependent development** (Cardoso, 1979; Alvin So 1990; Smith 2008)."[12]

Immanuel Wallerstein (1930–) has traced the rise of what he calls a **Modern World System (MWS)** back to the 15th century and the emergence of capitalism in Europe. He argued that the spread of commercialism, and later industrial capitalism, came through European domination of the rest of the world and the spread of an unequal world system. This system is based on an interregional and transnational division of labor, separating states and regions into a "core" (rich), "semi-periphery," and "periphery" (poor or satellite). The states in the core focus on higher-skilled, capital-intensive production, and the rest of the world focuses on low-skilled, labor-intensive production (and extraction of raw materials). The MWS allows individual states to gain or lose their position in the periphery, semi-periphery, and core divisions.

According to MWS theory, some countries, like the Republic of Korea, Taiwan, Brazil, and Mexico, have seen their power and status rise in recent decades, while many in sub-Saharan Africa and South Asia have struggled to maintain their position. Similarly, the Soviet Union lost its position at the end of the Cold War, and the Russian Federation today is in a weaker position with respect to its power and status. The MWS has also seen some states rise in power and status to become **hegemons**, or dominant powers, only to eventually lose that position. Historically, the status of hegemon passed from the Netherlands to the United Kingdom and then most recently to the United States. Therefore, MWS theorists see constant fluidity in the hierarchical structure of the international capitalist system.[13]

Multinational Corporations (MNCs) are central players in both Dependency and MWS theories. MNCs possess enormous wealth and (measured in annual revenues) are often more powerful than many states. For example, of the world's 100 largest economic entities in 2009, 44 were MNCs. The combined revenues of these MNCs were larger than the combined economies of the poorest 155 states (Keys and Malnight 2010).[14] The concentration of so much wealth in the hands of corporate leaders makes them economically and politically very powerful. Multinational corporations can offer billions of dollars in investment projects in LDCs and can also use their financial clout to gain concessions from states. They can even dictate their investment terms and conditions.

In order to maximize profits, MNCs also champion the cause of free trade, as well as the deregulation of finance and investment. Corporations naturally prefer access to markets with abundant cheap labor, free from organized labor unions. They are concerned only with their own profits and care little about job creation in the markets in which they invest. Investments by MNCs do not then necessarily correlate to higher employment in LDCs. For example, the contribution of the top 100 companies to global employment in 2009 fell far short of their combined economic clout. Together, they employed 13.5 million people, just 0.4% of the world's economically active population (Keys and Malnight 2010).[15]

Nor are MNCs concerned with the nature of the political systems in which they operate. Indeed, authoritarian regimes may actually be more attractive to MNCs, since such regimes can easily quell internal political and civil opposition to foreign investments. Democratic states, on the other hand, must remain transparent and accountable to the demands of their citizens, including the interests of local business communities.

Critics of MWS theory point out that the evidence from MNCs participation in the global political economy tells of a more complex story. MNCs are central to the economic viability of the capitalist economies, and many government-owned corporations also compete with MNCs for their share of the global market, for example, in the global oil market. The ownership of MNCs stocks and assets and the nationality (the place of its domicile or headquarter) of MNCs are also important in international disputes over their function and meeting contractual obligations. It would then be hard to imagine the global economy without the MNCs. Therefore, the role of MNCs in the global economy remains a matter of debate and paradigmatic controversy.

5.2 Early 20th Century IPE

By the end of the 1800s, the world was beginning to witness dramatic changes in the global political economy. The unification of the German provinces into a new German Empire had created a powerful new state in the center of Europe in 1871. The unification of the Italian city-states into a united Italy during the 1860s was another important event. So, too, was the Spanish-American War of 1898, which effectively made the United States a world-class power. The Russo-Japanese conflict of 1904–1905 also led to the defeat of a major European power at the hands of a rising Asian country with its own expansionist ambitions.

All these events occurred at the expense of the United Kingdom, which at this point was a declining global power. The Ottoman Empire, the only non-European Great Power, had been in decline for some time. By the end of the 1800s the European powers had also completed their colonization of the African continent (Africa was 90% colonized by the end of the century).

Between the 1870s and the beginning of WWI in 1914 the prices of major commodities had fallen and global trade had increased. The colonial powers continued to spread the world economy to states like China and India. As these events took place, new industries were developing that were changing the character of industrial life itself. With increasing input from oil, chemical, electricity, and auto industries, the principle of economies of scale became more widespread. The late 19th century in particular was a period of unparalleled prosperity for Great Britain; it controlled nearly a third of all global industrial output, with its nearest rival the United States still lagging far behind; its trade was also worth double that of France.

Europe, however, saw the reemergence of protectionism prior to WWI, while the United States, except for its immediate sphere of influence—the Central and South American subcontinent—remained largely disengaged from world affairs. The short 10-week long Spanish-American War was fought initially over the American intervention in the Cuban war of independence, but resulted in a major war with Spain. The 1898 Treaty of Paris allowed temporary American control of Cuba and indefinite colonial authority over Puerto Rico, Guam, and the Philippines. The United States also agreed to pay Spain a sum of $20 million for its acquisition of these territories.

The U.S. intervention in World War I in support of its allies, Britain and France, was slow to occur, but still had drastic effects on the American economy and society. The United States had remained neutral prior to April 6, 1917, although it had been an important supplier to Britain and other Allied powers. The war saw a dramatic expansion of the U.S. government in an effort to harness the war effort and a significant increase in the size of its military. However, President Woodrow Wilson's position that America had to play a role to make the world safe for democracy did not survive beyond his presidency, as the United States plunged back into a more isolationist policy after the war.

World War I resulted in nearly 40 million military and civilian casualties in Europe, and at least 2 million died from diseases. A further 6 million went missing and were presumed dead. It is still one of the deadliest conflicts in human history. Another important trademark of the conflict was that about two-thirds of the military deaths were in battle, unlike the conflicts that took place in the 19th century, when the majority of deaths were due to disease. The Spanish flu pandemic (from January 1918 to December 1920) also killed between 20 and 50 million people, making it one of the deadliest outbreaks of natural disease in human history (White 2011).[16]

The interwar period (1920–1939) saw the fragile German democracy slowly degenerate into Nazism, while Italy also experienced the rise of fascism. In Asia, Japan turned to militarism and wars of aggression, while China continued to experience "warlordism," instability, and civil war until the eventual communist victory in 1949. British and French colonial rule and ambitions in the Middle East, Africa, and Asia continued, while their economies suffered from the devastations of World War I and even became partially dependent on war reparations from Germany. War and militarism also took its toll: Italy invaded Ethiopia (1935), Germany reoccupied the Rhineland (1936), Japan invaded China (1937), Germany took over the Sudetenland in Czechoslovakia (1938), and Spain was devastated by civil war (1936–1939).

The U.S. economy, on the other hand, had experienced growth as a result of the demands of the war, leaving it as the world's strongest economy. The United States became the creditor nation of the world, while Britain, for the first time since the beginning of the industrial revolution, became a debtor nation. The U.S. economy, however, had slowed by 1927, and the stock market became overvalued with inflated prices, leading to the collapse of the market in the fall of 1929.

Scholars disagree on what actually caused the **Great Depression (1929–1939)**,[17] but the worldwide protectionist response to the crisis resulted in a collapse of global trade and devastated

Image © Patricia Hofmeester, 2013. Used under license from Shutterstock, Inc.

Figure 5.7. Franklin Delano Roosevelt Presidential Memorial, depression era breadline statue.

the economies of the major states. Economic nationalism, like the Smoot-Hawley Tariff Act of 1930, caused U.S. trade to drop by half, further exacerbating and prolonging the depression. Financial collapse and slowdown in the economy led to high unemployment, poverty, low profits, declining prices or **deflation**, plunging farm incomes, and lost opportunities for economic growth and personal advancement.

The U.S. economic policy under president Franklin Delano Roosevelt, elected in 1932, relied on government interventionist policy and **deficit spending** to stimulate economic activity. The Keynesian answer to the depression involved the U.S. government's spending vast amounts of money on the **economic infrastructure**, creating millions of jobs, and regulations overseeing the functioning of banks and financial institutions. The New Deal turned the depression around and introduced a new era of government involvement in the economy. The extent of government involvement in the economy through regulations and fiscal policy remains a point of contention even today among economists, political scientists, and politicians.

5.3 Post-War International Institutions, Agreements, and Principles

The devastation caused by World War II in Europe, as well as Japan and other Asian countries, left the United States as the single most important economy in the world. In 1945 the U.S. Gross National Product (GNP) was as great as half the world's. The European and Japanese economies were laid in ruin and were susceptible to communism. In response to the Soviet Union's economic challenge, the United States set in motion a series of international agreements, organizations and institutions to help with the reconstruction of the world economy. These included the creation of NATO in 1949, followed by security cooperation treaties with Australia and New Zealand (1952), South Korea (1953), Japan (1954 and 1960), Southeast Asian countries (SEATO 1964), Middle East (CENRO/Baghdad Pact 1955), the United Kingdom (1958) and a host of other agreements dealing with nuclear testing, nonproliferation, and arms reduction.

The Bretton Woods System

The gathering of 44 major trading states in Bretton Woods, New Hampshire, in 1944 was in essence a meeting to decide on the future political economy of the world. The Bretton Woods system (**BW**) refers to post World War II economic system that fixed exchange rates and liberalized multilateral trade with the help of new institutions, including the **General Agreement on Tariffs and Trade (GATT)**, the **International Monetary Fund (IMF)**, and the **International Bank for Reconstruction and Development (IBRD)**, commonly known as the World Bank. The legacies of these experiences are still with us today, albeit with profound changes in the global political economy since then.

Under the Bretton Woods Agreement, the United States fixed the price of the dollar at *$35* per ounce of gold, which meant freely buying gold from, and selling gold to, official bodies at that price. The fixed exchange rate used gold as a reserve asset, and only the United States was required to convert its domestic currency into gold. The value of the yen was also fixed at 360 yen per dollar under the Bretton Woods System that was sustained until 1971. The United States was at the center of the Bretton Woods system, playing the role of world banker, running balance-of-payments deficits, and supplying dollar reserves to other countries.

As the world's banker, the United States engaged in maturity transformation, accumulating short-term dollar liabilities while lending long-term, on net, to the rest of the world. Under BW, if one U.S. trading partner was concerned about inflation (U.S. dollar worth less), it could have always asked for gold instead, but since inflation was so low, at least until later in the 1960s, the dollar was in essence as good as gold. Other countries also pegged their currencies against the dollar, making dollar the de facto trade currency.[18] Therefore, U.S. trading partners began to collect and keep assets in dollar.

The United States further helped the cause of Bretton Woods and European and Japanese economic recovery through its foreign aid and the **Marshall Plan**, also known as the European Economic Recovery Plan. Japan received U.S. aid, and the Marshall Plan also endowed Europe with $13 billion on top of $12 billion in American aid to Europe between the end of the war and the start of the Plan. The Soviet Union and its allies, however, rejected the Marshall Plan and remained outside the BW system.

The fixed exchange rate ensured rapid economic recovery in Europe and Japan and as a bonus "internationalized" dollar as the currency of choice for investors and consumers alike. In West Germany, France, Italy, and even in Great Britain, the level of economic productivity, GDP per capita, exceeded the best performance of the interwar period by the early 1950s. The Japanese economic pie grew at an annual rate of 10% from the mid-1950s until the Arab oil shocks of the early 1970s. The Japanese then managed to maintain much more modest but steady growth rates until the early 1990s.[19] Liberal economists therefore believe the fixed exchange rate greatly contributed to ensuring international competitiveness.

Figure 5.8. Gold bars on dollar bills, symbolic photo for gold reserves, exchange rates, investment, security.

The Bretton Woods system increasingly became difficult to sustain, as European and Japanese economies recovered from the devastation of WWII and some emerging economies, the NICs also began to compete for their share of international trade. Rising prices and inflation and inadequate level of gold held as reserves in the United States were other major concerns for the United States. By 1960, there were more dollars in circulation overseas than the United States had gold to redeem (Dellas and Tavalas 2011).[20] Therefore, in 1968, the United States rescinded its promise to pay in gold and effectively removed itself from the gold standard. Moreover, the United States ran its first trade deficit since before World War I in 1971 because of increased competition from Europe and the NICs, totaling $2.3 billion. Once the Nixon administration took the United States off BW system, the dollar was devalued by 10% by the end of 1971, and by 1975 all major currencies were floating freely.

The international monetary system since the demise of the Bretton Woods has operated on **floating exchange rates** among all major trading partners. Gold is no longer the basis for exchange rate but it remains an important psychological (and real) backup for many countries. The U.S. dollar and other **hard currencies** are considered as reliable sources for savings and investment and are therefore in demand by people and investors everywhere. Many developing countries also rely on their reserve of hard currencies for trade and investment and major international trade transactions are done in U.S. dollar, euro, and the Japanese yen.

Central banks, in charge of **monetary policy**, oversee and manage the supply of money in the economy in major industrial countries, including the United States and other countries of the **Organization for Economic Cooperation and Development (OECD)**. They play a central role in the management of international economy and trade. The governments in the United States, Europe, Japan, and other major economies must now share their power with the central bank. On the other hand, **fiscal policy**—government policy dealing with revenues and expenditures such as taxation and public policy expenditures—can travel so far in managing today's complex economy. Fiscal policies are also political by definition and are thus slower in impacting the economy.

The post–Cold War times have witnessed increasingly serious global financial crises, e.g., 1997 Asia, 2000 dot-com in the United States, and the December 2007 to present global housing and financial crisis that have raised serious questions about the causes and consequences of such events. The increasing economic power of China and the inclusion of its currency, Renminbi or the Yuan, in the IMF Special Drawing Rights (SDR) Basket of currencies in September 2016 make major currency competition more fierce, with important consequences for the stability of global political economy. While the future of global financial situation at the time of this writing still remains uncertain, the management of the post–Bretton Woods global economy, trade, and finance systems seems far more daunting than the Bretton Woods years.

The International Monetary Fund and World Bank

The 44 countries attending the Bretton woods meeting in 1944 agreed to the creation of the IMF and the **International Bank for Reconstruction and Development (IBRD)**. What is known as the World Bank (established in 1946) is part of the World Bank Group that includes IBRD, the **International Development Association (IDA), the International Finance Corporation (IFC)**, the **International Centre for Settlement of Investment Disputes (ICSID)**, and the **Multilateral Investment Guarantee Agency (MIGA)**. IBRD raises most of its funds in the world's financial markets. According to its website, "this has allowed it to provide more than $500 billion in loans to alleviate poverty around the world since 1946, with its shareholder governments paying in about $14 billion in capital."[21] IBRD makes loans for development projects and has lent out billions of dollars to countries in need of low-rate loans to help their cause of social and economic development. The IDA, created in 1960, usually makes no-interest loans to the poorest LDCs. The IFC provides loans to promote private sector in LDCs, and the United States provides about 23% of its capital, and had 22.65% voting rights on IFC board in 2013. Japan (5.64%), Germany (5.15%), France (4.84%), and the UK (4.84%) are other major contributors (IFC online).[22] The primary purpose of ICSID is to provide facilities for conciliation and arbitration of international investment disputes. *MIGA's mission is to promote* **foreign direct investment (FDI)** into developing countries to help support economic growth, reduce poverty, and improve people's lives.

The IMF membership after the dissolution of the Soviet Union and the joining of new member states reached 170. In 2012, membership had climbed to 188 countries, matching the number of member states of the World Bank in 2013. IMF is headquartered in Washington, DC, and currently has a staff of 2,300. It provides credits to countries with short-term difficulties with their balance of payment. The Executive Board is responsible for conducting the day-to-day business of the IMF, and it is composed of 24 Directors who are appointed or elected by member countries or by groups of countries. The Managing Director serves as its Chairman. IMF relies primarily on its quota subscriptions (membership fees) paid by members in accordance with the size of their economies, valued at $215 billion in 2001. IMF increased its quota system contributions in January 2016 and accordingly, "as of September 2017, 181 of the 189 members had made their quota payments, accounting for over 99 percent of the total quota increases, and total quotas stood at SDR475 billion (about US$675 billion)."[23] IMF also keeps gold reserves and can under severe restrictions borrow money, but not from private markets.

The right to vote under the quota system is dominated by a few countries and remains a controversial point. In 2010, the share of the United States was 16.5% and the Group of Seven industrial countries—United States, Canada, the United Kingdom, France, Germany, Italy, and Japan—held a 41.2% of the total. The voting share of the 27 members of the European members was 29.4%, while the entire African continent's share was a mere 5.7% (IMF 2011).[24]

The World Bank, like the IMF, has adopted a weighted system of voting. A quota is assigned, equivalent to the country's subscription to the Fund. This determines its voting power in the Fund. Five Executive Directors are appointed by the members with the five largest numbers of shares (currently the United States, Japan, Germany, France, and the United Kingdom). China, the Russian Federation, and Saudi Arabia each elects its own Executive Director. In IBRD, the share of leading countries is United States (15.23%), Japan (8.97%), Germany (4.49%), France (4.25%), and the UK (4.25%). The five countries' total share of voting rights is 37.19% in 2013.[25]

These BW institutions have survived the end of the Cold War and are still important global institutions, helping with global governance. IMF and the World Bank are associated with the United Nations. Other than being central global financial and economic institutions and helping the cause of development (or underdevelopment, as the Radical School would postulate), they also contribute to international law and rules and norms of cooperation in tackling global financial and economic problems. There are calls for reforms in the structure of these institutions to make them better represent the changing global community and the needs of billions of people who live in the developing world but who are still deprived of fundamental human necessities. For example, many developing countries feel vulnerable to the IMF **conditionality rule**—IMF conditions for lending money that are pro-market capitalism and oppose public ownership or control of economic resources. IMF conditions such as "cut in government subsidies," "freeze on wages," or "devaluation of national currency" can help with the borrowing country's balance of payments, but they also hurt people since such policies lead to higher prices and unemployment.

Liberals and Radicals view these institutions and their role in IPE in different ways. For Liberals, IMF and World Bank, along with the UN and GATT, have been indispensable for the success of world economy after WWII and have helped spread economic and social stability and prosperity to LDCs. For Radicals, these institutions have been instruments in the hands of U.S. and other Western capitalist countries to continue the exploitation of LDCs through economic opening, privatization, and free trade and with little or no regard for the true national development of **human capital** in these countries. Global institutions, particularly the IMF, the WB, and the World Trade Organization (WTO), in recent years have been subject to criticism. We will further discuss the views of liberals and radicals below.

The General Agreement on Tariffs and Trade (GATT)

To avoid protectionism of the late 1920s and early 1930s, 23 countries signed the **General Agreement on Tariffs and Trade (GATT)** in 1948 and with the goal of the eventual removal of all tariffs on traded goods.[26] GATT was to gradually remove tariff barriers among countries, thus facilitating trade and avoiding trade war that in the 1930s had resulted in reduced trade and recession between the United States and Europe. The United States had introduced the **Smoot-Hawley tariffs** in 1930, resulting in retaliatory tariffs from its trading partners. The original intention behind U.S. tariff legislation was to protect domestic farmers from foreign agricultural imports. Republican presidential candidate Herbert Hoover during the 1928 election campaign had pledged to help the beleaguered farmers by raising tariff levels on agricultural products. With new tariffs protecting agriculture, however, there were new calls for increased protection from industrial sector and special interest groups.

Image © Ryan Rodrick Beiler, 2013. Used under license from Shutterstock, Inc.

Figure 5.9. Riot police are positioned to confront protesters during World Bank and IMF meetings on April 16, 2000, in Washington, DC.

Twenty-six countries adopted their own tariffs within one and a half year. Consequently, U.S. imports from Europe declined from a 1929 high of $1,334 million to just $390 million in 1932, while U.S. exports to Europe fell from $2,341 million in 1929 to $784 million in 1932. World trade declined by some 66% between 1929 and 1934. It was only with the 1934 Reciprocal Trade Agreements Act that American commercial policy generally emphasized trade liberalization over protectionism (U.S. Department of State).[27]

GATT principles only dealt with global trade in goods, excluding trade in services, e.g., banking, insurance, shipping, and communication, technology, and intellectual property rights. Furthermore, GATT negotiations in textile and agriculture proved difficult because each country tried protecting its farmers from outside competition through farm subsidies and other forms of protection. Many countries also considered food production as a matter of national security and therefore resisted policies that might lead to food import dependency or drastic reductions in food commodity production. Another major taunting factor in GATT negotiations was the issue of **nontariff barriers (NTBs).** As countries reduced their tariffs on traded goods, they replaced them with NTBs such as **quotas** and **embargos.** Finally, being a *general agreement* on tariffs and trade, GATT lacked the necessary mechanisms to resolve disputes in trade among trading partners.

The eighth and final round of GATT negotiations, also known as the Uruguay Round (1986–1994), was the most ambitious round and hoped to expand GATT to important new areas such as services, capital, textiles, agriculture, and intellectual property. It paved the way for the creation of the **World Trade Organization (WTO)**. WTO was officially commenced in 1995 and aimed to supervise and liberalize global trade. It is endowed with a framework for negotiating and formalizing trade agreements, and with a dispute resolution process that help enforce participants' adherence to WTO agreements. There are 164 members and 47 parties and observers in the organization as of July 2016, covering over 96% of global trade in 2017.[28] WTO rules and regulations are extensive, covering over 26,000 pages. These rules are expected to facilitate an incremental approach to gradually reach free global trade in goods and services, including historically controversial areas of trade like agriculture and textile, banking and insurance, and intellectual property rights.

The General Council is the WTO's highest-level decision-making body in Geneva, meeting regularly to carry out the functions of the WTO. It has representatives from all member governments and has the authority to act on behalf of the ministerial conference, which only meets about every two years. The General Council also meets, under different rules, as the **Dispute Settlement Body (DSB)** and as the Trade Policy Review Body. After the General Council, the top layer of the organizational structure is the **Ministerial Conference**. Settling disputes under WTO rules is the responsibility of the DSB, which consists of all WTO members. Countries in dispute have the right to appeal a panel's ruling. The Appellate Body was established in 1995 under Article 17 of the Understanding on Rules and Procedures Governing the Settlement of Disputes (DSU) (WTO Website). [29]

5.4 Post-War IPE

As discussed above, the international political economy after World War II witnessed the rise of the United States as a superpower and the leader of NATO, locked in a bipolar world competition with its arch competitor, the Soviet Union and its Warsaw Pact allies. The map of the world then was drastically different; a vast majority of countries were yet to gain independence. The United States was the richest and most powerful country on earth with an economy of about one-half of the world's and, until 1949, the sole possessor of nuclear weapons. As such, the United States set the tone for a liberal international political economy: It initiated the Bretton-Woods system, the GATT, NATO, the UN and military pacts, and agreements with its major allies such as Japan, Taiwan, South Korea, Australia and New Zealand, and Iran and Saudi Arabia.

The Bretton Woods period (1945–1971) saw the recovery of the European and Japanese economies, together with the consolidation of political stability and democracy. For example, in West Germany, France, Italy, and Great Britain, by the early 1950s the level of GDP per capita had exceeded the best performance of the interwar period. By 1960 economic production in these countries was well above levels that would have been predicted by extrapolating pre-1939 or pre-1914 trends into the indefinite future (Bradford DeLong 1997).[30] The Japanese economy also grew at an annual 10% rate from the mid-1950s until the Arab oil shocks of the early 1970s. The Japanese then managed to maintain much more modest, but steady growth rates, until the early 1990s (Lucien Ellington 2004).[31]

Only 51 independent states joined the United Nations in 1945, but that number had grown to 193 by 2013. The majority of the world's population in 1945 still lived under colonial rule and yearned for independence. Moreover, most newly independent countries found themselves caught up in the rivalry between the two superpowers, which limited their options in setting a truly independent course for their national economic and political development. Many leaders in LDCs tried to devise independent national economic plans, but found themselves pulled in different directions by the United States and Soviet Union.

Basically, the United States viewed communism as **totalitarianism**, or the state control of ideological, economic, and political orientations and activities of its people, and thus as antithetical to U.S. national and global interests. Conversely, the Soviet Union equated capitalism with **imperialism** and exploitation and thus perceived it to be opposed to its own interests and those of the rest of the world. Choosing either path to national development and international relations meant automatic hostility from the opposing camp. This significantly limited LDCs' access to global economic and financial resources and sometimes even resulted in both overt and covert foreign interventions. Famous cases of the latter included U.S. and Soviet interventions in Iran (1953), Guatemala (1954), Hungary (1956), Congo (1960–1966), Cuba (1961, 1962), Czechoslovakia (1968), Vietnam (1962–1975), Chile (1973), and Afghanistan (1979–1989).

The strife for independent policy helped the creation of the **nonalignment movement**—countries technically aligned with neither the capitalist nor the communist camp—that has survived the Cold War until the present day. Furthermore, the newly independent countries differed in their experimentation with national development and some performed a great deal better than others. The success of the NICs in rapid socioeconomic growth and political democracy proved that rapid economic growth and national development was possible even during the Cold War bipolar world. The NICs, along with some other emerging countries, have continued to experience rapid national development and increasingly gaining international prestige and influence after the Cold War, including, among others, South Korea, Taiwan, Singapore, Indonesia, Brazil, Argentina, Chile, and later China and India.

The global political economy is facing grave challenges at the time of this writing in October 2017. Among these are the still slow recovery from the 2008-10 housing and financial crisis and recession in the United States and Europe; the U.S. declared and still ongoing **war on terrorism**

Figure 5.10.   Cold War divided states and businesses (1945–1989).

Image © Minerva Studio, 2013. Used under license from Shutterstock, Inc.

since September 11, 2001; the rise of **BRICS** (Brazil, Russia, India, China, and South Africa) as an economic bloc along with other emerging economies like Mexico, Turkey, Indonesia, Malaysia, and Iran; and, social upheaval across much of the Arab World asking for political opening and socioeconomic justice, the **Arab Spring**, that has unfortunately tuned into an 'Arab Winter' of civil and political instability in places like Iraq, Libya, Syria, and Yemen. The North Korean and Iranian nuclear programs and the threat of nuclear weapons proliferation, political instability, war, and poverty in the sub-Saharan African region, e.g., Somalia, the Sudan, the Democratic Republic of the Congo, Zimbabwe, are among other challenges facing the international community. The Trump demonstration threatens in late October 2017 to decertify the Iran nuclear agreement, also known as JCPOA or the Joint Comprehensive Plan of Action, between Iran and the P5+1 (Germany). A possible demise of the nuclear agreement can damage any prospects for a nuclear agreement with North Korea and can also damage U.S. reputation and prestige, and soft power on the global stage.

What do IPE Liberals and Radicals think about IPE events since 1945? To what degree the hegemonic leadership of the United States contributed to the stability and prosperity of the world during the Cold War period? How did the bipolar Cold War system shape global political economy and how did it impact the fortunes of LDCs? Are we witnessing the emergence of what president George Herbert Bush called in the aftermath of first Persian Gulf War in 1991, a "**new world order**," and, if yes, how is it different from the "old order"? What do these major global events tell us about the present and the future trend in the global political economy? It would take volumes to answer these questions in detail, but here we can only hint at an overview of Liberal, Radical, and Mercantilist views on IPE development since WWII. We will focus here more on the global economic slowdown since late 2007. We hope students better appreciate the complexities of issues facing the global community and to see the utility in looking at global issues from different theoretical perspectives.

5.4.1 What Do Mercantilists, Liberals, and Radical Theorists Think about the Current Global Economic Slowdown?

Liberals see the current economic crisis since 2008 as the most serious challenge to IPE since the Great Depression but also are convinced that it can be resolved since **business cycles**—boom and bust in the market—are natural occurrences in capitalism. The world economy in the second decade of the 21st century has many tools in its possession, and with experiences learned from the past, it can resolve the crisis. There are disagreements, however, over what strategy to use to return the U.S. and EU economies back to health again. The economic crisis in the United States and Europe also concern people and states everywhere since the two poles, according to the IMF, were responsible in 2012 for about 40% of the world economic output, with GDP/PPP (GDP adjusted for purchasing power) of respectively $15,653 and $16,073 billion.

The United States and the EU countries have experienced economic slowdown and crisis since 2008. It began with the burst of the housing bubble in late 2007 and soon spread to the financial sector in the U.S. and the European markets. The housing market crisis was exacerbated by banks' and financial institutions' high-level risk-taking through speculative investment practices, subprime lending, and "innovative" investment mechanisms like "leveraging," and "credit default swaps." Banks and financial institutions in the United States had turned banking and investment through speculative behavior into some sort of a gambling enterprise some would refer to as **Casino Capitalism**. A combination of greed, deregulation, and absence of regulations in the financial market set the stage for brazen risk-taking by U.S. banks, money market funds, and other financial institutions that also engulfed European banks and financial institutions. Many government regulators and even investors in the United States and in Europe could not even understand the magnitude of risks involved in investment schemes cooked up by giant financial institutions, banks and insurance companies like the Lehman Brothers, Bear Stearns, Morgan Stanley, JP Morgan Chase, Citicorp, Bank of America, and the American Insurance Group (AIG). In the end, it all came crumbling down, creating the most massive and unbelievable private and public debt the world had ever seen (PBS 2012).[32]

In the United States, the Emergency Economic Stabilization Act of 2008, the bailout plan, authorized the United States Secretary of the Treasury to spend up to US$700 billion to purchase "distressed assets," especially mortgage-backed securities, and make capital injections into banks. By February 2009, the U.S. government stimulus package reached $937 billion. Other countries also initiated their own stimulus packages, including China ($586 billion), Germany ($103 billion), UK ($29 billion), and India ($4 billion). The large amount of borrowing by governments and private banks and financial institutions to avoid total breakdown of the entire American and European financial systems soared and that, in combination with all household debt, created unprecedented levels of global debt.

According to the World Bank, government debt to GDP in the 17 Euro-zone countries rose from an average of 56% in 2008 to 76% in 2011 (World Bank 2013).[33] For the 10 largest mature economies (Australia, Canada, France, Germany, Italy, Japan, Spain, South Korea, UK, and United States), total debt stood at nearly 350% of GDP in 2011. The total debt was even higher if one considers the economies of the PIIGS countries (Portugal, Ireland, Italy, Spain, and Greece) the worst hit by the debt crisis (Pasquali and Aridas 2013).[34] Moreover, the combined stock of developing countries' external debt rose from $4.4 trillion in 2010 to $4.9 trillion at the end of 2011 (World Bank 2013)[35].

At the time of this writing in October 2017, the U.S. economy is still experiencing a "soft" economic growth and unemployment rate of 4.2%, while the stock market has soared to a record high. Initially, from May 2008 to March 2009 stock prices dropped more than 50% (NYT August 2011),[36] but the stock market has made a comeback and the Standard & Poor's 500-stock index is now only 0.5% away from its 2007 high of 1565.[37] Nevertheless, the 2007–2008 economic recession in the United States grew into the 2008–2012 global recession (Isidore 2008).[38] Governments in United States and Europe, and elsewhere, have spent trillions of dollars of borrowed taxpayers' and freshly printed money to rescue their economies. The European Union countries still face years of austerity and hardship ahead before a full recovery. Economic austerity plans has already resulted in demonstrations and unrest in Greece, Spain, Cyprus, Italy, France, and elsewhere. The very survival of the EU has come under question and the next few years seems everything but easy for the Europeans, especially after the result of the British popular referendum on July 23, 2016 to leave the European Union, what is known as Brexit.

Notwithstanding the economic crisis, events since the advent of the Arab Spring in 2011 have resulted in millions of new refugees around the world, many of whom finding Europe as their final destination. The refugee and migration flow into Europe of mostly Syrian, Iraqi, Somali, and Afghani origin since 2011 have instigated further uncertainties and anxiety over nationalism, the state of the economy, and the overall EU cohesion.

For Liberals, the global economic crisis represents the folly of human behavior. Business cycles are natural and integral parts of market capitalism and occur to correct the market. Markets have integral self-correcting mechanisms based on supply and demand and boom and bust in the market are thus expected. Admittedly, the current crisis is deeper and more widespread and is only paralleled to the Great Depression of the1930s in its magnitude. But, there are many factors contributing to the current crisis, including, among others, the extent and effectiveness of government regulations, fiscal policy, and monetary policy overseen by the Central Bank (the Federal Reserve Board of Governors in the United States, the Fed). The overexuberant banks who lent money at subprime rates to increase profitability, the "greedy" home buyers who hoped to make a quick return on their money in the housing market, and the "enthusiastic" consumers with access to "cheap money" because of lower interest rates channeled through the Fed's **Quantitative Easing (QE)** monetary policy, were all rational actors who made bad decisions. As such, there were no conspiracies by capitalists to create the crisis to somehow exploit the market for higher rates of profits or to dismantle welfare policies of the state as in Europe. The globalization of international economies, trade, finance, and investment capital along with technological innovations in communications, information technology, and transportation simply means a truly interconnected world. The spread of the housing and financial crisis from the United States to Europe is not surprising; given the right policies, the crisis will come to an end.

There are disagreements among liberal economists over the "right" set of policies to end the global economic crisis. While some have advocated economic austerity plans along with economic stimulus packages to reduce government expenditures and control national debt burden, as in Europe, others in the United States have strongly asked for a Keynesian approach to overcome the crisis. Nobel Prize-winning economist Paul Krugman has been a strong advocate of a deficit spending approach to stimulate demand and economic growth without fearing the soaring government expenditures through borrowing and printing money by the Fed. He believes austerity plans, as implemented in the EU, are exactly the wrong economic policy. The United States must spend its way out of the current crisis (Krugman 2012).[39] Others have been cautious about "unlimited" government spending through bailout plans and stimulus packages, fearing the debt burden will erode confidence in the dollar and lead to a more serious economic crisis, maybe even depression. In the end, government bailouts in the United States and in Europe, as well as in China, India, and elsewhere, have been implemented to bring an end to global economic slowdown.

The Liberal take of the current crisis is in line with the overall understanding of the nature and the fundamentals of capitalism. There are disagreements among Liberals (and conservatives) over the extent of government involvement in the economy, but capitalism as a mode of production is accepted as the best way to manage the economy. Despite the current crisis and previous booms and busts in the U.S. economy, capitalism has proven resilient and has brought impressive rates of economic growth and prosperity across the world in the post–WII era. Capitalism has survived the onslaught of communism and has proven efficient in increasing productivity and economic growth, technology and innovation, trade and investment and spreading globalization around the world despite cultural and national differences. The United States led the capitalist world post–WWII and helped the world economy to recover and capitalism and trade to spread globally.

Liberals still hold that the Bretton Woods system and its institutions, the GATT, and the creation of WTO (discussed above) were instrumental in helping Europe and Japan to rise up from the devastation of WWII and to help spread prosperity to many developing countries through trade, investment, aid, and technology transfer. In the post–Cold War era since 1989, the world has become "flat" in terms of the playing fields, with all competitors having opportunity to compete in the global market. Capitalism, technology, and globalization are universal now (Friedman 2005).[40] Even the progressive critics of modern capitalism see it as the most effective mode of production.

There are disagreements among Liberals over how best manage capitalism: There are different shades of capitalism as exemplified by the U.S. form of capitalism compared to Northern European examples of Finland, Sweden, and Norway, or crony capitalism as exercised in some developing countries only to the benefit the rich and the powerful. The more cautious Liberal view sees the world bifurcated into two world of modern and traditional, not so much because of capitalism itself but due to misguided neo-liberalism, when lack of regulation and corporate power erode democracy (Barber 1995).[41]

The Radical school, be it Marxist/neo-Marxist, Dependency, or World System Theory, advocates see capitalism itself as the root-cause of the problem in the global political economy. Capitalism is by nature prone to create income and social inequality because it is based on the **Darwinian** idea of "survival of the fittest." Individuals and businesses alike compete over economic resources, and only those more capable do better and survive the competition: Social and economic inequality is natural to capitalism.

At global level, capitalist development leads to the separation of the world between the haves and have-nots in countries (core and periphery) or between rich and poor classes within and between countries (neo-Marxism). If Western colonial powers used brutal force, direct control, and exploitation to extract resources from colonized areas in Latin America, Africa, and Asia, the advanced capitalist states in North America and Europe have used free trade to open LDC markets for their minerals, natural resources, and cheap labor. Free trade is **neo-imperialism**. The global inequality within and among countries is thus inherent to capitalism and it is not accidental that there are tens of millions of people who live in poverty or at subsistence level worldwide (Sweezy 1946, Frank 1966, 1967; Amin 2009, 2010).[42]

The Radical perspective sees MNCs as agents of capitalism and in the business of accumulating profit but at the expense of the working class. MNCs seek markets with minerals and raw materials and cheap labor to invest not so much to help the cause of development in LDCs but to export their final products back to markets in the developed countries. Many LDCs thus find themselves producing commodities not for domestic markets but for export for consumption in the developed world. **The export-led industrialization** in many of the NICs and other emerging countries also means the continuing international division of labor and specialization in production that is a hallmark of capitalism.

The IMF, World Bank, GATT, the World Trade Organization, and other such Western-dominated IGOs, have served the cause of a worldwide U.S.-led capitalist development in post–WWII. Capitalists in both the developed and the developing countries benefit from the global division of labor and specialization in commodities and trade but at the expense of exploitation of the laborers. Corporations' expansion overseas penetrates markets and people in LDCs through changing peoples' consumption habits and helping with the suppression of local wages. MNCs thus contribute to authoritarian rule in LDCs. Corporations can and have helped the overthrow of popular regimes opposed to Western capitalism as in Iran (1953), Guatemala (1954), and Chile (1973).

There are social and political consequences associated with development and with capitalist development in particular. Indeed, criticism of capitalism is not confined to the Radical Left but also **Progressives**, who are critical of **laissez faire capitalism** and the Western-dominated international political economy that has divided the planet into the **Global North** and the **Global South**. Philip McMichael, for example, in *Development of Social Change*, argues that the United States set the tone for the "Development Project" after World War II with worldwide consequences for the global division of labor. This is continued today with what he terms the "Globalization Project." The United States led the development project to establish the post-war global system through establishing the UN and the Bretton Woods system and institutions, NATO and other military alliances, foreign and food aid, and the promotion of market capitalism in opposing communism.

The development project led to uneven patterns of development, food dependency, and authoritarian rule, and global division of labor with LDCs serving for the most part the interest of advanced countries. Globalization also is not a "natural" or "neutral" phenomenon, and it is a project because of the politics of globalization. Powerful international financial institutions, banks, corporations, states, and even NGOs construct and manage global markets. (McMichael 2012).[43] Only those LDCs vital to U.S. security concerns performed better in the development and globalization projects and slowly joined the rank of the NICs and developed countries, like Taiwan, Singapore, South Korea, Mexico, Argentina, and Brazil (McMichael 2012, Chapter 6).

Like the classical Mercantilist, **Neo-mercantilists** today share with realism the belief that economics must be in the service of politics, therefore, the supremacy of politics over economic matters. Neo-mercantilists encourage exports over imports, control over capital movement, and centralization of currency decisions in the hands of central government. It also encourages policies that increase the level of foreign reserves held by the government, allowing more effective monetary and fiscal policy. For neo-mercantilists the question is not whether free trade is good or bad, but if it serves the national interest of the country, e.g., creating or saving jobs and promoting economic growth. Trade and budget deficits and national debt are harmful to national interest, and policymakers must pursue those economic policies that promote national strength and not the narrow interest of special interest groups.

The notion that the state should intervene in the economy to promote national development is an old one and has been practiced widely over past centuries. Even the United States after 1815 used protection, subsidy, and other mercantilist measures to promote national development. In the aftermath of the World War II, Japan demonstrated its mercantilist economic "miracle" in the early 1960s, and the rest of the developing world began to heed Singapore's Lee Kuan Yew's advice to "look east" for guidance on how to achieve fast economic growth (Prestowitz 2013).[44] The success of the NICs in Southeast Asia and South America are also cited as important examples testifying to the success of mercantilism in promoting national development.

Mercantilist policies remain popular in many LDCs despite the "triumph" of liberal thoughts in the West in the age of globalization. The return of the New Left in South America in Venezuela, Brazil, Argentina, Ecuador, and Bolivia has seen an expanded role of the government in the economy in these countries. Venezuela, Bolivia, and Argentina have even nationalized some foreign companies in their efforts to control the economy through government control. In April 2012 Argentina's Christina Kirchner Fernandez government nationalized YPF, subsidiary of Spanish Repsol oil company, followed by Bolivia's nationalization of a Spanish-owned electric company on May 3, 2012. Still, economic crisis, corruption, and political upheaval in Brazil, Argentina, Venezuela, Cuba, and Bolivia since 2013 have undermined the survival of the "New Left" governments in South America that began to emerge earlier in 1999.[45] Only time will tell if Neo-mercantilism will endure in the age of globalization.

Key Terms

absolute advantage
absolute income gap
Adam Smith
Alexander Hamilton
Arab Spring
Association of Southeast Asian Nations (ASEAN)
autarky
balance of trade
balance of trade deficit
balance of trade surplus
bourgeoisie
Bretton Woods
BRICS
business cycles
cartel
casino capitalism
Comparative advantage
conditionality rule
convergence theory
Darwinian survival of the fittest
David Ricardo
deficit spending
deflation
dependency theory
Dispute Settlement Body
dumping
economic infrastructure

embargoes
export-led industrialization
Fernando Cardoso
fiscal policy
floating exchange rate
foreign direct investment
General Agreements on Tariffs and Trade (GATT)
General Council
George Friedrich List
Global North
Global South
globalization
Great Depression
hard currencies
hegemon
human capital
Immanuel Wallerstein
imperialism
industrialization
Inflation
International Bank for Reconstruction and Development (IBRD)
International Monetary Fund (IMF)
International Trade Organization (ITO)
Invisible hand
John Maynard Keynes
laissez faire capitalism

Lesser Developed Countries (LDCs)
Maoism
Marshall Plan
Ministerial Conference
mode of production
modernization theory
monetary policy
neo-imperialism
Neo-mercantilists
New world order
Newly Industrializing Countries (NICs)
non-aligned movement
non-tariff barriers (NTBs)
North Atlantic Treaty Organization (NATO)
Organization for Economic Cooperation and Development (OECD)
over-production
Patrick Buchanan
Paul Baran
predatory practices

price-fixing
proletariat
Quantitative Easing
quotas
relative income gap
Smooth-Hawley tariffs
specialization
Totalitarianism
under-consumption
United Nations (UN)
V. I. Lenin
variable-sum
Warsaw Pact
Wealth of Nations
win-lose
win-win
World Bank
World System Theory
World Trade Organization (WTO)
zero-sum

End Notes

1. Business Dictionary at www.businessdictionary.com/definition/globalization.html

2. Thomas Friedman, *Lexus and the Olive Tree: Understanding Globalization* (New York: Farrar, Straus and Giroux, 1999), p. 7.

3. "Summary of the Trans-Pacific Partnership Agreement." USTR. October 4, 2015. Retrieved October 15, 2017. https://ustr.gov/about-us/policy-offices/pressoffice/ press-releases/2015/october/ summary-trans-pacific-partnership

4. Adam Smith, *The Wealth of Nations: An Inquiry into the Nature & Causes of the Wealth of Nations* (New York: Bantam Classics, 2003).

5. Nick Fraser, John Maynard Keynes: "Can the great economist save the world?" The Independent, November 8, 2008, http://www.independent.co.uk/news/business/analysis-and-features/john-maynardkeynes-can-the-great-economist-save-the-world-994416.html. Retrieved October 17, 2017.

6. See Paul Krugman's New York Times blog posts, "The Conscience of a Liberal." https://krugman. blogs.nytimes.com/. Retrieved October 19, 2017

7. Karl Marx and Friedrich Engels, *The Communist Manifesto*, 1848.

8. Vladimir Lenin, *Imperialism, the Highest Stage of Capitalism*, 1917.

9. Timothy Cheek, *Mao Zedong and China's Revolutions* (New York: Macmillan, 2002).

10. Paul Baran, The Political Economy of Growth, *Monthly Review*, 1957.

11. Andre Gunder Frank, Capitalism and Underdevelopment in Latin America: Historical Studies of Chile and Brazil, *Monthly Review*, 1967.

12. Fernando Henrique Cardoso and Faletto Enzo, *Dependency and Development in Latin America* (Berkeley: University of California Press, 1979); Alvin Y So, *Social Change and Development: Modernization, Dependency and World-System Theories* Sage, 1990); Mitchell A. Seligson and John Passe-Smith, eds., *Development and Underdevelopment: The Political Economy of Global Inequality*, 4th ed., (Boulder, CO: Lynne Rienner, 2008).

13. See among others, Immanuel Wallerstein, *The Modern World-System I: Capitalist Agriculture and the Origins of the European World-Economy in the Sixteenth Century* (New York: Academic Press, 1974); Immanuel Wallerstein, *The Modern World-System II* (New York, Academic Press); Immanuel Wallerstein (1980). *The Modern World-System III* (San Diego: Academic Press, 1989); Daniel Chirot, *Social Change in the Twentieth Century* (New York: Harcourt Brace Jovanovich, 1977).

14. Tracey Keys and Thomas W. Malnight, Corporate Clout: The Influence of the World's Largest 100 Economic Entities, Global Trends, www.globaltrends.com/images/stories/corporate%20 clout%20the%20worlds%20100%20largest%20economic%20entities.pdf

15. Ibid.

16. *Matthew White, Source List and Detailed Death Tolls for the Primary Megadeaths of the Twentieth Century* at http://necrometrics.com/20c5m.htm

17. For different perspectives, see Barry Eichengreen, *Golden Fetters: The Gold Standard and the Great Depression, 1919–1939* (Oxford, UK: Oxford University Press, 1992); Milton Friedman, *Capitalism and Freedom* (Chicago: University of Chicago Press, 1962); Milton Freedman, Capitalism and Friedman, *The Wall Street Journal*, November 17, 2006. http://online.wsj.com/ public/page/news-opinion-commentary.html

18. Harris Dellas and George S. Tavlas, The Revived Bretton Woods System, Liquidity Creation, and Asset Price Bubbles, *Cato Journal* 31(3) (Fall 2011). www.cato.org/pubs/journal/cj31n3/ cj31n3-4.pdf

19. Lucien Ellington, *The Japanese Economic Miracle*, Stanford Program on International and Cross-Cultural Education, 2004 (http://spice.stanford.edu/docs/122)

20. Harris Dellas and George S. Tavlas, The Revived Bretton Woods System, Liquidity Creation, and Asset Price Bubbles, *Cato Journal*, 2011. www.cato.org/pubs/journal/cj31n3/cj31n3-4.pdf

21. http://www.worldbank.org/en/who-we-are/ibrd. Retrieved October 19, 2017. Accessed October 19, 2017.

22. International Finance Corporation, *Voting Rights of Directors*, http://siteresources.worldbank. org/BODINT/Resources/278027-1215524804501/IFCEDsVotingTable.pdf

23. http://www.imf.org/en/About/Factsheets/Sheets/2016/07/14/12/21/IMF-Quotas. Retrieved October 20, 2017.

24. International Monetary Fund, *Quota and Voting Shares Before and After Implementation of Reforms Agreed in 2008 and 2010*, at www.imf.org/external/np/sec/pr/2011/pdfs/quota_tbl.pdf

25. World Bank, *International Bank for Reconstruction and Development Voting Power of Executive Directors*, http://siteresources.worldbank.org/BODINT/Resources/278027-1215524804501/ IBRDEDs VotingTable.pdf

26. These countries were: Australia, Belgium, Brazil, Burma, Canada, Ceylon, Chile, China, Cuba, the Czechoslovak Republic, France, India, Lebanon, Luxembourg, Netherlands, New Zealand, Norway, Pakistan, Southern Rhodesia, Syria, South Africa, the United Kingdom, and the United States.

27. U. S. Department of State http://future.state.gov/when/timeline/1921_timeline/smoot_ tariff.html

28. https://www.wto.org/english/thewto_e/acc_e/cbt_course_e/c1s1p1_e.htm. Retrieved October 20, 2017.

29. World Trade Organization, WTO, www.wto.org/english/thewto_e/whatis_e/tif_e/org2_e. htm

30. J. Bradford DeLong, Post-WWII Western European Exceptionalism: The Economic Dimension, 1997. www.j-bradford-delong.net/econ_articles/ucla/ucla_marshall2.html) (14 January 2002).

31. Lucien Ellington, *The Japanese Economic Miracle*, Stanford Program on International and Cross-Cultural Education, 2004 (http://spice.stanford.edu/docs/122)

32. For a good review of the causes and the consequences of the global financial crisis see, the Public Broadcasting System (PBS) documentary, *Money, Power, and Wall Street*, 2012.

33. International Bank for Reconstruction and Development (The World Bank), 2013. http://data.worldbank.org/sites/default/files/ids-2013.pdf

34. Valentina Pasquali and Tina Aridas, *Global Finance*, 2013 www.gfmag.com/tools/global-database/economic-data/11855-total-debt-to-gdp.html#axzz2QwdnRkUk

35. International Bank for Reconstruction and Development (The World Bank), 2013. http://data.worldbank.org/sites/default/files/ids-2013.pdf, p. 2.

36. The Stock Market Then and Down, *New York Times*, August 10, 2011, www.nytimes.com/interactive/2011/08/11/business/economy/20110811-the-stock-market-then-and-now.html?_r=0

37. Anatole Kaletsky, Don't Worry about a Stock Market Drop, *New York Times*, March 14, 2013 http://blogs.reuters.com/anatole-kaletsky/2013/03/14/dont-worry-about-a-stock-market-drop/

38. Chris Isidore, It's Official: Recession since Dec. '07, CNNMoney.com, December 1, 2008 http://money.cnn.com/2008/12/01/news/economy/recession/

39. Paul Krugman, *End This Depression Now* (New York: W.W. Norton and Company, 2012).

40. Friedman, Thomas, *The World Is Flat: A Brief History of the Twenty-First Century* (New York: Farrar, Straus and Giroux, 2005).

41. Benjamin Barber, *Jihad vs McWorld: How Globalism and Tribalism* Are Reshaping the World (New York: Ballantine Books, 1995).

42. Paul Sweezy, *The Theory of Capitalist Development* (London: D. Dobson, 1946); *The Dynamics of US Capitalism: Corporate Structure, Inflation, Credit, Gold, and the Dollar* (New York: Monthly Review Press, 1972); Andre Gunder Frank, *The Development of Underdevelopment* (New York: Monthly Review Press, 1966); *Capitalism and Underdevelopment in Latin America* (New York: Monthly Review Press, 1967); Samir Amin, "A Critique of Stiglitz Report: The Limits of Liberal Orthodoxy," *Pambazuka Report*, 446 (2009) www.pambazuka.org/en/category/features/58453; *Global History: A View from the South* (Oxford, UK: Pambazuka Press, 2010).

43. Philip McMichael, *Development and Social Change: A Global Perspective* (Washington, DC: Sage, 2012).

44. Clyde Prestowitz, Triumph of the Mercantilists, *Foreign Policy* (Thursday, May 9, 2013). http://prestowitz.foreignpolicy.com/posts/2013/05/09/triumph_of_the_mercantilists

45. Sabatini, Christopher, "The Sad Death of the Latin American Left," Foreign Affairs, December 10, 2015. Retrieved October 20, 2019. http://foreignpolicy.com/2015/12/10/venezuelabrazil-chavez-maduro-rousseff-lula/

BIBLIOGRAPHY

Abbas, M. "The Long Overdue Palestinian State." *New York Times*, May 16, 2011.

Abootalebi, A. R., "Nationalism, Power Politics, and Pluralism in Divided Societies," in Fonkem Achankeng, ed. *Nationalism and Intra-State Conflicts in the Postcolonial World*, Lanham, Maryland: Lexington Books, 2015, pp. 113–130.

Al Jazeera. "Iran Rejects Women Presidential Hopefuls." *Al Jazeera*, May 17, 2013. www.Al Jazeera. com/news/Middle East/2013/05/2013 51754634102939.html.

Alvin Y. S., *Social Change and Development: Modernization, Dependency and World-System Theories*. Newbury Park, California: Sage, 1990.

Amin, S., "A Critique of Stiglitz Report: The Limits of Liberal Orthodoxy," *Pambazuka Report*, 446, 2009. www.pambazuka.org/en/category/features/58453.

—, *Global History: A View from the South*. Oxford, UK: Pambazuka Press, 2010.

Associated Press. "*UN Body Calls for End to Cuban Embargo.*" November 8, 2005. http://www. msnbc.msn.com/id/9969997/ns/world_news-americas/t/un-body-calls-end-cuban-embargo/ (accessed June 22, 2011).

Atran, S. "Genesis of Suicide Terrorism." *Science* 299, 2003: 1534–1539.

Balaam, D. N. and Michael V. *Introduction to International Political Economy*. 4th ed. Upper Saddle River, NJ: Pearson, 2008.

Baran, P., "*The Political Economy of Growth*." *Monthly Review Press*, 1957.

Barber, B., *Jihad vs McWorld: How Globalism and Tribalism Are Reshaping the World*. New York: Ballantine Books, 1995.

BBC News. "China Claims Success Inpatrolling Disputed Islnds." *BBC News*, September 17, 2012. www.bbc.co.uk/news/world-asia-china-19620013?print=true.

BBC News. "*Germany's Chancellor Merkel Urges EU Political Union.*" *BBC News*, June 7, 2012. http:// www.bbc.co.uk/news/world-europe-18350977 (accessed August 1, 2012).

Blagojevic, B. "Causes of Ethnic Conlfict: A Conceptual Framework." *Journal of Global Change and Governance*, 2009.

Blanchard, C. M. *The Islamic Traditions of Wahhabism and Salafiyya*. Congressional Research Service Report for Congress, Washington: The Library of Congress, 2008.

Bloom, L. *When Will the US Stop Mass Incarceration?*, July 3, 2012.

Brochmann, M., Rod, J. K., and Gleditsch, N. P. "International Borders and Conflict Revisited." *Conflict Management and Peace Science* 29, no. 2, 2012: 170–194.

Brunnschweiler, C. N. and Bulte, E. H. "The Resource Curse Revisited and Revised: A Tale of Paradoxes and Red Herrings." *Journal of Environmental Economics and Management* 55, 2008: 248–264.

Callahan, P. *Logics American Foreign Policy*. New York: Pearson Longman, 2004.

Cardoso, F. H. and Faletto E., *Dependency and Development in Latin America*. Berkeley. University of California Press, 1979.

Cheek, T., *Mao Zedong and China's Revolutions*. New York: Macmillan, 2002.

Chimni, B. S. "Marxism and International Law: A Contemporary Analysis." *Economic and Political Weekly* 34, no. 6, February 1999: 337–349.

Chirot, D., *Social Change in the Twentieth Century*. New York: Harcourt Brace Jovanovich, 1977.

CIA. *United States*. n.d. https://www.cia.gov/library/publications/the-world-factbook/geos/ us.html (accessed June Friday, 2012).

Coulson, J. N. "Shariah." *Encyclopedia Britannica*. n.d. www.britannica.com/topic/538793/Shariah (accessed June 6, 2013).

Crenshaw, M. "The Causes of Terrorism." *Comparative Politics* 13, no. 4, 1981: 379–399.

Deal, N. J. "China's Nationalist Heritage." *The National Interest*, Jan/Feb 2013: 44–53.

Dellas, H. and George S. T., "The Revived Bretton Woods System, Liquidity Creation, and Asset Price Bubbles," *Cato Journal* 31, no. 3, Fall 2011. www.cato.org/pubs/journal/cj31n3/cj31n3-4. pdf

DeLong, J. B., "Post-WWII Western European Exceptionalism: The Economic Dimension," 1997. www.j-bradford-delong.net/econ_articles/ucla/ucla_marshall2.html

Dempsey, G. T. "Reasonable Doubt: The Case Against the Proposed International Criminal Court." *CATO Institute*. July 16, 1998. www.cato.org/pubs/pas/pa-31es.html.

Domitrovic, B., "Against the Gold Standard? That's Not Quite Ivy League," *Forbes*, July 14, 2017. https://www.forbes.com/sites/briandomitrovic/2017/07/14/against-the-gold-standard-thats-not-quite-ivy-league/#469e8f839d39 (accessed October 17, 2017).

Dormann, K. "The Geneva Conventions Today." *International Committee of the Red Cross.* July 09, 2009. http://www.icrc.org/eng/resources/documents/statement/geneva-conventions-statement-090709.htm (accessed August 02, 2012).

Doyle, M. W. "Kant, Liberal Legacies and Public Affairs." *Philosophy and Public Affairs* 12, no. 3, 1983: 205–235.

Doyle, M. W. "Three Pillars of the Liberal Peace." *American Political Science Review* 99, no. 3, 2005: 463–466.

Durac, V. and Francesco C., *Politics and Governance in the Middle East*, New York, Palgrave, 2015.

Duvall, T. "The New Feudalism: Globalization, the Market, and the Great Chain of Consumption." *New Political Science* 25, no. 1, 2003: 84.

ECHR. "Overview 1959–2011." *European Court of Human Rights*, February 2012. http://www.echr.coe.int/ECHR/EN/Header/The+Court/Introduction/Information+documents/ (accessed August 03, 2012).

Eichengreen, B., *Golden Fetters: The Gold Standard and the Great Depression, 1919–1939.* Oxford, UK: Oxford University Press, 1992.

Ellington, L., "The Japanese Economic Miracle," *Stanford Program on International and Cross-Cultural Education*, 2004. http://spice.stanford.edu/docs/122

Erickson, A. S. and Adam P. L. "A Player, but Not a Superpower." *Foreign Policy*, March 7, 2013. http://www.foreignpolicy.com/articles/2013/03/07/a_player_but_no_superpower_china_military.

European Central Bank. *European Central Bank*, n.d. http://www.ecb.int/ecb/html/index.en.html (accessed July 02 and 03, 2012).

—. *The Economy*, n.d. http://europa.eu/about-eu/facts-figures/economy/index_en.htm (accessed June, 2012).

European Union. *European Parliament/About Parliament*, n.d. http://www.europarl.europa.eu/about-parliament/en/0080a6d3d8/Ordinary-legislative-procedure.html (accessed July 03, 2012).

—. *European Parliament/About Parliament*, n.d. http://www.europarl.europa.eu/aboutparliament/en/0076b966cf/Powers-and-functions.html—. *European Commission*, n.d. http://europa.eu/about-eu/institutions-bodies/european-commission/index_en.htm (accessed July 03, 2012).

Finn, P. and Ellen N. "Obama Defends Sweeping Suveillance Efforts." *The Washington Post*, June 7, 2013.

Frank, A. G., "The Development of Underdevelopment." *Monthly Review Press*, 1966.

Frank, A. G., "*Capitalism and Underdevelopment in Latin America: Historical Studies of Chile and Brazil.*" *Monthly Review Press*, 1967.

—, "Capitalism and Underdevelopment in Latin America." *Monthly Review Press*, 1967.

Fraser, N., "John Maynard Keynes: Can the Great Economist Save the World?" *The Independent*, November 8, 2008. http://www.independent.co.uk/news/business/analysis-and-features/john-maynard-keynes-can-the-great-economist-save-the-world-994416.html (accessed October 17, 2017).

Frieden, J. A. and David, A. L., and Kenneth, A. S. *World Politics.* New York: W. W. Norton & Company, 2010.

Friedman, M., *Capitalism and Freedom.* Chicago: University of Chicago Press, 1962.

Friedman, T., *Lexus and the Olive Tree: Understanding Globalization.* New York: Farrar, Straus and Giroux, 1999.

Friedman, T., *The World Is Flat: A Brief History of the Twenty-First Century.* New York: Farrar, Straus and Giroux, 2005.

Fukuyama, F. "The End of History." *The National Interest,* 1989.

Gibler, D. M. "Bordering on Peace: Democracy, Territorial Issues and Conflict." *International Studies Quarterly* 51, 2007: 509–532.

Goldstein, J. S. "Think Again: War." *Foreign Policy,* September/October, 2011.

Goode, E. "Incarceration Rates for Blacks Have Fallen Sharply, Report Shows." *The New New York Times,* February 27, 2013.

Heneghan, T. "Blair—Religion to Be as Important as 20th Century Ideologies." *Faith World,* May 29, 2008. blogs.reuters.com/faithworld/2008/05/29/blair-religion-to-be-as-important-as-20th-century-ideologies/.

Huffington Post. "Pakistan Warns US Drone Strikes Are 'Red Line'." February 5, 2013.***

ICC. "Resolution RC/Res.6." *International Criminal Court.* June 11, 2010. http://www.icc-cpi.int/iccdocs/asp_docs/resolutions/rc-res.6-eng.pdf (accessed August 06, 2012).

—. "Rome Statute." *International Criminal Court,* 2011. http://www.icc-cpi.int/NR/rdonlyres/ADD16852-AEE9-4757-ABE7-9CDC7CF02886/283503/RomeStatutEng1.pdf (accessed August 06, 2012).

ICRC. "What Is International Humanitarian Law?" *International Committee of the Red Cross,* 2004. http://www.icrc.org/eng/resources/documents/legal-fact-sheet/humanitarian-law-factsheet.htm (accessed August 01, 2012).

Institute for Global Labour and Human Rights. *Bangladesh Garment Wages the Lowest in the World— Comparative Garment Worker Wages,* August 19, 2010. www.globallabourrights.or/alerts?id=0297.

International Bank for Reconstruction and Development (The World Bank), 2013, p. 2. http://data. worldbank.org/sites/default/files/ids-2013.pdf—, 2013. http://data. worldbank.org/sites/default/files/ids-2013.pdf

International Finance Corporation, "Voting Rights of Directors." n.d. http://siteresources.worldbank.org/ BODINT/Resources/278027-1215524804501/IFCEDsVotingTable.pdf

International Monetary Fund, "Quota and Voting Shares Before and After Implementation of Reforms Agreed in 2008 and 2010." www.imf.org/external/np/sec/pr/2011/pdfs/quota_tbl.pdf20Isidore, C., "It's Official: Recession since Dec. '07, "*CNNMoney.com,*" December 1, 2008. http:// money.cnn.com/2008/12/01/news/economy/recession/

Jackson, R. "Doctrinal War: Religion and Ideology in International Conflict." *The Monist* 89, no. 2, 2006: 274–300.

Janis, M. W. "Individuals as Subjects of International Law." *Cornell International Law Journal* 17, no. 61, 1984: 61–78.

Kaletsky, A., "Don't Worry about a Stock Market Drop," *New York Times,* March 14, 2013. http://blogs.reuters.com/anatole-kaletsky/2013/03/14/dont-worry-about-a-stock-marketdrop/

Kaufman, S. J. *Modern Hatreds: The Symbolic Politics of Ethnic War.* Ithaca: Cornell University Press, 2001.

Keach, B. "International Law: Illusion and Reality." *International Socialist Review,* no. 27, January/February, 2003.

Kerr, R. and Eirin M. *Peace and Justice: Seeking Accountability After War.* Cambridge: Polity Press, 2007.

Kersten, M. "The US and the ICC: Towards A Closer Relationship." *Justice in Conflict,* April 10, 2011. www.justiceinconflict.org/2011/04/10-the-us-and-the-icc-towards-a-acloser-relationship.

Klare, M. T. *Resource Wars: The New Landscape of Global Conflict.* New York: Henry Holt and Company, 2001.

—. "The Coming Resource Wars." *ZNET*, March 13th, 2006. www.zcommunications.org/the-coming-resource-wars-by-michael-t-klare (accessed April, 2013).

Krasner, S. D. "Abiding Sovereignty." *International Political Science Review* 22, no. 3, 2001: 229–251.

Krugman, P., *End This Depression Now.* New York: W.W. Norton & Company, 2012.

—, "The Conscience of a Liberal," *New York Times* (blog posts). https://krugman.blogs.nytimes.com/ (accessed October 19, 2017).

Layne, C. "Who Lost Iraq and Why It Matters: The Case for Offshore Balancing." *World Policy Journal* 34, no. 3, 2007: 38–52.

Lenin, V., *Imperialism, the Highest Stage of Capitalism*, 1917 (Rough Draft Printing, 2014).

Lynch, C. "Iceland, Iran Lose Bids to Join UN Security Council." *Washington Post*, October 18, 2008.

Mani, R. "Cure or Curse? The Role of Religion in Violent Conflict and Peaceful Governance." *Global Governance* 18, 2012: 149–169.

Marx, K. and Friedrich E., *The Communist Manifesto*, 1848. Los Angeles: Millennium Publications, 2015.

McClurg, S. C. and Young, J. K. *A Relational Political Science.* Working Paper, Carbondale: Southern Illinois University, 2010.

McMichael, P., *Development and Social Change: A Global Perspective.* Washington, DC: Sage, 2012.

McNamara, K. R. *The Eurocrisis and the Uncertain Future of European Integration.* New York: Council on Foreign Relations, 2010.

Mearsheimer, J. J. "The False Promise of International Institutions." *International Security* 19, no. 3, 1994/95: 13.

Mearsheimer, J. J. and Stephen M. W. "Keeping Saddam Hussein in a Box." *New York Times*, February 2, 2003.

Melvin, N. and Koning, R. D. "Resources and Armed Conflict." In *SIPRI Yearbook 2011: Armaments, Disarmament and International Security*. London: Oxford University Press, 2011.

Mingst, K. A. and Arreguin-Toft, I. M. *Essentials of International Relations*, 5th ed. New York: W. W. Norton & Company, 2011.

Morgenthau, H. J. *Politics Among Nations: The Struggle for Power and Peace*, 6th ed. Edited by K. W. Thompson. New York: Alfred A. Knopf, 1965.

Mueller, J. *Retreat from Doomsday: The Obsolescence of Major War.* New York: Basic Books, 1989.

—. "The Banality of "Ethnic War": Yugoslavia and Rwanda." *International Security* 25, no. 1, 2000: 42–70.

—. "War Has Almost Ceased to Exist: An Assessment." *Political Science Quarterly* 124, no. 2, 2009: 297–321.

Nasri, R. "US, Israeli Threats of Force Against Iran Are Illegal and Harm Chances for a Deal." *The Christian Science Monitor*, March 7, 2013.

National Center for Law and Economic Justice. *Poverty in the United States: A Snapshot.* n.d. www.NCLEJ.org/poverty-in-the-US.php.

New York Times, "The Stock Market, Then and Down," August 10, 2011. www.nytimes.com/interactive/2011/08/11/business/economy/20110811-the-stock-market-then-and-now.html?_r=0

Nichols, M. *Deadlocked UN Security Council Members lay blame over Syria.* July 25, 2012. http://www.reuters.com/article/2012/07/25/us-syria-crisis-un-idUSBRE86O1PX20120725 (accessed August 09, 2012).

Nye, J. *The Paradox of American Power.* Oxford University Press, 2002.

Nye, J. S., Jr. "Get Smart: Combining Hard and Soft Power." *Foreign Affairs* 88, no. 4, 2009: 160–163.

—. *The Future of Power.* New York: Public Affairs, 2011.

Obama, B. "Obama's Speech on Drone Policy." *The New York Times*, May 23, 2013.

Osborn, A. "Mass Rape Ruled as War Crime." *The Guardian*, February 22, 2001.

Osiander, A. "Sovereignty, International Relations and the Westphalian Myth." *International Organization* 55, no. 2, 2001: 251–287.

Oxford Dictionaries. *Oxford Dictionaries.* n.d. www.oxforddictionaries.com (accessed May 22, 2013).

Pape, R. A. *Cutting the Fuse: The Explosion of Global Suicide Terrorism and How to Stop It.* Chicago: The University of Chicago Press, 2010.

Paris, R. "Human Security: Paradigm Shift War Hot Air?" *International Security*, 2001: 87–102.

Peterson, S. "NPT 101: Is Iran Violating the Nuclear Treaty?" *The Christian Science Monitor*, May 4, 2010.

Pinker, S. *The Better Angels of Our Nature: Why Violence Has Declined.* New York: Penguin Group, 2011.

Posen, B.. "The Security Dilemma and Ethnic Conflict." *Survival* 35, no. 1, 1993: 27–47.

Prestowitz, C., "Triumph of the Mercantilists," *Foreign Policy*, May 9, 2013. http://prestowitz.foreignpolicy.com/posts/2013/05/09/triumph_of_the_mercantilists.

Ray, J. L., and Juliet K. *Global Politics.* New York: Houghton Mifflin Company, 2008.

Rivkin, D. B. and Casey, L. A. "The Legal Case Against Palestinian Statehood." *Wall Street Journal*, September 20, 2011.

Ross, M. L. "Blood Barrels: Why Oil Wealth Fuels Conflict." *Foreign Affairs* 87, no. 3, 2008: 2–8.

—. "Unbalanced Globalization in the Oil Exporting States." *American Political Science Association.* Seattle, 2011.

Rucker, P. "At US-China Shirt-Sleeves Summit, Formalities and Suspicions Were on Display." *The Washington Post*, June 9, 2013.

Russett, B. "Peace in the Twenty-First Century?" *Current History* 109, no. 723, 2010.

Rustad, S. A. and Binningsbø, H. M. "At Price Worth Fighting For? Natural Resources and Conflict Recurrence." *Journal of Peace Research* 49, no. 4, 2012: 531–546.

Seligson, M. A. and John P.-S., eds., *Development and Underdevelopment: The Political Economy of Global Inequality*, 4th ed., Boulder, CO: Lynne Rienner, 2008.

Shah, A. *Poverty Facts and Stats*, January 7, 2013. www.globalissues.org/article/26/poverty-facts-and-stats.

Smith, A., *The Wealth of Nations: An Inquiry into the Nature & Causes of the Wealth of Nations.* New York: Bantam Classics, 2003.

Smith, M. A. *Power in the Changing Global Order.* Cambridge: Polity, 2012.

Snyder, J., ed. *Religion and International Relations Theory (Religion, Culture, and Public Life).* New York: Columbia University Press, 2011.

Starr, H. "International Borders: What They Are, What They Mean, and Why We Should Care." *SAIS Review* 26, no. 1, 2006: 3–10.

Sweezy, P. L. *The Theory of Capitalist Development.* London: D. Dobson, 1946.

Sweezy, P. L. and Hary M., *The Dynamics of US Capitalism: Corporate Structure, Inflation, Credit, Gold, and the Dollar.* New York: Monthly Review Press, 1972.

Tawfeeq, M. and Hanna, J. "Iraq Mayhem 'Ready to Explode' into Why the Conflict, UN Official Says." *CNN.* May 30, 2013. www.CNN.com/2013/05/30/world/meast/Iraq- violence/.

The Economist. "Once More with the Feeling." *The Economist*, May 18, 2013.

The Times. "Andre Gunder Frank." *The Times*, February 24, 2005.

Themner, L. and Peter W. "Armed Conflicts, 1946-2011." *Journal of Peace Research* 49, no. 4, 2012: 565–575.

UN News Service. *Without Security Council Reform, UN Will Lose Credibility.* May 16, 2011. www.UN.org/apps/news/printnews.ASP?nid=38390 (accessed June 27, 2011).

United Nations. *ECOSOC.* n.d. http://www.un.org/en/ecosoc/about/ (accessed June 23, 2011).

—. *Global Issues: Refugees.* n.d. www.un.org/en/globalissues/refugees/ (accessed June 6, 2013).

—. *The Universal Declaration of Human Rights.* n.d. http://www.un.org/en/documents/udhr/hr_law.shtml (accessed August 02, 2012).

US Energy Information Administration. *South China Sea.* 2013.

Victor, D. G. "What Resource Wars?" *The National Interest* 52, 2007: 48–55.

Wall, R. "Global Defense Spending Falls as US Cuts Outpace China Growth." *Bllomberg.com.* April 14, 2013. http://www.bloomberg.com/news/2013-04-14/global-defense-spending-falls-as-u-s-cuts-outpace-china-growth.htmlWallerstein, I., *The Modern World—System I: Capitalist Agriculture and the Origins of the European World-Economy in the Sixteenth Century.* New York: Academic Press, 1974.

—, *The Modern World—System II.* New York, Academic Press, 1980.

—, *The Modern World—System III.* San Diego: Academic Press, 1989.

—, *The Modern World—System IV.* San Diego: Academic Press, 2011.

Walt, S. M. *War and Change in World Politics.* Cambridge: Cambridge University Press, 1981.

Walt, S. M. "Nationalism Rules." *Foreign Policy,* July 15, 2011.

Waltz, K. *Man, The State and War.* 1957.

Waltz, K. N. "Why Iran Should Get the Bomb." *Foreign Affairs,* July/August 2012.

Wimmer, A. "Introduction: Facing Ethnic Conflicts." In *Facing Ethnic Conflicts: Toward a New Realism.* Edited by A. Wimmer, R. J. Goldstone, D. Horowitz, U. Joras, and C. Schetter. Oxford: Rowman and Littlefield, 2004.

World Bank, "International Bank for Reconstruction and Development Voting Power of Executive Directors." http://siteresources.worldbank.org/BODINT/Resources/278027-1215524804501/IBRDEDs VotingTable.pdf

World Bank. *Involving Nongovernmental Organizations in Bank-Supported Activities.* n.d. http://go.worldbank.org/0WT7SICZY0 (accessed September 13, 2010).

World Health Organization. *10 Facts on Malaria.* March, 2013. www.who.int/features/factfiles/malaria/en/.

Zenko, M. *Reforming US Drone Strike Policies.* Special Report No. 65, New York: Council on Foreign Relations, 2013.

Index

CPSIA information can be obtained
at www.ICGtesting.com
Printed in the USA
FFOW01n0329060118
44383743-44111FF

9 781524 950453